ISSUES IN PHILOSOPHICAL COUNSELING

ISSUES IN
PHILOSOPHICAL
COUNSELING

Peter B. Raabe

Westport, Connecticut
London

Library of Congress Cataloging-in-Publication Data

Raabe, Peter B., 1949–
    Issues in philosophical counseling / Peter B. Raabe.
        p. cm.
    Includes bibliographical references and index.
    ISBN 0–275–97667–X (alk. paper)
    1. Philosophical counseling.   I. Title.
    BJ1595.5.R225 2002
    100—dc21   2001058943

British Library Cataloguing in Publication Data is available.

Library of Congress Catalog Card Number: 2001058943
ISBN: 0–275–97667–X

First published in 2002

Praeger Publishers, 88 Post Road West, Westport, CT 06881
An imprint of Greenwood Publishing Group, Inc.
www.praeger.com

Printed in the United States of America

The paper used in this book complies with the
Permanent Paper Standard issued by the National
Information Standards Organization (Z39.48–1984).

10 9 8 7 6 5 4 3 2 1

For the Raabe and the Russell families

"The medicines for the soul were discovered
by the ancients, but it is our job to find out
how to apply them and when."
Seneca (2 B.C.–65 A.D.)

Contents

Acknowledgments

I would like to express my overdue gratitude to my birth family for the questions stirred in me by their beliefs: Wenzel, Elisabeth, Cecilia, Renate, and Kurt Raabe, and Heinz Zambelli. I would also like to express my appreciation to my best friend Jim Owen for starting me on the road to philosophy by demonstrating to me, so many years ago, that there really are no wrong questions.

Thank you once again to my wife Anne and my son Tim, my immediate family, for their patience and support.

Thank you also to my intellectual family for their kind assistance, scholarly insights, willing participation, and permission to use portions of their interviews in many of the chapters that follow: Tim LeBon, Christopher Borst, Stephen R. Palmquist, Peter Koestenbaum, Stephen Hare, Gale Prawda, Leonard Angel, Justin Irwin, Shlomit Schuster, Jon Mills, Wanda Dawe, Michael Russell, Paul Sharkey, Eite Veening, Maria Colivato, Terry and Peter March, Vaughana Feary, Dennis F. Polis, Colin Clayton, David Hilditch, and Christian Perring.

I would like to thank Annegret Stopczyk for inviting me to speak at the Helene Stöcker Gesellschaft conference in Berlin and for her generosity in this regard; Dale Cannon for inviting me to explore philosophical counseling with the philosophy students and faculty of Western Oregon University, and his wife Jeanné for her hospitality; Yosef Wosk and Shamina Senaratne at Simon Fraser University for their ongoing support; Brian Burtch for his technical advice; Jim Sabin, acquisitions editor at Greenwood Publishing, for accepting my manuscript; Terri Jennings, production editor, for her careful work; the participants at the North Shore Philosophy Café for the stimulating informal discussions; Mike and Debbie

Wheeler for their encouragement; and Martin Hunt for the excellent web site he created for me at http://www.interchange.ubc.ca/raabe/.

My appreciation goes out as well to the many philosophy students and individuals from all over the world who have not only read or studied my first book but who have also shared their interests in philosophical counseling with me by e-mail. And, of course, I am indebted to my clients who continue to teach me so much, and without whose willingness to apply philosophy to the nonhypothetical problems in their own lives my work in philosophy would be merely academic.

Introduction

Since the publication of my first book I have received many e-mail messages and phone calls asking me about specific issues in philosophical counseling: Do you approve of counseling by e-mail? How should a philosophical counselor deal with a client who has been diagnosed as having a mental illness? What about the effects of prescription medication on a client? How do you respond when someone asks you, What is the meaning of life? Can you give me any advice on how to start a practice? and so on. I certainly don't claim to have the final answer to any of these questions but I know how hard it can be to find insights into them in the material that has been published in the field to date. There are also few suggestions and strategies for resolving the problems of everyday life in the writings of eminent philosophers who have concerned themselves primarily with hypothetical issues, trivial abstract analysis, and the development of grand philosophical systems. I therefore offer this volume as a starting point of philosophical inquiry into a number of common—perhaps even ordinary—but significant life issues, and as a companion to my first book.

While my book *Philosophical Counseling: Theory and Practice* dealt extensively with the theoretical underpinnings of the practice, the present volume focuses more on application. Some chapters were originally presented as papers at a conference of scholarly societies and associations whose doors were open to the general public, others were published in peer-reviewed professional journals, and still others were written specifically to instruct philosophical counselors in active practice. I hope that the easy readability and the largely nontheoretical orientation of these essays will make this book of interest not only to academics and practicing professionals but also to anyone not academically trained in philosophy and, even more important, to anyone struggling with the reality of these issues in his or her own personal life. My intention is for this book to fill the huge gap on the bookshelf located between the popular and the academic into which very few contemporary philosophers venture. I hope to show that it is indeed possible to write deeply about serious matters in a nontechnical style, and to fill that void between the shallow self-help and simplistic New Age books on the one end, and the arid, abstract, academic philosophy texts on the other.

Please bear in mind that philosophical counseling is a new field of practice, despite the fact that it is a revitalization of the original intent behind philosophy as that intent was stated by the ancients. In putting philosophy to use, Socrates approached the issues of life in his day with a certain amount of skepticism and doubt, deliberately questioning the familiar ways of thinking, and challenging so-called commonsense beliefs and popular opinion. With this book I also deliberately question and challenge the familiar ways—including the familiar psychological ways—we have of thinking about issues such as the differences between men and women, the supposed irrationality of the emotions, the use of psychotropic medication, what it means to be normal, the "value" of a terrible affliction, the meaning of suicide, the interpretation of dreams, and one's duty to oneself.

The first chapter begins with a discussion of the entire field of philosophy as it exists at the time of this writing. I'm sure this chapter will raise a few eyebrows; it certainly did when I first delivered it as a presentation paper at a national philosophy conference in Edmonton, Alberta, Canada. Although the paper was understood by some philosophers as an unwarranted attack on academic philosophy, my intention was, and still is, to bring attention to the fact that philosophy, as it is typically presented in classrooms today, is its own worst enemy. My argument is that philosophy, like most other fields of study, needs to have a practical side to it, a clinical component, a "technology" of philosophy, if you will, capable of counterbalancing the almost exclusively hypothetical approach to problem resolution found in academics, and able to give a credibility of utility to the abstract theoretical speculations which constitute its body of knowledge. Philosophical counseling must turn philosophy into an actual practice once again if philosophy is to survive in any meaningful way.

Chapter 2 is what I believe to be the most concise and clearly stated conception of philosophical counseling as I have argued it in my previous book. Chapter 3 examines how philosophical counseling actually works and proposes the hypothesis that philosophical counseling, by its very definition as being useful to real life, must go beyond its abstract and theoretical academic orientation and be instead an empirically oriented experimental endeavor. Chapter 4 is an interview with Peter Koestenbaum who was practicing what he has called clinical philosophy together with a number of psychotherapists some 30 years ago. Interestingly, the clinical philosophy Koestenbaum practiced back then is very similar to what is today called philosophical counseling. Chapter 5 compares and contrasts the dialectic that takes place within a philosophy café with the discursive process of a philosophical counseling session, while chapter 6 explores the benefits and hazards of counseling on the Internet. These early chapters are perhaps the most abstract and theoretically oriented in that they discuss, in broad strokes, what philosophical counseling is and ought to be.

Chapter 7 is the first of a number of chapters devoted to a closer look at issues I consider to be more personal. I have had many clients who have said to me, "I'm surprised that you're willing to talk with me about my personal problems. I always thought philosophers weren't into that." My response is to respectfully remind my clients (as well as myself) that the personal is always also philosophical, and that philosophy—whether political, moral, epistemological, or metaphysical—is always also personal.

Chapters 7 through 10 offer an insight into the nature of interpersonal dialogue as it is and might be conducted in a philosophical counseling encounter. Chapter 7 discusses social biases and misconceptions about sexual orientation. But more than being just a description, chapter 7 offers practical advice on how to respond to the six most common arguments used to condemn same-sex relationships. Chapter 8 brings up an issue that is often overlooked because of the current political climate in the Western world. With the pervasive fear of punishment for transgression against so-called political correctness, serious and in-depth discussion of the differences between men and women has all but disappeared from the popular media. But disregarding the different discursive styles between men and women in a counseling situation can be disastrous. It matters very much whether the counselor is a woman and the client is a man or vice versa, or whether both are of the same sex. And philosophical counselors must take into consideration that sex and gender are in fact very different things. This chapter discusses the influence of sex and gender differences in the counseling dynamic and illustrates how they were applied in one particular instance. Chapter 9 considers, among other things, the relationship between men and emotions, and between women and rationality. It argues that reason and the emotions are not at all located on opposite ends of the spectrum; thinking and feeling are intimately linked and equally important in the philosophical counseling process. And if you think that philosophical counseling is always only about a wise philosopher engrossed in somber thought or a serious discussion, chapter 10 says "think again," and argues otherwise.

The next four chapters examine the serious matter of physical and mental illnesses and how these relate to philosophical counseling. Chapters 11 and 12 critique the currently pervasive and popular trend in the field of psychotherapy of, first of all, diagnosing almost any feeling or thought deemed to be out of the ordinary as a mental illness, and then prescribing psychotropic drugs to act as their cure. These chapters discuss many of the issues surrounding the psychopharmacological approach to so-called mental health—such as the fallacy of assuming that because a chemical can be used to alter distressing feelings and thoughts in the mind that therefore the cause of such distress is always a chemical imbalance in the brain. The chapters compare the effectiveness of the use of drugs in treatment to counseling, and they show how medication can interfere with a person's motivation to work at resolving their own problems. In essence these chapters deal with the question of whether it is necessary to drug your brain in order to change your mind. Chapter 13 investigates the nebulous and controversial issue of what it is that constitutes a normal human being. Historically if a person was labeled "abnormal" by the community it often amounted to a death sentence. Today we understand that "normal" does not have to be so brutally defined, nor does it have to be as narrowly defined as it is in the ever-changing diagnostic manuals used by almost all psychotherapists. In fact there is good reason to celebrate those mental abnormalities and even physical afflictions, which were at one time reviled, because of the benefits they can bring to both the individual in question and society at large. This is the point that is argued in chapter 14.

Chapters 15 through 18 deal with a number of issues that can be quite frightening to the neophyte philosophical counselor. The issues are large and metaphysical, and because they are concrete—someone's life may be at stake—they can shock the philosopher who is faced with them into self-doubt and an apprehensive reluctance to deal with them. Chapter 15 reveals that there are a number of ways of effectively approaching the question of the meaning of life. This chapter is a somewhat expanded discussion of, and an explanatory complement to, the Appendix C found in my previous book. It offers an approach to the question of the meaning of life that goes beyond mere academic denial of the formal legitimacy of this question, and beyond the theological perspective, to one that is specifically suited to philosophical counseling. A philosophical counselor is also often faced with the client who has made poor life decisions and who has recently discovered, to his dismay, that there is not much of life left to him. While some cultures value and respect the aged, in our Western societies old age is considered a self-inflicted infirmity to be avoided at all costs. Chapter 16 offers some practical suggestions to the philosophical counselor who finds herself having to deal with a client who is afraid, or simply doesn't know how, to grow old gracefully. For example, the chapter considers issues such as the reconciliation of a younger self-image with advanced chronological age, the advantages of a necessarily slower pace of life, and the acceptance of an inevitable death. Chapter 17 goes on to discuss death in relation to the philosophical counselor who is faced with a client who admits to having suicidal thoughts. Counselors and therapists face an ethical dilemma whenever a client confesses to wanting to end his own life. Should the counselor try to talk the client out of committing suicide regardless of the client's reasons for wanting to do so? In order to decide what sort of help to offer the suicidal client, the philosophical counselor needs to understand why someone would want to stop living in the first place. To complicate these matters even more, the distressing life issues which can deaden the joy of life often overlap with the personal religious beliefs of both the counselor and the client. Chapter 18 addresses the question of how the nonbelieving philosophical counselor might deal with a very religious person, and, conversely, whether the counselor's religious convictions will compromise his efforts to establish an effectively therapeutic relationship with a client who holds contrary beliefs.

Chapter 19 examines various methods of dream interpretation. Dream interpretation is an approach to therapy that has been central to the psychoanalytic pursuit of mental health since its inception, and is still regarded today as essential to many of the numerous forms of psychotherapy. Freudian and Jungian methodology is critiqued, and an approach to dream interpretation is suggested that is more amenable to the assumptions, or rather intentional absence of assumptions, in philosophical counseling about the deeper functioning of the human mind.

The last two chapters focus attention on the philosophical counselor. Chapter 20 draws attention to a rarely discussed element within one of Kant's categorical imperatives: the duty one has to oneself. Most philosophers will readily agree with the deontological principle that a person should never use another as merely a means to an end, but what is rarely spoken of is Kant's warning that a person should never use himself or herself merely as a means either. This is especially relevant to counselors whose desire to be helpful to others makes them forget the duty they have to care for themselves. The final chapter offers sound advice from a number of practitioners to those wishing to establish their own practice. Although some suggestions may seem suited to only particular geopolitical regions, most can easily be universalized and adapted to conform to local customs, laws, and regulations.

As mentioned in the first chapter of this book, philosophy is not, and never has been, a solitary discipline. In order to practice what I preach I have requested and received input from philosophers and philosophical counselors from different parts of the world. Their participation in the writing of many of these chapters has allowed me to present points of view, arguments, and suggestions that would probably never have come to my own mind. For that I am very grateful, and I offer this volume not as a collection of my own definitive explanations but in the true spirit of philosophical counseling: as a shared exploration.

Chapter 1

The Man Who Saved the World
but Could Not Save Himself*

If it weren't for philosophical counseling, the ancient conception of philosophy as something that is put into practice by philosophers would now be completely meaningless.[1] That's because while philosophers have been teaching philosophy, they have over the centuries systematically given away to others, such as biologists, astronomers, and doctors, anything that ever became a practice in that field. The most recent, and perhaps distressing, example of this misplaced generosity was when philosophers gave the practice of philosophy to psychotherapists. But what does psychotherapy have to do with philosophy? And why do I claim that the idea of philosophy as something that is put into practice by philosophers would be completely meaningless if it weren't for philosophical counseling? Isn't philosophy practiced in colleges, universities, and even some high schools?

Philosophy has certainly *claimed* to be a practice, but it hasn't often lived up to this claim. Two centuries before Christ, Epicurus proclaimed that philosophy was meant to relieve human suffering.[2] Around the beginning of the Christian Era Seneca wrote in his letter to Lucilius,

Shall I tell you what philosophy holds out to humanity? Counsel. One person is facing death, another is vexed by poverty. . . . All mankind are stretching out their hands to you on every side. Lives have been ruined, lives that are on the way to ruin are appealing for some help; it is to you that they look for hope and assistance.[3]

*An earlier version of this chapter was presented as a paper at the Symposium on Public Philosophical Practices in Canada for the Canadian Philosophical Association's 44th Annual Congress, in conjunction with the Congress of the Social Sciences and Humanities, 2000, Edmonton, Alberta, May 24–May 31, 2000.

More recently, notable philosophers such as Friedrich Nietzsche, Ludwig Wittgenstein, John Dewey, and many others have similarly claimed that the value of philosophy lies in its application to real life. But they have also often complained that philosophy has gone off on a wrong track somewhere, and especially that contemporary academic philosophy is not the best, or even *any*, example of what it means to practice philosophy. For example, in 1920 John Dewey wrote,

The causes remain which brought philosophy into existence as an attempt to find an intelligent substitute for blind custom and blind impulse as guides to life and conduct. The attempt has not been successfully accomplished. Is there not reason for believing that the release of philosophy from its burdens of sterile metaphysics and sterile epistemology instead of depriving philosophy of problems and subject matter would open a way to questions of the most perplexing and the most significant sort?[4]

This confusion of academic philosophy with applied philosophy, the practice of philosophy, the practical application of philosophy, philosophical practice, philosophical praxis, and so on goes back a long way to a man who himself often claimed to be confused when engaged in one of the above. Socrates, as Plato portrayed him in his various dialogues, claimed, as many others have before him and since, that the ultimate aim of philosophy is to improve the human condition. Professor of philosophy Luis Navia sums it up nicely when he says that

all of his [Socrates'] activities, his conversations, his choices, and possibly even the most insignificant of his gestures were determined by the purpose that he set for his life, which was to understand the human self both in himself and in others, convinced that that understanding is attainable and that it is a necessary requirement for a good and happy life.[5]

Many philosophers believe that, despite the important work of the pre-Socratic philosophers, Socrates' approach to understanding the human self should be considered the starting point of philosophy as a practice. But it is the tragedy of Socrates' own life that exemplifies what has gone wrong with practice in philosophy. Socrates was sentenced to death on what may be called Athenian principles—that is, he was ordered to stop what he was doing, and ultimately sentenced to death, in order to uphold the conservative principles of Athenian law and morality. What Socrates did wrong was to accept his state's challenge to participate in a war of principles. He stood firm by his own, more liberal, principles—the foremost of which was that an unexamined life is not worth living.[6] He killed himself on principle instead of following the advice of those who loved him by which he could easily have saved himself, such as that it was unwise for him to adhere to the *logical* claim to a right to free speech in light of the very *emotional* accusation against him that he was corrupting the young citizens of Athens. What is worse, just for the sake of his principles he ignored the expressed needs of his friends and his family to have him remain alive. Of course, we now consider him a hero and a legendary man of principles, but by killing himself Socrates seems to have exhibited a lack of understanding of both the limits of logical argument and of himself as intimately connected to others.[7] Philosophy did not do for Socrates what it was supposed to do. It seems that Socrates had become so absorbed in discussing human beings in the abstract, and in examining 'the person' as a universal concept that he became unable to save the one thing that is always infinitely more important than any abstract theoretical principles about humanity: his own life. Socrates' work as a philosopher was meant to rescue Athenians from living according to unreasonable religious dogma, unjustified cultural and political traditions, and unexamined personal habits. With his philosophy he was out to save the world. But he couldn't save himself.

Recall that in several dialogues, such as *Crito*, *Gorgias*, and *Republic*, Socrates suggests that the philosopher's role is analogous to the physician's. As the physician cares for the body's health, the philosopher aims at improving the soul's; and not only his own but also the souls of others. This analogy breaks down miserably, though, when training in the two fields is compared. When a person goes to medical school she is trained in both theory and practice. It would be a sad state of affairs indeed if medicine were simply a theoretical discipline. But that is exactly the case with philosophy; and it is a sad state of affairs indeed. Theory in any field is always meant to inform its practice, except in the peculiar field of philosophy. Apparently, philosophers are uninterested in utilizing their knowledge; they do not concern themselves with the personal entanglements of any actual human life. Academic philosophy concerns itself primarily with fabricating abstractions out of the realities of life. As Ludwig Wittgenstein put it, philosophy leaves everything as it is.[8] While Plato praises the philosopher for his ability to think abstractly he has Socrates admit in his *Theaetetus* that the typical philosopher "is the object of general derision" because he is so far out of touch with real life that he doesn't even know who his next-door neighbor is.[9]

While Socrates sees philosophy as the greatest of arts,[10] and analogous to the practice of medicine and of the midwife,[11] he sees it at the same time as, paradoxically, removed from practical things and the particulars of human activity. But what sort of art is it that has no practice? What sort of medical practice does not venture beyond hypothesizing? What sort of midwife does not offer actual comfort to both mother and child? Academic philosophy has evaded these questions by simply abandoning its practice and instead steeping itself in the ideal of a never-ending quest for the 'ultimate Truth' with a capital T.

There is no denying that today's jobs in philosophy are primarily academic, requiring specialized graduate degrees. If we apply the Socratic medical analogy this would be like saying that jobs in medicine are primarily academic, requiring graduate degrees—surgeons teaching the next generation to become teachers of surgery so that they may teach the next generation to become teachers of surgery, and so on, operating on a few hypothetical cadavers to illustrate their theories, but without using their surgical skills to really help alleviate the suffering of living individuals in any meaningful way. Academic philosophy is like that: philosophy professors teach the next generation to become philosophy professors who teach the next generation to become philosophy professors, and so on, dissecting a few hypothetical dilemmas along the way to illustrate sweeping theories, but without ever using their philosophical skills to help others deal with the problems of their lives in any meaningful way.[12]

Miami University at one time found itself in the not-uncommon position of having to defend the continuation of its philosophy program. Students complained that getting a philosophy degree would not lead them to any meaningful occupation or profession outside the academy. So the university posted an essay on their web site which pointed out that jobs for which philosophy provides good background qualifications are available in a variety of fields. It announced that philosophy majors graduating recently from Miami University have gone on to further study or careers in such fields as law, government, medicine, education, administration, business, social work, the ministry, library work, and systems analysis.[13] Notice that they say that philosophy provides only *background* qualifications and that it can lead to a job in fields *other* than philosophy. What this message suggests is that academic philosophers give birth to children who must live in other people's houses in order to survive.

If we apply the Socratic medical analogy to this message it becomes absurd. Imagine Miami University posting an essay on their web site for medical students who have discovered that a degree in medicine doesn't lead to a meaningful job. It might read something like this: "Jobs for which a degree in medicine provides good background qualifications are available in a variety of fields. Medical students graduating recently from Miami University have gone on to further study or careers in such fields as law, government, education, administration, and many more." We would find this message patently absurd because it refers to a medical degree; why then don't we find it equally as absurd when it refers to a philosophy degree?

The problem with contemporary philosophy is that it has become, by self-definition, all talk and no action. But academic philosophers themselves are aware of the fact that if theoretical philosophy is to be useful it ought to have a practical side to it just as there is a practical side to the theories of medicine, psychology, law, physics, and so on. Professor of philosophy Amelie Rorty writes, "Philosophy is not, and never has been, a subject. It is, and should be, a variety of activities, performed in a variety of ways."[14] Other academic philosophers argue that business ethics and biomedical ethics are in fact applied philosophy. There are countless books and journal articles published in those fields. But Rorty points out that "unfortunately, with some exceptions in medical ethics, the coworkers and the audience for applied ethics tend to be fellow philosophers."[15] Rorty's point is that philosophers write papers that are typically only read by other philosophers, even when those papers claim to be concerned with applied philosophy, and when they're not intentionally written in a technical or theoretical style. This is not surprising since there has been very little attempt made by academic philosophers to encourage the general public to access their knowledge or expertise. Quite frankly, "applied philosophy" is an oxymoron when it is simply taught as a subject to students.

Philosophers who think corporations or institutions need their expertise in abstract reasoning are summarily dismissed by other professionals as presumptuous.

Philosophers who write academic papers on business ethics or biomedical ethics and expect their esoteric philosophical speculations to change conventional practices in those sectors are sadly idealistic. As Richard Shusterman puts it in his book *Practicing Philosophy*,

I am not claiming that America's professional philosophers have no political role or influence whatever. . . . Philosophers sometimes get a hearing on public issues. . . . My point is that influential policy initiatives are not coming out of philosophy departments.[16]

The world of business is transformed by people coming out of economic and commerce departments, not philosophy. The once-fashionable corporate trend of (curiously) having a philosopher on the corporate payroll to act as the company ethicist was a short-lived fad that is slowly becoming passé due to the ethical conflicts that it generates. For example, in January 2001 the Canadian government came under severe criticism for having an in-house ethicist evaluate accusations of an unethical conflict of interests that had been aimed at the Prime Minister. Opposition members in the House of Commons revealed through the national media that this supposedly impartial ethicist was himself caught in a conflict of interests because he could not risk seriously criticizing the Prime Minister since the Prime Minister signs his paychecks.

The world of politics does not have room for philosophers. Likewise, the worlds of business and medicine are typically modified by people extensively trained in business and medicine. What philosophers who specialize in so-called applied philosophy seem to have missed is that identifying yourself with an activity in a classroom, such as objectively *lecturing about* philosophy, or even dispassionately discussing the human condition, is not the same as personally *participating in* the actual activity of helping to change the human condition for the better. This is not to say that individual academic philosophers never engage in political activism or never participate in activities aimed at social change, but rather that the so-called practice of academic philosophy has a goal (teleology) that does not include transforming the human condition for the better. For example, as mentioned above, Richard Shusterman is the author of the book *Practicing Philosophy*. He is also a professor of philosophy and argues that "philosophy's solutions to life's riddles are not propositional knowledge but transformational practice."[17] But in trying to explain what he means by "transformational practice" he makes the common error of dividing philosophy into only two basic forms: (1) theory, which is what is done in academia, that is, "the formulation or criticism of general, systematic views about the world—including human nature, knowledge, and the institutions of human society;" and (2) philosophical practice as "an art of living," that is, as focusing on self-improvement as "a deliberate life practice that brings lives of beauty and happiness to its practitioners."[18] But Shusterman's admirable attempt to define philosophy as a practice, that is, as the development of an "art of living," promotes a decidedly *self-centered* and *personal* use of philosophy which brings happiness only to its primary practitioner. In his book *Contingency, Irony, and Solidarity* philosopher Richard Rorty also sees the activity of philosophy as being private,

that is thinking by oneself and only for oneself.[19] Again, applying Socrates' medical analogy this is like saying medicine has two basic forms: theory and self-application. This makes the doctor perennially his own patient. Where does this leave
the practice of medicine between two people, the cooperative effort between doctor and patient to improve the condition of the patient? One of the most famous
twentieth-century philosophers, Bertrand Russell, defines philosophy in his little
book *The Problems of Philosophy* this way:

Physical science, through the medium of inventions, is useful to innumerable people who
are wholly ignorant of it; thus the study of physical science is to be recommended, not only,
or primarily, because of the effect on the student, but rather because of the effect on mankind in general. This utility does not belong to philosophy. If the study of philosophy has
any value at all for others than students of philosophy, it must be only indirectly, through its
effects upon the lives of those who study it. It is in these effects, therefore, if anywhere, that
the value of philosophy must be primarily sought.[20]

Russell goes on to point out to his readers that philosophy has "properly" given
up all practical and solvable questions to the empirical disciplines. From this observation, that the world is divided into two types of questions—the practical or
solvable and the philosophical or unresolvable—he makes the normative assertion
that philosophy therefore *ought* to simply concern itself with the inherently unresolvable. Russell promotes the traditional (though not classical) academic idea,
and the pompous ideal of philosophy as merely solitary contemplation, as knowledge for its own sake, as self-application, as devoid of any shared utility, and as
useless for mankind for it does not and need not concern itself with lowly practical
matters which can simply be left to the manual laborers. In fact later, in his Lowell
lectures delivered in Boston in 1914, he says explicitly that the aim of philosophy
is the *theoretical* understanding of the world, "which is not a matter of great practical importance to animals, or to savages, or even to most civilized men."[21]

Russell's denial of philosophy's usefulness to anyone but the student of philosophy and Shusterman's self-application leave out the use of philosophy as *interpersonal* counsel or therapy, which is in fact where it all began. As mentioned earlier,
Epicurus said that philosophy was meant to relieve human suffering. For Epicurus
the pursuit of pure knowledge—theoretical philosophy—has no intrinsic value;
knowledge is only ever of instrumental value. (I agree.) Epicurus went on to say
"for just as there is no benefit in medicine if it does not drive out bodily diseases, so
there is no benefit in philosophy if it does not drive out the diseases of the soul."[22]
What are these diseases of the soul? Freud developed psychoanalysis to deal with
what he believed to be diseases of the soul. But a number of Freud's contemporar-
ies and students disagreed with what they found to be the coldly clinical and
pseudo-scientific nature of his approach. Using the medical analogy, Freud's approach was, for them, too similar to surgery—the medical doctor operates on the
unconscious patient, while Doctor Freud operates on the patient's unconscious—and a number of psychoanalysts believed that not all individuals in distress were suffering from diseases requiring such major surgery. So they decided
to create various alternate approaches, which were less like surgery and perhaps

more analogous to physiotherapy, that came to be called psychotherapy. Some psychotherapists took a philosophical approach and labeled their specific methods with names such as Existential therapy, Cognitive therapy, Logo therapy, and Rational Emotive Behavior Therapy (REBT). While all this was going on most philosophers, watching from their academic retreats, simply sat back and allowed the practice of philosophy to be taught by psychotherapists to their students in clinical and counseling psychology, many of whom had little or no education in philosophy.[23] This is still the state of affairs today. The practice of philosophy, which is most helpful to individuals in sorting out the complexities of their lives, and resembles most clearly the ancient conception of a beneficial philosophical practice, is now the property of counseling psychology departments.[24]

Socrates insisted that understanding the human self and improving the human condition ought to be the goal of practice in philosophy, but with the advent of psychotherapy academic philosophers gave away to psychotherapists the very heart of philosophical practice when they allowed psychotherapists to claim it as their own. Academic philosophy has put today's philosophical counselors into the unenviable situation of having to explain why they propose to do what psychotherapists are already doing. The competitive academic environment which has mutated philosophy into a "blood sport"[25] has forced philosophers to stick to the academy's principles: examine the human condition only in abstraction, and claim to be midwives but keep your intellectual pursuits removed from participation in practical things and the particulars of human life. In his 1942 introductory address at the Conference for Psychology in Zurich, Switzerland, psychoanalyst Carl G. Jung saw academic philosophy as an outright embarrassment to psychotherapists. He told his audience,

I can hardly draw a veil over the fact that we psychotherapists ought really to be philosophers or philosophic doctors—or rather that we already are so, though we are unwilling to admit it because of the glaring contrast between our work and what passes for philosophy in the universities.[26]

The low point for philosophy must surely have been the logical positivism fad, when symbolic logic was invented to serve as an infallible mathematical language for arriving at the 'Truth,' when morality was considered a nondiscussible issue, and when the practice of philosophy consisted of having students answer questions like, "When applying the rule 'universal introduction' why can we not substitute the variable that is bound by the new universal quantifier for a constant that occurs in an undischarged assumption?"[27] How does the answer to this question correlate with the betterment of a human life? Is this any better than asking how many angels can dance on the head of a pin? If philosophy is supposed to be the attempt to further our understanding *in order to improve the human condition* then much of what transpires in academic philosophy departments today should not be called philosophy.

What is worse than philosophy being reduced to a meaningless shuffling of symbols is philosophers themselves portraying the practice of philosophy as walk-

ing *alone* and thinking *alone*, and characterizing the philosopher as a reflective individual whose need for *solitude* in practicing philosophy brings him to *separate*
himself from others into a "peculiar *isolation*."[28] But to claim that philosophers
function alone, either intellectually or emotionally, is an arrogant male fantasy.
Real life has a wonderful way of intruding upon philosophy. Spouses and children
and siblings and colleagues and lovers and the butcher, the baker, and the candle-
stick maker all have a way of influencing even the most abstract notions within the
philosopher's supposedly solitary contemplations. In the words of anthropologist
Clifford Geertz, "Human thought is consummately social: social in its origins, social in its function, social in its forms, social in its applications."[29]

Perhaps even worse than the portrayal of the philosopher as acting alone is the
ironic tendency of some academic philosophers themselves to trivialize a philosopher's expertise. For example, Gadamer, who is described by his publicist as "one
of the leading philosophers of the twentieth century,"[30] says that philosophy "must
be seen as a natural propensity within us all rather than some sort of professional
skill or ability."[31] Isn't this like saying the practice of law or medicine must be seen
as a natural propensity within us all rather than some sort of professional skill or
ability? Taken to its logical (and absurd) conclusion this means that individuals
who have spent many years enduring the expense and hardships of academic study
in order to achieve a prestigious postgraduate degree in philosophy (Gadamer himself is professor emeritus of philosophy) have simply wasted their time since they
have gained nothing beyond that "natural propensity" which is already within us
all.

But then it is understandable why philosophers are themselves often reluctant to
claim that they have any sort of professional skill or ability, especially in a practical sense. After all, a philosophy degree has no practicum requirement. Philosophy
as practiced in academia has been reduced to teaching, to publishing books, and to
providing articles for peer-reviewed journals that fail to offer any kind of remuner-
ation to their contributors. Furthermore, many of those books and articles are co-
gently argued but unbelievably trivial in content.[32] Contemporary philosophical
writings in the "publish or perish" academic environment are largely abstractions,
presented in an almost incomprehensibly affected style, containing innumerable
references to obscure papers and volumes, and resulting in self-referential conclusions completely removed from the most basic realities of life. Too many good
philosophers have spent too much time and too many words discussing too many
issues that have too little relevance to too few human lives. Philosophy departments offer their students courses in logic, metaphysics, epistemology, the philosophy of religion, and so on but nothing on the philosophy of human relations. In
fact, mainstream academic philosophy has effectively ignored half the human population: women.[33] Philosophy has also become so specialized that much of what is
done by philosophers is irrelevant even to other philosophers.[34] Academic philosophers find themselves forced to perpetuate the myth that they are engaged in 'the
pursuit of Truth,' 'pure philosophy' or 'knowledge for its own sake,' overlooking
the fact that in ancient times 'the pursuit of Truth' referred primarily to *natural*
philosophy (science), and concealing the fact that 'pure philosophy' and 'knowl-

edge for its own sake' are simply euphemisms for 'uselessness' when looked at from a practical perspective.

By giving away everything that is practical and useful, philosophers have necessarily become enchanted with pretentious pseudo-problems. They have busied themselves with diminishing the issues of everyday life into abstract academic absurdities in which theoretical persons achieve ideal moral objectivity while standing behind hypothetical curtains, and the philosopher is never himself at risk in the ubiquitous "lifeboat dilemma" or "desert island" predicament. Philosophy in the classroom does not consist in helping students come to a better understanding of themselves—that is largely left to counseling psychology departments. Philosophy in the classroom consists of helping philosophy students become better philosophy students. There never was, and never will be, therapy for the soul in a philosophy classroom, because the students' personal struggles with life are defined as irrelevant to academic disputation and scholastic achievement.

If Socrates were to visit us today he might conclude that philosophy has saved the Western world. For the most part we no longer live according to unreasonable religious dogma, unjustified cultural and political traditions, and unexamined personal habits. But if Socrates were to visit an academic philosophy department he would see that philosophy has done poorly at saving itself. Academic philosophy is devoid of both practice and experimentation; it is merely the process of teaching and learning academic process, even in so-called applied courses. Socrates would wonder where interpersonal philosophical practice is to be found if not in colleges and universities. Until the advent of philosophical counseling, interpersonal philosophical practice was not found anywhere.

But American pragmatist philosopher Nicholas Rescher warns that we should not belittle intellectual pursuits. Rescher argues that while skeptics from antiquity have always said,

forget about those abstruse theoretical issues; focus on your practical needs, they overlook the crucial fact that an intellectual accommodation to the world is itself one of our deepest practical needs—that in a position of ignorance or cognitive dissonance we cannot function satisfactorily. We are creatures for whom intellectual comfort is no less crucial than physical comfort.[35]

Philosophical counseling offers the kind of "intellectual accommodation to the world" and "intellectual comfort" that Rescher is talking about, without holding mere intellectualization as all there is to the practice of philosophy. This intellectualization is all that philosophy is as it is practiced in most contemporary academic philosophy departments, and that is what is wrong with philosophy. Philosophical counseling is the regenerated practical arm of philosophy that was amputated by academics.

If Socrates were to visit a philosophical counselor today he would notice that it is philosophical counseling that is saving the practice of philosophy. While Socrates would see that teaching is sometimes part of the counseling process, he would also witness the fact that philosophy is being practiced as he portrayed it with his analogy to the practice of medicine: he would see a cooperative search between two individuals for an improved condition. And if Socrates were to consult a philosophical counselor today concerning the war of principles in which he was engaged with the state of Athens, he might find himself being gently invited to reconsider whether the principle he holds so dear—that an unexamined life is not worth living—is in fact true, and more importantly, that it is worth dying for. In this way the practice of philosophy might help to save the man.[36]

NOTES

1. I would include the growing phenomenon of the philosophy cafés as a recent development of philosophical practice, but for the sake of clarity and focus I will not discuss them in this chapter. For a discussion of the similarities and differences between philosophical counseling and philosophy cafés see chapter 5 in this volume entitled "Counseling and the Café."

2. *The Epicurus Reader.* Brad Inwood and L. P. Gerson, trans. Cambridge: Hackett, 1994. 99.

3. Ibid., section 48.

4. See Dewey, John. *Reconstruction in Philosophy.* (1920) Boston: Beacon Press, 1957. 126.

5. Navia, Luis E. *The Adventure of Philosophy.* Westport, Conn.: Praeger, 1999. 55.

6. Plato. *Apology.* 38a. Clitophon says Socrates believes, "someone who doesn't know how to use his soul is better off putting his soul to rest and not living at all." *Clitophon* 408b in *Plato: Complete Works.* John M. Cooper and D. S. Hutchison, eds. Indianapolis: Hackett, 1997.

7. This is a charitable interpretation. A more cynical view would be that he simply didn't care how his death affected others.

8. Wittgenstein, Ludwig. *Philosophical Investigations.* G.E.M. Anscombe, trans. Oxford: Blackwell, 1958. 124.

9. Plato. *Theaetetus.* 173d–177b.

10. Plato. *Phaedo.* 61a.

11. Ibid., 149 sq.

12. In Plato's dialogue titled "Clitophon" Clitophon exhibits similar concerns when he asks Socrates, "Will this be our life-long work, simply to convert to the pursuit of virtues those who have not yet been converted so that they in turn may convert others?" (*Plato: Complete Works.* John M. Cooper and D. S. Hutchison, eds. Indianapolis: Hackett, 1997. 968). In his book *Philosophy as a Way of Life* Pierre Hadot criticizes university philosophy as being made up of professors who train professors, professionals training professionals, and specialists training other specialists. He also quotes Schopenhauer as saying, "Generally speaking, university philosophy is mere fencing in front of a mirror." (Oxford: Blackwell, 1995. 270–271).

13. The essay is from the Miami University philosophy department web sites at http://www.muohio.edu/~phlcwis/jobs.html.

14. Rorty, Amelie Oksenberg. "Socrates and Sophia Perform the Philosophic Turn." *The Institution of Philosophy.* Avner Cohen and Marcelo Dascal, eds. La Salle, Ill.: Open Court, 1989. 271.

15. Ibid., 275.

16. Shusterman, Richard. *Practicing Philosophy.* New York: Routledge, 1997. 212n.

17. Ibid., 25.

18. Ibid., 2, 3.

19. Rorty, Richard. *Contingency, Irony, and Solidarity.* Cambridge: Cambridge University Press, 1989.

20. Russell, Bertrand. *The Problems of Philosophy* (1912). London: Allen and Unwin, 1966. Chapter XV, "The Value of Philosophy."

21. Russell, Bertrand. *Our Knowledge of the External World* (1914). New York: Routledge, 1993. 36.

22. *The Epicurus Reader.* 98.

23. For a more detailed discussion of the relationship between philosophy and psychotherapy please see my book *Philosophical Counseling: Theory and Practice.* Westport, Conn.: Praeger, 2001.

24. The rehabilitative critical/creative thinking program in the prisons of British Columbia is administered by psychologists.

25. See Norman Swartz's essay "Philosophy as a Blood Sport" on the Internet at http://www.sfu.ca/philosophy/swartz/blood_sport.htm. See also *The Oxford Companion to Philosophy* which defines philosophy as follows: "Philosophy is a collaborative pursuit. . . . The form of the collaboration involved, though, is not cooperative, like that of a surgical team, but competitive, a business of critical argument" (Oxford: Oxford University Press, 1995. 670).

26. Jung, Carl G. "Psychotherapy and a Philosophy of Life." In *Essays on Contemporary Events.* R.F.C. Hull, trans. Princeton, N.J.: Princeton University Press, 1989. 45.

27. This comes from an actual Philosophy 220 examination.

28. Gadamer, Hans-Georg. *The Enigma of Health.* Stanford, Calif.: Stanford University Press, 1996. 93. Italics added for emphasis.

29. Geertz, Clifford. *The Interpretation of Cultures.* New York: Basic Books, 1973. 360.

30. Gadamer, back cover.

31. Ibid., 93.

32. On close inspection even highly regarded works such as Immanuel Kant's gigantic *Groundwork of the Metaphysics of Morals* and John Rawls' huge *A Theory of Justice* (Cambridge, Mass.: Harvard University Press, 1971) offer little more than a secularization of ancient religious principles and a repackaging of commonsense fairness.

33. Crimshaw, Jean. *Philosophy and Feminist Thinking.* Minneapolis: University of Minnesota Press, 1993. 2.

34. For a discussion of what some philosophers are doing to offset the perceived uselessness of contemporary philosophy see Michael Lopez's article "Philosophy Going Mainstream" first published on December 1, 1989 in the *Times Union* and republished online as "Philosophical Differences" at http://www.TimesUnion.com.

35. *The Strife of Systems: An Essay on the Grounds and Implications of Philosophical Diversity.* 160. Quoted in *A Dictionary of Philosophical Quotations.* A. J. Ayer and Jane O'Grady, eds. Oxford, U.K.: Blackwell, 1994. 376.

36. Not surprisingly, this paper created quite a backlash from a number of academic philosophers when parts of it were published in a newspaper and on a university web site. Not only did those disgruntled scholars take issue with the arguments made in the paper, some of them also posted vicious personal attacks on me on public e-mail discussion lists questioning the legitimacy of my academic credentials. The following messages were sent by individuals defending me against these personal attacks. They were received in the form of

private e-mail correspondence. I have changed the signatures of the correspondents out of respect for their privacy.

Dear Dr. Raabe,

I just wanted to write a quick note to let you know how much I appreciate what you said. I am writing in private, not on the forum because, alas, I see the forum also taking part too often in "academic" philosophy and I have grown weary of quibbling. I was beginning to think that I was the only person who was dismayed at how far philosophy has strayed into 'intellectual masturbation'. Reading some of the abstracts & papers that the A.P.A. [American Philosophical Association] and other journals print I have often wondered what practical application they have to the general public. In any case I am usually too busy to write responses but I felt I just had to make time to let you know—not that it matters to you. I hope one day we might meet at some conference or symposium. Just in case you are wondering, I teach medical ethics, and my thesis was on the ethical & social implications of psychiatric ideology.
A. B. Ph.D.

Peter:

I just read your presentation on the U of Alberta website and could not agree with you more. One can carry it one step further. Many philosophers who have chosen to apply philosophy in the form of bioethics continue with the same mistake, of dealing with abstract issues to the detriment of real life suffering. One example of this is on issues of autonomy where endless debates around such issues as assisting suicide, telling the full truth even where that will be detrimental, etc. continue to whirl. Without passing judgement on the merits of any particular position, my point is that many of these arguments are abstractions from principles (that often compete with other principles) that do not help (and may harm) individual patients. This is not directly related to philosophic counseling, but it relates to the issue of pure academic thinking, regardless of consequences vs. considering the broader canvas of how this may impact patients' lives.
Y. Z. MD

Chapter 2

Philosophical Counseling
in Brief

In the eighteenth century the German philosopher Immanuel Kant wrote a very long and difficult to digest 600-page book titled *Critique of Pure Reason*.[1] Two years later Kant felt obligated to write another, but relatively shorter, book (only 250 pages) in which he tried to explain what it was he had tried to explain in his previous book. And, of course, he believed it deserved a much longer title: *Prolegomena to Any Future Metaphysics That Can Qualify as a Science*. Twentieth-century philosopher Paul Carus translated Kant's *Prolegomena* from the original German into English. In his explanatory essay on the meaning and significance of Kant's profuse philosophizing Carus begins with the following words:

Philosophy is frequently regarded as idle verbiage; and the great mass of the average productions of this branch of human endeavor would seem to justify the statement. . . . While philosophical books, essays, lectures, and lessons may be intricate and long-winded, there is at the core of all the questions under discussion a public interest of a practical nature.[2]

The problem, as every scholar who has ever read any philosophy knows, is the difficulty of finding even the tiniest core of practical information that might be useful to real life in the pleonastic minutia contained within that moldering mountain of abstract, abstruse, analytical, and absurdly long-winded books, essays, and lecture papers. Academic philosophy, as it has been conducted in the West from the Middle Ages until the end of the twentieth century, has not in fact been overly concerned with providing clear and easily comprehended practical wisdom. Philosophical counseling, on the other hand, goes directly to the heart of philosophical issues and concerns that are not only of general public interest but also of personal relevance and significance to a particular individual. Philosophical counseling offers both the best available theoretical information and the most practical approaches to nonacademic problems to individuals searching for relief from the difficulties of their own real-life situations.

Many essays have been written about philosophical counseling in the last two decades, and recently a number of books have been published on the topic, but the information in them has often been contradictory and seemingly mutually exclusive. The following questions still remain: What exactly is philosophical counseling? How does philosophical counseling compare with other forms of philosophy and other types of counseling? and, What should a general theory of philosophical counseling include? I therefore offer the following, nonexhaustive summary of what philosophical counseling *is not* and what it is.

- *Philosophical counseling is not academic philosophy.* It is not a systematic analytic examination or discussion of the historical roots and development of metaphysical, epistemological, ethical, religious, or political thought. It is not the practice of "pure" philosophy; it is not simply "thinking about thinking"; it is not concerned with academic philosophy's stereotypical and hopelessly ambiguous 'love of wisdom,' nor is it engaged in the 'pursuit of Truth' (natural philosophy or science); it does not take the stance of a detached observer; it is not removed from social and cultural contexts; and it does not focus on the examination of the contents of primary source texts (exegesis) and their "correct" interpretation (hermeneutics). It does not approach philosophical texts as literary studies, but rather uses texts as a source of diverse perspectives on various issues; and yet it is not merely the application of wisdom gleaned from ancient texts. Philosophical counseling is the practice of *being* philosophical, of utilizing various methods of philosophical inquiry to help others to *develop* wisdom in their approach to issues and problems. It does not exercise the competitive approach so prevalent in academia (dialectical dismantling), nor is it merely critical (deconstruction). It is both actively constructive and proactive. And yet it does not replace academic philosophy; instead it instantiates what has been learned in the classroom. Philosophical counseling is a collaborative, creative (maieutic) dialogue between two individuals—one of whom (the counselor) has been extensively trained in both the history and the practice of philosophy, and another (the client) who wishes to draw on this expertise—whose goal is to improve the life of the client.

- *Philosophical counseling is not teaching.* It is not concerned with having people learn the history of philosophy. Yet it can and does involve teaching at times. Unlike teaching in a classroom, philosophical counseling does not primarily concern the direct (didactic) transmission of knowledge from an expert to a novice, or from the 'knower' to the one seeking knowledge. But at times a client does want to learn from the philosophical counselor such things as critical and creative thinking skills, what famous philosophers have said on various issues, how to make an ethical decision, and so on. Philosophical counseling becomes teaching (pedagogy) when the client asks to learn due to a personal *Entwicklungsdrang* (literally, the urge to develop), and when the counseling relationship is intentionally focused on the exchange of information and abilities. And it teaches both client and counselor at that extraordinary moment when their combined thinking creates an original insight (dialectical synthesis).

- *Philosophical counseling is not applied philosophy.* Applied philosophy is a largely academic endeavor involving the insertion of preconceptualized formulas, recipes, and principles for correct thought and action into hypothetical, and predominantly moral, di-lemmas. Philosophical counseling is an activity or process that develops meaningful and useful insights and puts those insights to use in significant real-life issues in order to alle-viate suffering, distress, and confusion. It is the agreed-upon cooperation between two individuals (or sometimes a number of individuals in a group) to establish an investiga-tive atmosphere which is meant, in one stage of the process, to lead to the resolution of immediate personal problems and concerns.[3]

- *A philosophical counselor is not a consultant philosopher.* Consultant philosophers typ-ically work in the world of commerce, industry, and government, whether it is with profit-oriented corporations or nonprofit institutions such as schools and hospitals. While the aim of consultant philosophers is to help a business or institution establish op-erating parameters in the form of a mission statement, a code of ethics, or a situational precedent, philosophical counselors are concerned with relieving, and preventing the re-currence of, the personal and often very private confusion and problems of individual clients. And while consultant philosophers can often handle a client's concerns monologically, philosophical counseling is always a dialogical endeavor between at least two individuals.

- *Philosophical counseling in group is not a philosophy café.* A philosophy café is not meant to be therapeutic, while philosophical counseling is. The purpose of a discussion within a philosophy café is for the participants to come to a greater understanding of the many elements within any one issue or topic. While it is an exchange of ideas for per-sonal edification, discussion in a philosophy café is not necessarily aimed at coming to a definitive conclusion, and it is never intended to solve the personal problems of individ-ual participants, although it may. A philosophical counseling group, on the other hand, is in fact focused on resolving some problem. A philosophical counseling group is en-gaged in a discussion that will help individuals gain new perspectives and insights into their own personal issues of concern, develop a course of thinking and acting, and hope-fully end the suffering those issues have caused. The philosophy café is always focused on the single issue under discussion rather than on individual participants, while the philosophical counseling group is equally focused on both the many issues raised by the group and on the welfare of the attendant individuals.

- *Philosophical counseling is not therapy.* It is not therapy in the medical sense in that there is no scrutiny of the sufferer's mental condition by a professional diagnostician, no labeling of neurobiological diseases of the brain or psychological syndromes of the mind according to some treatment manual, and no administration of a predetermined curative treatment. In other words, any informal evaluation of a problem that may occur in philo-sophical counseling transpires outside the scientific paradigm of the diagnosing of neurobiological illnesses and their predetermined cure. Philosophical counseling does not pathologize interpersonal conflicts and moral dilemmas. It does not define extraordi-nary people as abnormal nor does it define ordinary people as sick, damaged, abused, or traumatized after having endured extraordinary experiences.[4] Philosophical counseling emphasizes the individual's strength and the present, not supposed weaknesses and the past. There is no demand that the client contractually commit to a predetermined time span or minimum number of sessions with the counselor.[5] While philosophical counsel-ing does not consider symptomatic relief its goal, it can be rehabilitative, and clearly therapeutic in its effect.

- *Philosophical counseling is not psychotherapy.* It does not assume that a person is, as Carl Jung put it, "a prisoner of the unconscious."[6] It sees human beings as capable of making moral choices that override so-called unconscious desires. Philosophical counselors do not pretend to understand the unconscious (if such a thing exists) or to be able to interpret it, and therefore to know people better than they know themselves. Philosophical counseling does not define the client as a patient with a mental illness, nor as a person whose adult life has been predetermined by deeply buried childhood experiences.[7] It does not interpret thoughts or feelings as symptoms. It does not assume that all anxiety, depression, distress, and confusion are manifest symptoms of some abnormality in the brain, or an unfulfilled sexual fantasy hidden in the mind. While psychotherapy "essentially . . . endeavors to understand and change the emotional forces within an individual,"[8] philosophical counselors recognize that anxiety, depression, and other emotional states are absolutely appropriate—as well as reasonable and rational—reactions to various significant life situations. Philosophical counselors realize that, while medication may at times be helpful, not all negative emotional states are the result of internal causes (endogenous aetiology) that necessarily require pharmaceutical or psychoanalytic intervention, but that there are often external forces (exogenous reasons) for an individual's distress—such as a hostile political climate manifested in familial or sociocultural limitations to personal freedom, poverty, racism, sexism, homophobia, bigotry, and so on—for which the most appropriate philosophical discussion is aimed at determining both survival strategies and corrective political action. While philosophical counseling is informed by psychological theories and clinical discoveries, it is not concerned with making the unconscious conscious, with the revelation of forbidden childhood wishes, with transference or counter-transference, with projection or introjection, with resistance or denial, with regression or repression, with reading meaning into free associations (mind reading), or with treating so-called irrational and hidden intrapsychic conflict. It does not attempt to analyze, as Freud so famously put it, the "psychopathology of everyday life."[9] Philosophical counselors are not restricted to following any particular school or method; philosophical inquiry is generally much broader in scope than psychotherapy. And philosophical counselors do not consider themselves the omniscient experts on whom clients must remain perpetually intellectually and emotionally dependent. Instead, philosophical counselors offer to teach their clients those philosophical abilities and dispositions that will help them avoid or prevent problems in the future.

- *Philosophical counseling is not a scientific endeavor.* It is not concerned with empirically evaluating competing hypotheses about the human condition, whether organic or psychological, or with phenomenologically classifying symptoms, or with detecting or observing diseases, or with objectively measuring abnormalities, nor with cataloguing naturalistic causes, or with formulating recipes meant to standardize diagnosing, prognostication, or treatment (algorithmic strategies). Neither does it construct theories about the human condition, human thinking, or human behavior from the hypotheses of the social sciences and then generalize from one client to all others; nor does it simply apply given universal theories to an individual. Philosophical counseling is philosophic in nature. It questions theories—especially those concerning human individuals—and their generalizability. It is a unique hermeneutic of each individual, a shared and reciprocal critical and creative inquiry into the life problems specific to a given person. It is a joint attempt to come to a better understanding of the issues involved in that problem (heuristic), and a cooperative search for its resolution on both an intellectual (cognitive) and emotional (affective) level. In this sense, while not strictly scientific, philosophical counseling is nevertheless experimental.

- *Philosophical counseling is not religious or New Age.* Philosophical counselors do not promote any particular religion or spirituality as 'The Truth'; they are not concerned with teaching their clients what to believe, and do not advocate any belief system as the right one. Rather than making the sort of authoritative truth claims typical of the modernist practice of the behavioral sciences, philosophical counseling takes a more postmodern approach in that, as philosopher Pauline Rosenau said, it "affirms the gentler practices of listening, questioning, and speaking."[10] Philosophical counselors are generally eclectic in their approach, rarely focusing on one philosopher or philosophic system as the exclusive source of insight and information. Philosophical counselors do not promote the resolution of human problems by means of supernatural or occult practices. They do not rely on divine revelation or channeling dead Masters as legitimate epistemic endeavors within a counseling session, nor do they consider any of the psychic approaches (such as astrology, reading tarot cards, tea leaves, auras, or palm lines, numerology, alchemy, crystals, pyramids, Runes, ceremonial magic, exorcism, past life regression, or gazing at a crystal ball) as significantly reliable and efficacious means of client counseling. But philosophical counseling can and often does include an examination of the relationship between the client's religious or spiritual beliefs and his secular worldview (which also consists of beliefs and values) in order to help the client resolve or avoid problems that may arise when beliefs conflict with the demands of life.

* *Philosophical counseling is not a casual conversation.* It is not the sort of spontaneous discussion a person might have with a friend. It is polemical in that it is a critical inquiry into existing modes of thinking and so-called common sense. It is a focused dialogical exchange between a trained and highly educated philosopher and a client, a deeply thoughtful and respectful discourse which always has as its guiding premise both the improvement of the client's personal condition and the betterment of his life. It is therefore a catalyst for individual development, a venue for social criticism with social emancipatory potential. Although a philosophical counseling dialogue may not contain the jargon or the combative verbal attacks typically found in an academic encounter, the counselor's philosophic background is always present, subtly generating each question and informing every exploration.

It is important to note that philosophical counseling does not dismiss all talk of mental illness as unfounded or nonsensical. It is equally important to understand that "mental illness" is a generic term which I believe refers to at least three very different kinds of causal factors: (1) endogenous causes, internally produced by neurological malfunctions, congenital defects, disease, environmental toxins, serious injury, or abuse of drugs which prevent normal cognitive and affective (thinking and feeling) functioning; (2) severe exogenous causes, externally produced by factors such as child abuse, traumatic experiences, and prolonged stress which interfere with normal living by producing anxiety, depression, and so on, and which, if unaltered over a long period of time, can result in permanent "ruts" in neural pathways causing obsessive and antisocial behavior; and (3) the distress and confusion suffered as a result of unresolved everyday life problems and concerns which may be bettered termed "reasons" than "causes." (See Figure 2.1.)

Philosophical counseling is not at all appropriate for individuals suffering from the sort of mental illness described in 1. Individuals in this category may be incapable of rational thinking and discussion at an adult level, and may require long-term institutional care and extensive pharmacological intervention just to function. Obviously, individuals who are said to have mental illness of the sort described in 3 are well suited for philosophical counseling and may benefit substantially from it, sometimes even from a minimal number of sessions. It is the

Figure 2.1
Illustrative Ratio of Kinds of Mental Illnesses

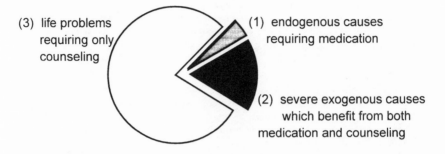

(3) life problems requiring only counseling

(1) endogenous causes requiring medication

(2) severe exogenous causes which benefit from both medication and counseling

individuals in category 2 over which there is presently a great deal of disagreement and controversy. Psychotherapists are often too ready to diagnose the person who has been suffering from exogenous stressors as being in category 1. Medication is frequently prescribed to treat a supposedly classifiable mental disorder before an effort has been made to inquire into possible reasons for this person's distress (more will be said about medication in chapters 11 and 12). The so-called symptoms exhibited by the client's thought patterns and behavior are too readily taken to be evidence of the sort of malfunctioning brain found in category 1. In fact even individuals in category 3 who are merely struggling with everyday problems can sometimes find themselves medicated before they are adequately listened to.

For the philosophical counselor a client in category 2 can present a very demanding challenge. For example, while many individuals who suffered from poor parenting as children will have grown into completely normal adults, others will have developed the problems associated with what psychotherapists diagnose as schizophrenia.[11] Some individuals in this category may be quite able to carry on a rational discussion. Others will be able to do so only when they are taking carefully regulated prescription medication as part of their daily routine. Philosophical counseling can complement the existing drug therapy for this sort of client. Other individuals in category 2 may appear to be rational in the early stages of counseling, but they may later come to exhibit problematic behavior, such as repetitive dialogue, an inability to focus on topic and concentrate on the counseling discussion, random and bizarre thought patterns, incoherent and rambling utterances, an inability to think and speak logically, and so on, which may be medication-induced or the result of abnormally patterned thinking "ruts" in the neural pathways. This type of client may receive no benefit whatsoever from philosophical counseling since the intellectual and affective responses conducive to a meaningful and beneficial philosophical dialogue are not available to them. The philosophical counselor must consider carefully whether accepting a person perceived to be in category 2 as a client, and taking payment from him for counseling, is in fact ethically justified. This is not an easy task considering the scarcity of discussion and information about mental illness in the current philosophical counseling literature.

The philosophical counselor often deals with individuals who are dissatisfied with other forms of counseling they have had. She sees individuals whose minds are sound but whose thinking is confused or obstructed. The philosophical counselor understands that most individuals live by many forgotten and often unexamined (rather than unconscious) assumptions and values that can affect thinking and behavior in puzzling or distressing ways. She also sees a person's thinking as being informed by childhood memories and experiences but not determined by them. Through a series of dialogues the philosophical counselor helps the client become aware of hidden biases, unspoken assumptions, and conflicting values which may be preventing an inquiry into alternative perspectives that could help ease the problem. But the philosophical counselor's aim is not simply to resolve a client's immediate problem and then send him on his way. The philosophical counselor also offers to educate the client in more effective ways of thinking so that if this type of problem arises again the client will be better able to deal with it on his own.

Granted, cognitive approaches in psychotherapy, such as Rational Emotive Behavior Therapy (REBT), Logotherapy, and existential psychotherapy, seem to already be doing some of the philosophical work philosophical counseling claims to do. But these approaches were developed in the 1950s when psychotherapists were the only ones interested in applying philosophy to counseling and willing to work with a nonacademic population on nonhypothetical (real life) problems. Today there are a growing number of philosophers willing and able to work with ordinary people.

It is generally agreed that to become a *philosophical* counselor it is necessary to have achieved at least a Master's degree in philosophy. The philosophical counselor will thereby be far more competent in discussing existential, ethical, political, and logical problems than counselors and therapists trained primarily in psychology. To undertake such an exploration, a few philosophical counselors prefer to use the reasoning of a single philosopher or philosophical system. Most, however, take a more eclectic approach, knowing that specialization in one area of philosophy restricts a counselor's effectiveness when his client's needs or concerns shift over time. The key to philosophical counseling generally is its client-centered and open-ended nature, one which does not manipulate the client's thinking so as to bring him to accept some particular philosophy as 'The Truth.' The philosophical counselor's intention is to help his client reach any reasonable and morally permissible goal the client has set for himself.

Apart from being of great help to the average person, philosophical counseling can also be of immense value to professional psychotherapists. After all, philosophy is the foundation from which all other fields of thought were developed. Philosophy is not simply the transmission of a body of knowledge; it is the activity of constantly broadening and deepening one's understanding by means of thinking and discussion. The term "philosophical counseling" may therefore be correctly interpreted as either the name of a discrete practice with formal credentials or as the abilities and disposition underlying other counseling methodologies. Philosophers have an extraordinarily rich repertoire of theoretical perspectives at their disposals, and are especially adept at seeing not only the problems in a client's reasoning but the implications and assumptions behind the theories guiding all of the various psychological therapies. The philosophical counselor is therefore well prepared to facilitate an inquiry into both the content and the process of reasoning which may have resulted in either personal or professional difficulties for the psychotherapist.

Socrates' personal belief that the unexamined life is not worth living is, for people who are happy with their lives, an extreme exaggeration (like saying a life without music is not worth living). But it is certainly true that the examination of a *troubled* life by means of philosophical counseling can lead to living a better life. And while most philosophical counselors will admit that a philosophical examination of a life is not an exact science, many counseling encounters contain an element common to scientific research: experimentation.

NOTES

1. Kant, Immanuel. *Critique of Pure Reason* (1781). Norman Kemp Smith, trans. New York: St. Martin's, 1965.

2. Kant, Immanuel. *Prolegomena to Any Future Metaphysics That Can Qualify as a Science* (1783). Paul Carus, trans. Chicago: Open Court, 1993.

3. A detailed discussion of the four stages in philosophical counseling, and a more in-depth discussion of what philosophical counseling is, can be found in my book *Philosophical Counseling: Theory and Practice* (Westport, Conn.: Praeger, 2001).

4. Some of the points in this section are adapted from Tana Dineen's book *Manufacturing Victims.* Montreal: Robert Davies Publishing, 1996.

5. For an indication of the typical scope of treatment expected to be received by patients of psychiatrists and psychoanalysts it is instructive to examine what Horst Kächele and Rainer Richter present (in their essay "Germany and Austria" in *The Challenge to Psychoanalysis and Psychotherapy.* London: Jessica Kingsley Publishers, 1999. 53) as the payment schedule agreed upon by the German medical insurance system: (1) Initial interview and evaluation—up to 6 sessions; (2) Psychodynamic short-term therapy—up to 25 sessions; (3) Psychodynamic middle-term therapy—up to 50 sessions; (4) Psychodynamic long-term therapy—up to 80 sessions; (5) Psychoanalytic therapy—up to 300 sessions.

6. Jung, Carl G. "Psychotherapy and a Philosophy of Life." In *Essays on Contemporary Events.* R.F.C. Hull, trans. Princeton, N.J.: Princeton University Press, 1989. 45.

7. Although not a philosophical counselor, Professor of Pediatrics and Psychiatry Michael Lewis argues convincingly that childhood experiences neither determine who we become nor limit what we are able to do in his book *Altering Fate: Why the Past Does Not Predict the Future.* New York: Guilford Press, 1997.

8. Schill, Stefan de. *Crucial Choices—Crucial Changes: The Resurrection of Psychotherapy.* Amherst, N.Y.: Prometheus Books, 2000. 85.

9. See Sigmund Freud's "Psychopathology of Everyday Life" (1904). In *The Basic Writings of Sigmund Freud.* A. A. Brill, trans. and ed. New York: The Modern Library, 1995.

10. Rosenau, Pauline Marie. *Post-Modernism and the Social Sciences.* Princeton, N.J.: Princeton University Press, 1992. 90.

11. The question of what causes schizophrenia is still a very contentious issue. It is currently fashionable to hold that it is a neurobiological disorder. This justifies pharmaceutical treatments but ignores evidence to the contrary.

Chapter 3

Experimental Philosophy

Philosophical counseling is necessarily experimental philosophy. The idea of experimental philosophy is an exciting notion which conjures up the image of an archetypal philosopher with his white beard brushing thick books, stirring simmering words, and measuring quicksilver premises like an alchemist distilling the wisdom of the ages into a dram of 'Truth.' Unfortunately, there is no experimental philosophy in academia. The word "experiment" signifies some form of practical, empirical activity that adjudicates among competing hypotheses; philosophy in academia has been diminished to the realm of pure intellectual speculation. This is not to say that scientific experimentation has no intellectual aspect. A scientific experiment always begins with a reasoned supposition, a hypothesis, and then proceeds from there, by means of an empirical test, to its verification or falsification. Academic philosophy, on the other hand, begins and ends in abstract hypothesizing; conceptualized realities rest on a priori (without reference to experience) conclusions which are never tested empirically to determine their veracity or workability in real-life applications.

Experimentation was the enlightenment (or modernist) philosopher's answer to the question of how to arrive at epistemic certainty, and from this the field of natural philosophy—later known as science—emerged to separate itself from the purely rationalistic method of philosophy.[1] Empirical science—which has come to include everything from physics (natural science) to psychology (social science)—was held to be the best means for determining the 'Truth' about the world and for advancing from this a posteriori (based on experience) arguments with the causal power to change the world and the people in it. So-called pure philosophy came to be referred to as "armchair philosophizing" and "mental gymnastics" be-

cause it left the rolled-up-sleeves approach of the examination of real-world matters to others, and concerned itself almost exclusively with devising grand
theoretical systems of little or no practical usefulness. Eighteenth-century German
philosopher Immanuel Kant is one of few philosophers to have actually used the
term "experimental philosophy." In his *Critique of Pure Reason* Kant spoke of experimental philosophy as being the final means for deciding a dispute and as the
practical experience which can remove misunderstanding from discussions. But
Kant did not claim that experimental philosophy was useful only in determining
the truth about concrete matters in the natural world, he maintained that moral philosophy ought to "present its principles, together with their practical consequences, one and all *in concreto* in what are at least possible experiences; and the
misunderstanding due to abstraction is thereby avoided."[2]

Twentieth-century American philosopher John Dewey wrote similarly,

Knowing, for the experimental sciences, means a certain kind of intelligently conducted doing; it ceases to be contemplative and becomes in a true sense practical. Now this implies
that philosophy, unless it is to undergo a complete break with the authorizing spirit of science, must also alter its nature. It must assume a practical nature; it must become operative
and experimental. . . . The change does not mean a lowering in dignity of philosophy from a
lofty plane to one of gross utilitarianism. It signifies that the prime function of philosophy is
that of rationalizing the *possibilities* of experience, especially collective human experience.[3]

Yet, despite the fact that both Kant and Dewey speak of experimentation in philosophy, they referred to "possible experiences" and the "possibilities of experience" which are not at all like the sort of concrete experiences encountered in the
empirical experimentation one would find in a scientific laboratory. What then
could it mean for philosophy to be experimental but not in the strict scientific sense
of that term? And why would philosophical counseling be *necessarily* experimental?

Experimentation in the empirical sciences involves a number of clearly defined
procedures which must be carefully followed for their conclusion to be, as Dewey
puts it, "in the authorizing spirit of science." Scientists generally agree that the essential ingredients of any experiment must include the following:

1. A verifiable (or falsifiable) hypothesis.
2. A sincere doubt in the experimenter's mind of the truth of that hypothesis.
3. A purpose to the experiment.
4. The method or design of the experiment.
5. The experimenter's act of choosing which objects or assumptions/beliefs to operate on.
6. The act by which the experimenter modifies those objects.
7. The object's reaction to the experimenter's act.
8. The recognition of the teaching of the experiment. What has been learned, or what con-
    clusion may be reached?[4]

It is generally accepted that the purpose of any experiment is discovery, but the discovery of what? To say experiments in science aim to "discover the truth" is as vague and unhelpful as saying that philosophy is 'the pursuit of Truth,' or worse, that the practice of philosophy is 'the love of wisdom.' Perhaps a better way to state it is to say that experimentation is meant to discover which out of a number of possible answers is or are the best to any one, or several, of a number of questions such as How? Why? When? or Where? Forensic science even tackles the question of Who?

Scientists structure and control their experiments very carefully not only out of the desire to discover which answer is the correct one out of a number of possible alternatives (the truth), but also out of fear. The fear inherent in all science is not the fear of simply being factually wrong but the fear of being in error and having that error result in terrible harm to fellow human beings. For example, most scientists would hold that it is simply not enough to hypothesize, argue, and reach a conclusion by means of intellectual discussion to determine what a safe level of X radiation might be for a human being. Scientists rightly insist on empirical evidence, that is, evidence by means of tests and experiments, to verify their a priori ratiocinations. Their experiments would include tracking the results of a number of tests on living nonhuman organisms such as mice, probably in a number of different laboratory locations, with a variety of dosages of X rays, and over an extended period of time, to ensure that the conclusions reached about safe dosages of X rays would be as close as humanly and statistically possible to certainty that there would be no harm to humans.

Philosophical counselors have similar fears. They do not fear that they will be merely factually wrong (miss 'the Truth') but rather that what has been agreed upon in a counseling session as the best approach to resolving a particular issue or concern may in fact turn out to cause terrible emotional or even physical harm to the client. The desire to avoid harm is the primary reason why practitioners generally approach philosophical counseling as *necessarily* experimental philosophy. A second reason is that, according to one of the defining postulates of philosophical counseling, the life experience of each individual client is unique, and therefore no solution to one client's problems can be wholly generalized or universalized to solve the problems of other clients. This means philosophical counseling cannot and does not offer predetermined or ready-made solutions to anyone. Each personal problem presented by the client calls for its own investigation into the reasons behind it, and each problem requires that the client actually try out in practice (experiment with) the various possible approaches to its alleviation as discussed in the counselor's office.

But the concept of experimental philosophy in philosophical counseling creates somewhat of an ambiguity. In both the natural science and the social science laboratories the word "experiment" suggests a test perpetrated upon a test subject by the experimenter—often at a substantial cost to the test subject (including its life) but without any direct benefit to that subject—for the sake of verifying the veracity of a particular hypothesis. This is the sense in which a typical scientific experiment is carried out on a laboratory mouse. But this is not how an experiment is carried out in philosophical counseling. After all, a client is not a mouse! Experimentation in philosophical counseling is always carried out by counselor and client working together to find out if a hypothetical approach to alleviating the client's actual problem will work in practice. The counselor suggests a number of interpretations in his understanding of the client's problem and asks the client to determine which one(s) seems to her to be the most correct. Then the counselor suggests various approaches to alleviating the problem and asks which one(s) the client believes will work the best. In this sense the counselor is conducting an experiment every time he asks which of the options discussed the client wishes to pursue, rather than simply dictating what the client ought to do. But the client will also be conducting experiments when she tests *in real-life situations* those approaches discussed in the counseling office in order to determine which is (or are) in fact the most effective, acceptable, and workable in alleviating her problem. These real-life experiments take what is done in philosophical counseling beyond the notoriously unresolvable hypothetical thought experiments so familiar to students of academic philosophy and in fact settle the question empirically as to which action or argument will exert the most causal power in the material world. And to be truly helpful to the client, experimentation in philosophical counseling always moves from being merely objective (viewing problems from an impersonal perspective) to being not subjective, but nonobjective (including oneself in the situation), and from being merely analytical (reductively critiquing the issues and concerns) to being constructive (inductively deciding on alternative ways of thinking or acting).

Saying that philosophical counseling is necessarily experimental philosophy obviously does not mean that it is the kind of experimentation in which an individual is wired up to computers and observed in a laboratory, nor does it mean that the experimentation is hit-or-miss or trial-and-error any more than experimentation in medical science or psychology is hit-or-miss or trial-and-error. The philosophical counselor always approaches the client and the client's problem with the utmost respect, and with both professional care and thoroughness. The counselor keeps an open mind; he offers to the client what he believes are the best hypotheses among the various available options without stating categorically and paternalistically that they just are the best.

For example, a client may say to the philosophical counselor, "Bill and I used to be really close friends. He would call me a couple of times a week. But he only called once after my accident, and he hasn't called in the three weeks since then. He's turned out to be a bad friend."

The counselor does *not* respond with an absolute statement like, "Bill is probably just busy with his own life, or he doesn't want to disturb you during your convalescence. So he's not a bad friend." This would be taking an authoritarian, and even paternalistic, approach since the counselor is saying, "You're wrong, and here's the correct interpretation of the situation. . . . " Instead, the counselor offers alternate possibilities as hypotheses to be tested by the client.

The counselor might say something like, "Do you think Bill might be just too busy with his own life at the moment?" In this way the counselor is experimenting by merely offering a possibility to the client which the client can then apply to what she knows about Bill to determine if this might be the case. The client's application of the possibility suggested by the counselor is itself an experiment. If the client answers, "Bill never mentioned being busy the last time we talked," the counselor might then ask, "Do you think he just wants to give you time to recover fully from the accident?" This question is then a second experiment testing another possibility. The counselor's questions are like the hypotheses used in empirical experiments—Hypothesis 1: Bill is busy; Hypothesis 2: Bill is giving you time to recover. Each hypothesis is the basis for a joint experiment conducted by the counselor and the client. This a priori experimentation will not only help the client come to a particular understanding of Bill's behavior, it will also help the client decide on a course of action: either (a) call Bill, or (b) wait for him to call, or perhaps even (c) terminate the friendship. The experimentation may then shift to an empirical or concrete approach: after deciding on a course of action the client attempts to interact with Bill and then reports back to the counselor how the experiment went. For example, the client might say, "After we discussed the situation, I decided I should try calling Bill. I called him twice but each time he said he was too busy to talk with me." This tracking of developments adds information to the situation and serves to focus further a posteriori discussion on why Bill might be doing what he is doing, and what the client might do in the future. Of course this is a very simple case, but this experimental approach is in fact a very effective collaborative approach to even the most serious life situations.

William James said that the whole function of philosophy "ought to be to find out what definite difference it will make to you and me, at definite instants of our life, if this world-formula or that world-formula be the true one."[5] In philosophical counseling an experiment is rarely, if ever, undertaken to decide such grandiose issues as which "world-formula be the true one." Philosophical counseling is not concerned with formulating vast theories about how to understand or run the world, and it is not an attempt to reach some ultimate or absolute 'Truth.' But it does improve the world to some extent in that it helps individual sufferers to make decisions that will alleviate their suffering, prevent or avoid harm to themselves and others in the future, or help create the most all-around beneficial outcome to a situation. As mentioned in chapter 2, philosophical counseling harks back to antiquity. Historian and philosopher Martha Nussbaum points out that for the pre-Socratic Epicureans and Stoics the philosopher's arguments were meant to have practical value in the life of the philosopher's discussion partners, and that they were "appropriately assessed as arguments in connection with their causal power" in alleviating human misery.[6] In other words, the cogency of an argument did not depend merely on the logic of its propositional constructs but materially on its effect in the resolution of concrete human existential problems.

In philosophical counseling the "causal power" of the various hypotheses for problem resolution which have been arrived at inductively through discourse are tested and tracked empirically in life to determine the answer to the client's question, Which one of the seemingly plausible and workable alternatives we have considered will work best in the client's situation? Discourse can only arrive at hypotheses; experimentation (both in thought and in reality) is employed to verify

the effectiveness of reasoned conclusions about oneself, the world, and one's relation to the world in everyday application. Experimental philosophy in philosophical counseling aims most often not at epistemic certainty but at the empirical
adjudication of competing hypotheses in order to find the one with the most practical value.

So what exactly does experimental philosophy look like in the context of philosophical counseling? As mentioned earlier, in science the experimenter begins
with (1) *a verifiable (or falsifiable) hypothesis.* The philosophical counselor and
his client also begin with the formulation of a hypothesis. This may take the form
of a statement such as, I have no right to complain about how badly my husband is
treating me, or I should choose the career that pays the best, or There is no purpose
in life. These statements point the way to tests or experiments that can then be conducted to overcome the subjectivism that often accompanies suffering and distress, and the perspectivism or lack of "peripheral vision" (the limitations and
biases inherent in one's own point of view) that is inherited from family, peers, and
society. Imagination is therefor essential for producing the sort of hypotheses that
can alter for the better the client's habitual and routine thinking whose narrow perspective has so far been unhelpful.

Natural science demands that there be (2) *a sincere doubt in the experimenter's
mind of the truth of that hypothesis.* French philosopher and scientist Jules Henri
Poincaré argued that it is simply impossible to conduct an experiment without preconceived ideas, but this does not mean experimentation in philosophical counseling needs to be overly skeptical.[7] The philosophical counselor and his client
always hypothesize with the idea that "this might work to solve the problem" and
experimentation proceeds from there. The purpose of hypothesizing in philosophical counseling, and (3) *the purpose of the experiment* is first to settle on the hypothesis that will have the most direct effect in terms of improving the life of the client.
Experimental philosophy in philosophical counseling is always aimed at the ideal
of 'the good life' as envisioned by the client, which the philosophical counselor
understands to be reasonably possible and morally permissible. The (4) *method or
design of the experiment* in philosophical counseling is geared toward producing
results that can be applied to the client's real-life situation. Experimentation is
conducted first analytically by determining the exact nature of the client's prob-
lem(s), then a priori by creatively imagining the outcomes to various approaches to
the problem, then by analogy to similar situations, then possibly by acting out the
imagined scenarios in the safety of the counseling office, and finally by trying
out—empirical experimentation—what is believed to be the best approach in the
client's actual life situation and tracking the results. During the next visit to the
counselor's office discussion focuses on the outcomes of the experiment so that
improvements can be made.

While in the science laboratory the course of the experiment is determined by
(5) *the experimenter's act of choosing which objects or assumptions/beliefs to operate on,* in philosophical counseling the client and philosophical counselor work
together in choosing which of the client's problems to operate on. This will decide
(6) *the act by which the experimenter* (both the counselor and the client) *modifies*

those objects or problems. While experimental philosophy is, as Dewey put it, a "trial of ideas,"[8] it is even more when employed in philosophical counseling. The counselor and the client put their ideas to the test in order to observe (7) *the object's reaction to the experimenter's act* and to learn from this the best course of action to take. Experimentation in philosophical counseling proceeds by abductive reasoning, that is, by an examination of all the norms that guided the formulation of the hypotheses and deciding which hypothesis may be abandoned and which may be taken seriously. Through a process of elimination the course of action that is chosen for similar future situations is the one that works better than the rest at the time of the experiment.

The ultimate end of any experiment is (8) *the recognition of the teaching of the experiment.* Natural scientists and some philosophers claim that their aim is to reach the conclusion which is the absolute 'Truth.' Philosophical counseling does not have such a vague and lofty goal. The philosophical counselor and his client aim at something more like finding which of a number of assumptions and beliefs are reasonably justified, which alternatives for action will prove to be the most beneficial to the client and others, and which hypothesis will be the most useful. Certainly, the client may present a hypothesis to be tested such as, "This man doesn't love me anymore" for which the goal in philosophical counseling may indeed be to find the truth of the matter. But in most instances the goal is not 'Truth' as such but rather a practical answer to an existential or moral question of some sort. The approach in experimental philosophy and philosophical counseling is pragmatic; the goal is to determine what is best to think or to do. As the ancient philosopher Seneca put it, "The medicines for the soul were discovered by the ancients, but it is our job to find out how to apply them and when."[9] The choice as to which is the best course of action is based on the evidence of the test or experiment, and even when an experiment has failed (in that an experimental course of action did not bring the desired good results) it is not an absolute failure since the client and counselor stand to learn from it. The outcome of the experiment clearly allows for the verification or falsification of beliefs and assumptions, and the client's approach to life can be altered or even corrected according to what the experiment has revealed.

As in empirical science, experimental philosophy (which I am arguing is the essence of philosophical counseling) allows the counselor and client to go beyond just establishing facts about the world, and enables the client to choose one course of action from among many, based on predictions of probable beneficial future outcomes. Experimental philosophy clarifies both the personal and the practical in ontology (being), epistemology (beliefs and knowing), meaning (emotive and descriptive), politics (relationship with others), religion (relationship with a higher power), and ethics (avoiding harm or doing good). But more than that, the results of experimentation in philosophical counseling produce knowledge that is much more certain and conclusive than the a priori hypothesizing common to academic philosophy, and therefore has the potential to create in the client the confidence to think and act, and to change thinking and actions, in accordance with that knowledge.

Experimental philosophy is an efficacious combination of intellectual philosophizing with concrete experience. As John Dewey put it, experimental philosophy is

a philosophy which no longer puts experience in opposition to rational knowledge and explanation. Experience is no longer a mere summarizing of what has been done in a more or less chance way in the past; it is a deliberate control of what is done with reference to making what happens to us and what we do to things as fertile as possible of suggestions (of suggested meanings) and a means for trying out the validity of the suggestions. When trying, or experimenting, ceases to be blinded by impulse or custom, when it is guided by an aim and conducted by measure and method, it becomes reasonable—rational.[10]

The reasonable and rational process of philosophical counseling demands that the counselor refrain from simply stating categorically for the client what ought to be done, and that he instead ask questions and offer suggestions which do not presume to lead to absolute 'Truth.' Clearly, experimental philosophy in philosophical counseling is not a radical idea. It is nothing more than the spirit of inquiry and exploration already present in most counseling encounters which focuses not merely on analysis and critique but also in helping the client come to a firm conclusion regarding which course of action is likely to bring the best results. Experimental philosophy takes philosophical counseling out of both the realm of academic philosophy—which concerns itself almost exclusively with producing a priori deductive and inductive conceptualizations notoriously lacking in conclusiveness—and the medical approach so dominant in psychotherapy—in which the client is subjected to a clinical diagnosis and treated according to a predetermined scientific formula. Philosophical counseling as experimental philosophy is truly unique in the field of philosophy in that it uses the empirical approach to knowledge in order to resolve the actual (not just hypothetical) issues and concerns of suffering human beings. Yet, while today's conception of philosophical counseling is rarely, if ever, oriented according to the medical model so prevalent in psychotherapy, there was a time when philosophical counseling was much more closely allied with psychotherapy than it is today, and when it was in fact called "clinical philosophy."

NOTES

1. The *Old English Dictionary* (OED2) defines experimental philosophy as: "(a) the philosophy which insists on experiment as the necessary foundation and test of all reasoned conclusions; (b) physics or 'natural philosophy' as studied or demonstrated by means of experiments (now rare)." As late as 1819 the term "experimental philosophy" was still used to denote what we would today call science. The OED2, under "experimental philosophy," cites an essay in *Pantologia* as stating, "Experimental Philosophy is an investigation of the wisdom of God in the works and laws of nature."

2. Kant, Immanuel. *Critique of Pure Reason* (1781). Norman Kemp Smith, trans. New York: St. Martin's, 1965. 396. Italics are in the original.

3. Dewey, John. *Reconstruction in Philosophy* (1920). Boston: Beacon Press, 1957. 121–122.

4. Adapted from Charles S. Pierce, *Selected Writings* (1905). Philip P. Wiener, ed. New York: Dover, 1966. 193–194.

5. James, William. *Pragmatism* (1907). New York: Dover, 1995. 20.

6. Nussbaum, Martha. *The Therapy of Desire*. Princeton, N.J.: Princeton University Press, 1994. 329.

7. Poincaré, Henri. *Science and Hypothesis* (1905). New York: Dover, 1952. 143.

8. Dewey, John. *Democracy and Education. The Philosophy Source* CD. Daniel Kolak, ed. Belmont, Calif.: Wadsworth, 2000.

9. Quoted in Nussbaum. 336.

10. Dewey, *Democracy and Education.*

Chapter 4

Clinical Philosophy

As an academic discipline psychology, like physics, is of no help to anyone. Physics becomes useful when it is applied in engineering. Psychology becomes useful when it is turned into practice as psychoanalysis or psychotherapy, that is, when it becomes clinical. Philosophy suffers the same fate of uselessness when it is merely studied as an academic subject. But what is the philosophical equivalent of *clinical* psychology?

A few, but very few, philosophers have at various times argued that there ought to be a clinical application of philosophy that serves the same purpose as clinical psychology. But for many philosophers the word "clinical" in clinical philosophy conjures up an image of the worst kind of institutionalized curative procedures in which paternalistic experts, applying their powerful "medical gaze," as Michel Foucault called it, dispense healing to the grateful sufferers. And for many philosophers today the idea of philosophy being combined with psychotherapy, and philosophical counselors working hand-in-hand in clinical practice with psychotherapists, is simply unimaginable. What then prompted the development of clinical philosophy some 30 years ago? And why are clinical philosophers and philosophy clinics not a prevalent feature in today's therapeutic community?

In the 1970s Peter Koestenbaum, at that time professor of philosophy at San Jose State College in California, attempted to advance the integration of philosophy and psychotherapy with the publication of *The Vitality of Death: Essays in Existential Psychology and Philosophy* (1971), followed by a 570-page volume entitled *The New Image of the Person: The Theory and Practice of Clinical Philosophy* (1978). In the latter book Koestenbaum defined clinical philosophy as "the confluence of a combined phenomenological model of being and existential personality theory with depth psychotherapy." Koestenbaum argued that when the medical model of the person (which he referred to elsewhere as the ghost-in-the-machine theory) is the standard of normalcy and the basis of treatment, healing becomes a very limited activity. From the perspective of clinical philosophy the medical model is a form of "cultural pathology." The "philosophic as 'cure,' " he called it, is to overturn the model itself on which the putative cures of conventional therapy are based.

Koestenbaum sought to help establish clinical philosophy "as a bona fide discipline, with both theoretical and practical orientations." He pointed out that many patients treated at that time with conventional therapy or medicine "are in truth people who suffer from philosophical conditions, rather than psychological diseases. They suffer from the basic problems of life (such as responsibility, love, and death) and need philosophical insight and help." Koestenbaum wrote that it is "quite readily possible to diagnose a client philosophically, and as a result of that to propose a treatment strategy, a counseling direction, or even a didactic course." According to Koestenbaum clinical philosophy requires of the practitioner a solid background in philosophy, especially in what he called "the phenomenological model of being and the existential personality theory, and in psychology and psychiatry, especially clinical practice and experience in psychotherapy."

Koestenbaum is now 74 years old. I e-mailed him several questions which he was kind enough to answer.

RAABE: In *The New Image of the Person* you discuss what you call clinical philosophy. You consider clinical philosophy not as a replacement for psychotherapy but as an addition to it. Because of this some philosophers argue that clinical philosophy is not true philosophical counseling (which they separate completely from psychotherapy). How would you respond to this?

KOESTENBAUM: I see clinical philosophy as a presuppositionless (to the degree possible) description of what it means to exist as a human being in the world. I think Heidegger in his own way attempted that in *Being and Time*, and, earlier, so did Descartes in his *Meditations* and in his *Discourse on Method*. Clinical philosophy is an attempt to do precisely that. No one can claim perfection. The project, however, is worthy.

Psychotherapy illuminates the structure of consciousness and of human relations. It divulges how consciousness works, especially in such areas as embarrassment, anxiety, growth, projection, effusive joy, reconciliation, hope, and other forms of insight. It opens up the possibility of layers of awareness, even of the peculiar mechanism of the unconscious, so cleverly assailed by Sartre. Psychotherapy enlarges the field for phenomenological investigation of the inward life, of intersubjectivity, and of its impact on externality.

Psychotherapy is only accidentally connected with "healing." It is better to conceive of it as an inspired way of learning more about oneself as an individual but even more about how the mind works. This is particularly true if we dwell on the unusual fact that in psychotherapy we see that consciousness reflects on itself, that we think about thinking and feel about feeling. This phenomenon of "reflexivity" is a universal philosophical conundrum that tells us something about the unique nature as well as the peculiar limits of knowledge.

Once we are aware of the deep structures of human existence, through this kind of a presuppositionless analysis of what it feels to be us, we can develop, expand, and act on them as a way to help us become stronger as persons. We can teach and dialogue intelligently. This would be called philosophical counseling, in my way of thinking. The differentiator is the power of philosophic insight, philosophical vocabulary, philosophical depth and perspicuity. This leads to character, to inner strength, to the willingness to risk, and no longer to be anxious about anxiety or guilty about guilt, but just plain anxious and guilty.

I think we need not be fussy about borders. Life is a seamless experience, and disciplines foster a divisiveness required for clarity and precision but which can distort the ambiguities of real experience.

RAABE: What got you, a philosopher, motivated to develop the theory and practice of clinical philosophy?

KOESTENBAUM: When you study phenomenology and existentialism you recognize that you are face to face with some inspired and penetrating insights into what it means to be human. You are grateful for the sharp minds that have come up with trenchant observations of inner states and ways of being in the world. They talk about anxiety and free will, about your sense of identity and uniqueness and the inevitability of death. They talk about authentic and neurotic guilt. And they make the effort to let you in on their discoveries of inner landscapes. You may not agree with them. There is no problem with that. All you need to do is to improve on their descriptions of the human condition. We will all benefit from that.

I worked on this thirty years ago, and it became immediately obvious that psychiatric descriptions of these inner states benefited from philosophic deepening, and, of course, vice versa. The initiative was taken by psychiatrists, and for years we had joint conferences and journals. It was a fruitful time for both professions. My two long books, *The Vitality of Death* and *The New Image of the Person* try to chronicle the development of these philosophic-psychiatric ideas.

I found my home in bringing together the depth of psychiatry with the depth of philosophy. You could always tell the training: psychiatrists wrote differently from philosophers. The only one who could write in the style of both combined was Rollo May.

I have been using the power of the combined disciplines for helping people manage their business issues. It has been a long struggle. I feel I am in the midst of it, trying to find applications, be in touch with what is real, serve my clients well, and maintain my integrity with respect to values. It is a great adventure. I feel I have made progress, but, believe me, the real tasks still lie ahead.

RAABE: What would you say to those psychologists and psychotherapists who argue that philosophers don't belong in counseling?

KOESTENBAUM: It's odd to use the expression "belong." There is behind such talk a territorial dispute that has more to do with vested interests (which are understandable, of course) than with intellectual integrity. There are competent people in both fields. And there are mature people in both fields. And there are charlatans and inept people in both fields as well. In a free society, people can be where they wish to be, as long as they are totally honest about what they do and what their credentials and qualifications are, and do not violate the laws. The question is, what are their underlying issues and what can we learn from them?

RAABE: We don't hear much about clinical philosophy, either in university philosophy departments or in counseling departments. Why do you think that is?

KOESTENBAUM: Two reasons: (1) Those of us interested in the field and committed to it do not spend enough energy, seriousness, and both developmental and marketing effort in bringing the subject matter out to the public's attention. *Mea culpa* is answer one. (2) When stuck, the rule is to analyze the resistance. We face the same obstacles that Freud did. There are two differences: we don't have a Freud (volunteers are welcome), and the age we live in shoots great men and women, opting instead for mediocrity. In Freud's day, both fortunately and unfortunately, the Great Man theme was alive. We do not want a cult. We want integrity and professionalism. And that takes personal courage and sacrifice.

What Koestenbaum has here described as clinical philosophy is called "philosophical practice" or "philosophical counseling" by others. Regardless of what it is called, the desired end is the same: an improvement in the life of the client. But for some the term "philosophical practice" also includes discussion in a public forum known as a philosophers' café or a philosophy café. While the operant element in both philosophical counseling and the philosophy café is philosophical dialogue, they each have features that make them unique and quite dissimilar. It is important for a philosophical counselor to understand their similarities and differences.

Chapter 5

Counseling and the Café

The students in an undergraduate philosophy class are discussing Socrates' decision to drink the cup of hemlock in his hand. Suddenly, in the middle of an argument about whether an autonomous individual has the intrinsic right to decide when to die, a student stands up and blurts out that s/he has tried to commit suicide on two different occasions.

The attempt of a member of the class to bring up an intimate personal matter is not an uncommon experience for those instructors who teach philosophy courses that seem to have some relevance to real life. The same kind of incident occurs every now and then at philosophy cafés. In cafés where the participants themselves suggest the topics of discussion serious personal concerns are sometimes offered as topics or are raised in the course of the evening's discourse. Some participants interpret certain topics—such as, Am I responsible for the actions of my children or my spouse? What determines the value of a human being? Can an adult live by the rules learned as a child? Can the world be divided into inferior and superior people? What is a midlife crisis? Does my job define who I am? and What is the meaning of life?—as an invitation to use the intellectual resources and empathy of group members to resolve painful problems in their own lives.

But a philosophy class is not the proper place to talk about events in one's own life. Or is it? And a philosophy café is not a group counseling session. Or is it? In the café that I facilitate in North Vancouver we often exchange personal experiences with the evening's discussion topic. The intention behind this exchange is twofold: first, it allows participants to see how many different ways the evening's topic can be interpreted. One of the most fascinating evenings was when participants shared their experiences of evil. Second, it brings philosophy "down to earth" by allowing the topic to be more than merely a theoretical discussion. If a philosophy café is an attempt to bring philosophy to the general public then why not allow participants to offer personal examples? Of course, offering personal examples which are meant to illustrate or broaden the topic of discussion is very different from a participant's attempts to have the group alleviate a personal problem.

Steve Palmquist, facilitator of a philosophy café in Hong Kong and philosophical counselor, says he likes to encourage people to "explore their own insights at a deeper level, to think clearly about the implications of their beliefs, to recognize their prejudices for what they are, and to consider the potential advantages of other ways of thinking." This is exactly what's done in philosophical counseling, but Palmquist is in fact talking about how he runs his philosophy café. Does this similarity of process mean a philosophical counseling session is nothing more than a one-on-one version of a philosophy café discussion? Is "philosophy café" just a fancy new name for group counseling?

For Stephen Hare, past president of the Canadian Society for Philosophical Practice (CSPP), a philosophy café is "a well-mannered and regulated dialogue among strangers and slight acquaintances held in some semi-public setting, in which the participants are free to come and go, and where people agree to share a single dialogue, in a somewhat disciplined although completely non-technical way, about some aspect of human life which is raised at the outset in the form of a general proposition or question."

As discussed in chapter 2, philosophical counseling consists of a trained philosopher helping an individual deal with a problem or an issue that is of concern to that individual. But it is also done in groups. This is when the line between philosophical counseling and a philosophy café can become very fuzzy. Some of the differences between philosophical counseling and a philosophy café are quite obvious: philosophical counseling is held in private, not in some semipublic setting; in philosophical counseling the client makes a tacit agreement to remain in discussion with the counselor until the end of the scheduled hour,[1] while participants at a café make no agreement to remain in the group and often come and go freely; in philosophical counseling the topic of discussion always focuses on the client's personal problems or concerns, while in a philosophy café the topic may be theoretical, completely imaginary, and at times even facetious[2]; counseling sessions that span a number of weeks or even months may at times deal repeatedly with only one issue, while the topics discussed in a philosophy café are intentionally different each time; and the shared dialogue in philosophical counseling may not necessarily remain on one topic or question throughout even a single session, while in each philosophy café every effort is made to stay on the topic designated for that evening.

A somewhat less obvious difference is that the philosophical counselor will encourage a particular level of intimacy and self-disclosure in a counseling session, while in a philosophy café, according to Hare, "I make a point of avoiding a certain kind of intimacy. . . . If people want to be anonymous—and if they want to remain silent—they are free to do so; if they want to be more personal they are free to make an offering but not to try to make it a formal point of procedure. No one is pressured to introduce himself or herself, or to speak except for clarification." In this sense a philosophy café is more like a classroom where participation is not forced, and discussion of private personal issues is considered inappropriate. Active participation and discussion of private matters are, of course, exactly the point of philosophical counseling. If the client remains silent philosophical counseling cannot take place.

Palmquist admits that the philosophical counselor and the moderator or facilitator of a philosophy café will often perform a similar function. When either session is going well the counselor/moderator need do nothing more than guide the client's/participant's own brainstorming, directing it to clearer and deeper forms of expression and understanding. But Palmquist believes it is unacceptable to regard a philosophy café as a group counseling session. An important difference is that when he is facilitating a café discussion Palmquist sees his job as helping the group to reconcile or synthesize the many opposing viewpoints presented by participants, while in a counseling session he helps the client to carefully analyze the numerous potentially opposing perspectives in order to settle on the most beneficial.

Gale Prawda suggests that the differences and similarities between a philosophy café and philosophical counseling become more apparent when one examines the motivation or intention of participants. Prawda is an American philosopher living in Paris, a philosophical counselor, and the originator of English-language philosophy cafés in both Paris and London. While philosophical counseling allows the client to focus exclusively on personal issues and concerns, Prawda sees the philosophy café as giving participants a nontherapeutic experience.

"Some enjoy the friendliness and unique experience of being able to gather together with others to discuss an issue communally and to try and make some sense out of it. A philosophy café gives them an opportunity to exchange ideas, to share in thinking together, to develop themselves personally from some of the thoughts, and to develop their own critical faculties of thinking. . . . Some just come for the simple joy philosophy can bring and the intellectual stimulation. . . . There are also quite a few psychotherapists, sociologists, writers, scientists, etc. coming to hear and see other perspectives in these dialogues/discussions. For them philosophy cafés help add to their professional baggage either in form or content." One of Prawda's participants described the café experience as "an antidote to brain pollution."

Although there is currently a debate in France as to what a philosophy café is and how it should be conducted, Prawda points out that when Marc Sautet began the movement "his intention was to use the maieutic approach [helping others to bring their ideas to birth] in dealing with daily-life problems/questions and to treat these subjects with a critical eye." But isn't dealing with "daily-life problems" more fitting as the content of a philosophical counseling session than of a philosophy café?

Like many other facilitators of philosophy cafés, Prawda sees a difference in the purpose of discussions held in philosophical counseling and in philosophy cafés. In the philosophy café discussion is both the goal as well as its own intrinsic reward, while in philosophical counseling discussion is typically a means to an end, or an extrinsic goal: the mitigation of the client's suffering or distress through the resolution of some life problem.

"If one is thinking along the lines of group therapy, I'd suggest a Socratic dialogue format rather than a philosophy café. The advantage to a Socratic dialogue comes from the unlimited time available over a number of sessions and a limit on the number of participants, as well as the rigorous emphasis on the discussion topic. This will be more beneficial to participants individually whereas philosophy cafés are limited in time as well as in their therapeutic effect on the large number of participants."

Prawda maintains that philosophical counseling allows "real dialogue" while discussion in a philosophy café is often "quasi-diluted" because so many disparate points of view are offered. Philosophy cafés are also limited in the amount of time that can be spent on one topic—usually one meeting of about two hours—whereas philosophical counseling sessions can dwell on one issue as long as the client feels the need, or discussion can come back to the same problem as often as the client wishes. However, that being said, Prawda points out that philosophy cafés can nonetheless complement counseling. One participant of his philosophy cafés became a client for a few sessions and went back to the philosophy café "with opened eyes and developed even further. . . . For her the 'philo café' seemed to be an extension and a complement to the work we covered in our [counseling] sessions."

Leonard Angel, philosopher in Vancouver, Canada, points out that the "philosophers tea" which he hosts once a month is in fact a fusion of personal and academic discussion topics which constitute "a bridge between the purely academic life and the personal quest for fulfillment." In other words, while the activity within a philosophy café and philosophical counseling are often perceived to be very different in intent, they need not be mutually exclusive in their effect. Despite the fact that philosophy cafés are not meant to be group counseling sessions, participation in a philosophy café may result in meaningful insights into real life, and therefore personal counsel to some participants. When an individual gains a useful insight into a personal problem within a philosophical counseling setting it is clearly due to the efforts of the counselor and that individual whose intentions were to cooperatively arrive at such an insight; but when an individual gains a useful insight into a personal problem while attending a philosophy café it is usually only due to good luck.

Useful insights into personal problems are gained not only by participating as part of the group in attendance at a philosophy café or by a face-to-face meeting with a philosophical counselor. They may be gained also in a much more remote manner.

NOTES

1. The length of a counseling session is typically one hour but it may vary.
2. The topic of our December 2000 philosophy café was "Does Santa Claus Exist?"

Chapter 6

E-mail Counseling

Just as technology has changed most other areas of our lives, it has changed the nature of practical philosophy and philosophical counseling. While most of us think of counseling as being a face-to-face and often very intimate dialogue, telephones, computers, and video cameras have allowed consultations to take place between individuals who may never meet each other in person. In this chapter I want to focus specifically on the benefits and risks of counseling by e-mail.

A quick search on the web reveals a growing list of web sites offering online counseling services mostly geared to a psychotherapeutic approach. Interactions are of two types: the first is one-time visits—in which the client asks a question and the counselor gives a detailed response. The second is ongoing—in which the counselor and client form a relationship that allows inquiry to explore deeply into the client's concerns. Some philosophical counselors feel that if their practice does not include online counseling and an "office" in cyberspace they are not only losing potential clients and revenue, they are also missing a ride on the wave of the future. But is e-mail counseling a sign of things to come? Counselors who believe their clients have benefited from counseling by e-mail are happy to extol its virtues to anyone willing to listen. But what about those things that can go wrong?

Justin Irwin, communications officer for a crisis hotline organization in the United Kingdom called the Samaritans, says their e-mail service "has been growing rapidly." Irwin is quick to point out that he would not consider their e-mail service as counseling, but rather "non-directive, non-judgmental emotional support offered by helping the 'caller' explore their emotions or feelings behind any particular problem they might be going through." In 1997 the U.K. Samaritans received about 7,500 messages; by 1998 that had grown to over 15,000. In 1999 it was close to 30,000. Irwin points out that e-mail callers are twice as likely to express suicidal feelings as those who call by telephone. This may be due to the fact that more than half of their e-mail callers are under the age of 25—the age group most likely to attempt suicide. But Irwin thinks it's also due to the nature of the medium being used. E-mail eliminates a face-to-face, or even phone-to-phone discussion. The young and naturally inhibited may find it easier to express suicidal ideation and feelings online than on the phone.

U.K. philosophical counselor Tim LeBon says his experience with e-mail counseling has been very good. The act of writing seems to him to be more appropriate than verbal dialogue for assessing arguments and mapping out one's ideas. It encourages both client and counselor to think deeply in trying to work out their responses. It also allows them the time necessary to do this—time in quantities rarely available in formally arranged office appointments.

There is general agreement that what recommends e-mail counseling over all other mediums is the fact that client and counselor can connect over vast distances at very little expense. E-mail counseling does not require the counselor to organize appointments, rent an office space, allow for travel time, or purchase a professional wardrobe. It does not call for the client to be physically present—a requirement that the physically challenged, or extremely shy, nervous, or easily embarrassed client may find difficult to meet. The absence of a physical appearance also means that the client-counselor relationship will not be negatively affected by the counselor's race, sex, age, and so on. Furthermore, both client and counselor can reflect back over printouts of past sessions. A hard copy allows them also to make notes directly on the printed page—gathering questions and insights that can serve as catalysts for future discussions. Online counseling also allows the counselor the time to reflect, and more importantly to conduct research into unfamiliar areas without losing "professional face" to the client. And the very act of articulating worries and concerns in a message can itself be therapeutic for the client. As one client put it, "Expressing myself in these emails is somewhat of a relief."

But Shlomit Schuster, a counselor in Israel, feels e-mail counseling is sadly lacking in communicative capability. She argues that if you're going to allow technology to act as the intermediary it should at least function at the voice or visual level. Tim LeBon agrees. He has found that e-mailing makes it harder for the counselor to pick up important nuances from the client, such as facial expressions, body language, tone of voice, and pauses and hesitations. This, he says, makes it more difficult to "work with the whole person."

But online counseling is still largely experimental, and there are better ways to get help. A most obvious flaw with e-mail counseling is that it is not available to anyone without a computer or Internet access. Even if such access exists, for online counseling to work both client and counselor must have a certain level of competency in their writing skills. If either can't express themselves clearly, or conversely if either is inclined to write long, unwieldy passages, the counseling relationship will soon deteriorate into frustration. E-mail messages need to be concise. Unfortunately this can lead the client to censor his thoughts, edit his writings, and eliminate important material for the sake of brevity. Spontaneity is lost to convenience.

Perhaps the second biggest drawback is that there is a lack of that physical closeness to a warm and caring human being that research has shown is vital to the effectiveness of all the helping professions. Most counselors who have counseled by e-mail agree that they prefer to explore the eyes of their clients rather than the pixels of their computer screens. In fact research has shown that the choice of therapeutic method often proves to be less essential to beneficial counseling outcomes than the warmth and caring found in the human connection between counselor and client.[1] Counselors also note that the use of humor as a part of therapy is very difficult to employ on the Internet. Merriment can be missed, or worse it can be misunderstood. A joke can read like the worst kind of callousness or insensitivity and can easily lead to the termination of a counseling relationship.

While a client may have the perception of an immediate connection with the counselor once the "Send Mail" button has been pressed, there is no guarantee there is actually a counselor present at the other end. A response from counselor to client and vice versa can take an excruciatingly long time. A sent message may also be intercepted. Cyberspace hackers feel no moral obligation to respect the privacy of others. And I imagine that a person using his employer's computer to send personal messages to a counselor has no legal right to confidentiality either.

For clients there is no legal protection against fraudulent counselors. But fraud works in both directions. At the moment there is also no legal recourse for the online counselor whose client fails to send the promised check in the mail. It's possible that payment may be reliably received only if the counselor has set up some sort of elaborate, carefully safeguarded electronic payment system (some counseling web sites accept credit card numbers and charge by the minute or by the message). Furthermore, there is no guarantee that the client isn't a fraud, that is, someone simply having a good laugh at the counselor's expense. There is no way to verify by e-mail that a client's distress is real. This could mean, for instance, that the rise in the number of suicidal e-mail messages received by the U.K. Samaritans could simply be due to young computer users having them on. There is no way to tell.

My own experience with online counseling has been mixed: frustrating at times, but sometimes very rewarding. The frustration has come from my volunteering to respond to e-mails received through a specialized web site offering information and advice to single mothers. It was set up as a sort of electronic message board which allows people to post anonymous questions, and to which I and several other professionals posted our responses. The problem was that we counselors never had any indication of whether our messages were appropriate or appreciated. In fact there was no way to know whether our carefully thought-out responses were ever even read, since they were not sent to the individual but simply posted on the public message board. It was like shooting arrows into the dark, never knowing if the message landed anywhere near the target. What was even worse was that some of the messages were written by women who appeared to be in severe crisis situations; they presented extremely serious problems, to the extent that sometimes the physical safety of the women and their children seemed in jeopardy. Sending out a single electronic piece of advice under these circumstances felt appallingly inadequate, and was therefore not only unrewarding but very stressful.

The interaction I have had, and continue to have, with individuals who have contacted me through my own philosophical counseling web site has been far more rewarding. After I respond to these messages with suggestions and advice, I will often receive a second message from that individual telling me that I have "hit the mark" regarding their problem, or that they appreciate my advice, and so on. I discovered from this that some sort of a reward for hard work is important if a counselor is to remain motivated to continue. Of course, money is one kind of reward for counseling work, but money doesn't provide the only kind of feedback needed to validate a counselor's efforts. Without some indication from those receiving the counselor's messages that the advice was helpful, even if money has exchanged hands, the counselor is soon likely to lose heart.

More rewarding still are clients with whom messages are exchanged over the course of a number of weeks. The few clients who have approached me for this sort of more extensive e-mail counseling were usually distressed but not in crisis situations. They were articulate and comfortable with the medium, and they didn't consider online counseling their only option. This made them ideal e-mail clients. And this exchange of a number of carefully worded messages over time, although not verbal, gives the counselor a sense of working with a person who is immediately present, rather than with an electronically posted message which may already have been long forgotten by its sender.

Clients have also occasionally used e-mail to verify information, change appointment times, or ask questions about specifics for which there was not enough time in the previous in-person counseling session, thereby using e-mail to supplement in-person counseling rather than to replace it. I don't consider the question of whether e-mail counseling will replace all face-to-face counseling in the future a serious question. Just like the telephone, e-mail can be very useful in altering the time and space between two people, but it will never replace the pleasure and the fusion of energy that occurs when two people meet in real time and in a real place.

The following is a small sampling of the many e-mails I have received through my web site from all over the world, and the messages I sent in reply. I have had a few clients who have corresponded with me and paid me for e-mail counseling for up to six months, but generally most people who contact me by e-mail expect only the one reply to their initial message. In order to retain the unique character of the messages received they are presented here with the spelling errors and grammatical mistakes found in the originals.

SUBJECT: CAREER DECISIONS

Dear Dr. Raabe,

To keep this short, as I suspect that you are overwhelmed with emails, my question is as follows. I am in the middle of making a difficult decision about my career. For ten years, I have worn many leadership "hats" in both the for-profit and non-profit sectors. Five years ago, I went back to school to complete a graduate degree. Since then, I have worked in publishing as a development editor and in academia as a project manager for a large environmental project. I moved across the country to undertake the project management position at a university.

Unfortunately, I did not work well with the director of the project (a long story), and thus decided to end my work there after the completion of my first yearly contract. Now, for the first time in years, I have had an opportunity to reflect on what is truly important to me in terms of career aspirations. Over the years, I have read widely in the areas of mentoring, leadership, career counseling and the like in search of answers to my quest to bring deeper meaning to my work life. Now I am considering shifting career directions to become a career counselor.

Yet I worry that this career shift in my thirties will threaten my financial security (i.e., I am still trying to pay student loans). Also, I have worked hard to make it to the mid/senior management level in the environmental field. Is there a method that you could suggest that would help me know if I am making a reasonable choice? I wonder whether I should continue trying to find deeper meaning and more meaningful contribution in my present field of service—the environmental field, or whether I should make a big change to a field that has always interested me. It is a very tough decision, and I would appreciate any advice that you could offer.

Thank you very much for your help.

Best wishes,

A.B.

Dear A.B.,

The situation you describe is certainly a difficult one. It's also classic in that it puts you into the situation (that many of us know so well) of having to make a choice between the comfort and security of staying where you are at the present moment or giving it all up for the sake of only the possibility of a better future elsewhere. Your choice isn't only between certainty and mere possibility it's also between staying with a job that you seem to be good at and successful at or going into a new field which you believe will make you much happier. Of course there's no guarantee that changing careers will in fact make you happier. And I think it's this uncertainty about the future that makes you hesitate.

One thing you may want to consider is your recent unhappy experience with the director of the environmental project. Is it possible that this experience has made you want to leave the field? Might it be the case that you'd still be enjoying that job (the work involved in it) if things had gone differently in your relationship with the director? What I'm saying is, the idea of self-employment can seem very enticing when you've just had a bad experience with an employer.

Regarding the question of financial security, consider the fact that you have already changed jobs a few times and, as far as I can tell, have managed to do OK financially. But, of course, being self-employed is a different ball game from having a steady position with an employer. I would suggest that before you make any life changes you do some market research to see whether being a self-employed career counselor is a viable career. I'm assuming that you're planning to become self-employed as a career consultant, but this doesn't necessarily have to be the case. You could become a career counselor in a high school, but then you'd be working for someone else again.

Since your decision isn't a moral or ethical one, you could simply take a pragmatic approach: make a list of all the pro's and con's for changing careers or staying with the one you have now and then see which has the longest pro's to recommend it.

While a consideration of the amount of money there is to be made at each job is important, there is another issue that you may also want to consider and that is the question of which decision would make you the happiest. And the way to answer this question is to ask yourself which would make you the happiest if someone else, for example me, made it for you? Imagine that I wrote to you, "You should stay at your job." Would this be a relief or a disappointment? Or if I wrote, "You should become a career counselor." Would this bring a rush of excitement or a sinking feeling in the pit of your stomach? Your answers to these two questions—the nature of your emotional reactions—will give you a clue as to what you really want to do. If you then do what you really want to do you'll be working at a job you love to do, which means you'll do a good job at it, people will notice, word will go around, and eventually you'll do fine financially. I hope this helps.

Best regards,

Peter

SUBJECT: SPIRITUALITY, SEXUALITY, AND RELIGION

Dr. Raabe:

I am a 30-year old doctoral student of philosophy. I've read about but never tried philosophical counseling before. I am hoping that you will be able to help me resolve a certain "cognitive dissonance" that I am currently experiencing.

I consider myself a spiritual person, seeking self-actualization through the insights of major religious traditions. However, I find that the moral prohibitions of those same traditions, especially with regard to sexuality, are not always consonant with what I understand to be the requirements of a healthy psyche. Thus, I am prevented from embarking full-sail on a spiritual journey by a nagging sense of guilt and doubt, which also prevents full enjoyment of a relationship which I otherwise see as beneficial.

I would certainly appreciate your perspective on this situation.

Sincerely,

Y. J.

Dear Ms. Y. J.

I think your problem stems from the difference that exists between your own spirituality and religious traditions. Your attempt to find self-actualization is certainly an aspect of spirituality but it is not necessarily part of most religious traditions. What we today call personal spirituality would have been considered punishable heresy in the past. Personal spirituality included mysticism which often differed radically from accepted social norms of conduct and beliefs, especially in the area of sexuality, and led to terrible persecution.

Religious traditions are never based on the personal spirituality of its members. Most religions have their origins in the personal spirituality of some master, but in order to function on a social level such spiritual beginnings are always adjusted to augment existing moral norms. As the term suggests, religious traditions are an attempt to reconcile personal spirituality with cultural and social traditions. The sexual norms of many masters were definitely not in line with the social norms of their day. Some promoted complete abstinence, others promoted polygamy or polyandry. But while the spiritual teachings of many masters have survived in the form of religious traditions, their thoughts on sexuality are generally abandoned in favour of the status quo (two heterosexual people joined for life). Most religions consider enlightenment as good, but they believe that too much enlightenment is bad for the masses and for social stability.

It seems to me the situation you find yourself in calls for a decision on your part between following your own spirituality or the religious traditions of your community. If you have been raised to believe strongly in the prevailing religious traditions it will be difficult for you to abandon them despite the fact that you may be able to argue they are wrong in light of the conclusions your personal spirituality has led you to. If the choice is clearly a dichotomy (either I follow my own beliefs and make my own decisions about sexuality or I follow religious traditions) then it will be difficult. But perhaps there are other options. For example, some former traditions have been abandoned by some religions in order to accommodate the changing times and growing pressure from their members. The clash between religious traditions and a healthy psyche is the classic clash between religion and science (or rationality). And religion has had to make many concessions to science since the 1700's.

You are only "prevented from embarking full-sail on a spiritual journey" as you put it if you believe that your spirituality is dependent on a traditional religious foundation. You might find it interesting to read what the 17th century British philosopher John Locke had to say regarding the differences between religious beliefs, religious practices and traditions, and spirituality in his *A Letter Concerning Toleration*. And, although she was addressing the issue of feminism's rejection of traditional male thinking, 20th century philosopher Janet Radcliffe Richards' words may be useful to you in thinking about the issue of following religious tradition as well. She wrote, "What is necessary is to insist on *splitting up the packages*, looking at the good and bad aspects of tradition and keeping what is good wherever we can."[2]

I hope this helps.

Regards,

Peter

SUBJECT: WHAT BELIEFS SHOULD CHILDREN BE TAUGHT?

Dr. Raabe,

I see you do Email counseling. Well, I currently think that if I had a child, I would make no mention of a supernatural power. I would answer any questions that my child may ask me about a god with an answer to the effect of: "some people do explain things in terms of a nonphysical power, but my way, and my suggestion, is to approach every phenomenon as if there were a physical explanation, even if humans have yet to discover it." However, the woman I love looks forward to sharing her religious faith with her children. She says she will bring them to church services and teach her beliefs. I am of course free to teach them what I think as well.

I have many questions about this, but I am having trouble asking even a single one. My questions have to do with my relationship with this woman and the healthiness of raising a child in such an environment.

Also, I wonder about compromising itself. I consider faithful religious beliefs to be based on fallacies. What would be the moral considerations about remaining loyal to a woman whom accepts what I consider profound untruths. Should I decide to raise children with her, what would be the moral considerations of compromising so that I agree to permit my child to be taught a profound lie by his or her mother.

Thank you, Dr. Raabe, for offering your service.
Sincerely,
R. T.

Dear R. T.

One of the most common reasons why people are attracted to each other is because they share common beliefs and values (not just in a religious sense). One of the most common causes of strife between individuals is conflicting beliefs and values. The raising of children also involves teaching beliefs and values. When the beliefs and values of the parents are out of sync there is potential for their child to grow up confused, lost, and sometimes angry.

I think it will be very difficult for you and the woman you love to remain loving and caring of each other when you see her as accepting of profound untruths, and of potentially teaching lies to your future children. Your use of the words "untruths" and "lies" when it comes to religious beliefs indicates that you have very negative feelings about religion. It might be instructive for you to inquire into why this is so. It might also be interesting for you to explore what the connection is between faith and truth (or lies). You'll find that rationality and logic don't automatically and necessarily consign religious faith to the category of untruths and lies. There are some very well-known philosophers whose thinking is considered to consist of impeccable rationality and logic, who none-the-less had a strong faith in God. The 18th century German philosopher Immanuel Kant is a good example.

You say you wonder about "the healthiness of raising children in such an environment." If you could accept religious beliefs simply as beliefs rather than lies, I wonder what harm you imagine will come to your children if your wife were to teach your children her beliefs? If you believe there is real potential harm then you should not marry a woman who will potentially harm your children. But if you think that there will be no "real" harm involved then it seems to be OK to marry.

The options you seem to have are (1) don't marry someone with beliefs and values that are radically different from yours and that may harm your future children, or (2) learn to be more tolerant of, and open to, beliefs and values that are different than yours so that you won't see them as mere untruths and lies.

Compromise in a loving relationship doesn't consist of simply tolerating or permitting the other to believe or do something. It consists of respecting and accepting the other's beliefs and values as completely as you respect and accept your own. This doesn't mean you have to believe the other's beliefs; it means not judging them as false.

I hope this helps.
Best regards,
Peter

SUBJECT: WHY ME?

Dear Sir,

I am a 4th year student of philosophy at a University. I am currently researching about philosophical counseling for a paper I plan to submit by the end of the semester. In light of this I wish to undergo Philosophical Counseling myself. What advice can you give people like me who are handicapped and ask the question, "Why me? Why did this happen to me?"

I know that Philosophical Counseling is a new field and I plan to contribute in my own small way to the growth of a project that may be of great help to my fellow handicaps.

Sincerely
L. L.

Dear L. L.

If you believe in a Supreme Being or a 'Cosmic Plan' then a physical handicap will raise the question "Why me?" or "Why did this happen to me?" in a particular way. In a sense it's asking "What have I done to deserve this?" But no mortal can know the mind of the Gods or know the 'Cosmic Plan' well enough to answer this question.

In the absence of a belief in a Supreme Being or a 'Cosmic Plan' to what happens to us here on earth, the question, "Why did this happen to me?" has the same meaning regardless of what aspect of your physical makeup you're referring to. In other words, you could ask, "Why did this happen to me?" in regards to the colour of your eyes, hair, or skin, your height, or even your sex. The answer, in the absence of a belief in a Supreme Being or 'Cosmic Plan,' is that there is no particular reason which can be given except that it's a function of biology. Your eyes, your hair, your skin just have the colour they do, and you just are as tall (or short) as you are and the sex you are simply because of the way your genes were arranged at conception. There is no one to blame or hold accountable, not any Supreme Being or 'Cosmic Plan' or even your parents (unless your affliction is the result of some harmful behaviour by your parents, such as alcoholism which leads to fetal alcohol syndrome).

But people don't usually ask "Why did this happen to me?" unless they're unhappy with themselves, unless they see their physical makeup either as a punishment, or a deficiency of some sort. And a person will see a handicap as a punishment or a deficiency if, when he compares himself to so-called 'normal' individuals, he believes that his own situation is of less value than those normal individuals. But it's important to remember that each individual, normal or otherwise, is unique in his/her physical makeup, and that this uniqueness of their physical makeup has a major impact on how they experience life. A normal individual may experience life a certain way, but the normal person who breaks a leg and must spend the next six weeks in a cast (thereby becoming temporarily handicapped) has the opportunity to experience various aspects of life that will never be experienced by the person who will never spend time in a cast. Of course, life in a cast is not pleasant, but the person in a cast will learn things about himself and about family, friends, and strangers that he would never have learned if he had not been forced to hobble around in a cast for six weeks. The same can be said about individuals who consider themselves permanently handicapped: they experience life in a way not available to 'normal' others.

So the trouble with being 'normal' (non-handicapped) is that the normal person never gets to experience life other than in a normal way. What normal people often don't realize is that they're missing out on an incredible array of experiences simply because they are normal. If normal people could see the richness of life experienced by the handicapped they would probably ask about their normalcy, "Why me? Why did this happen to me?"

Best regards
Peter

SUBJECT: SUICIDE

My friend, who was 18 years old, committed suicide about a month and a half ago. He killed himself in his fathers dressing room, the night before graduation. He had been an extremely strong believer in existentialism and studied philosophy endlessly. He had once told his mother that he felt others' pain at the age of six, (and I learnt this at his funeral) and he had once told another friend that he had felt that there were 'steps' in life, and every time that we ask a question, we were advanced to the next step. He felt that life was a true journey, and that he had completed all steps and felt that he should go on . . . which had eventually lead to suicide.

There had been this other side of him that had been involved in drugs, such as Mescaline, Pot, and even as far as drinking bennadryl to get this feeling where he feels paralyzed and looks at the world differently. There had been a lot that had happened to him though—he had recently been thrown out of his previous high school and his hopes of going to an Ivy League college diminished.

I write to you now, with hope for an explanation, because I carry a lot of guilt due to his death. I had seen him just hours before his suicide and wonder . . . I should have seen the signs, (his drug abuse) but it was something that I assumed that he had always done. He had been a somewhat new friend to me. He had told me that he had seen a psychiatrist every week, but that didn't help him with anything and that they just talked and then, a week before his suicide, he had been able to talk his parents into letting him discontinue his therapy.

I hope that you can give me some kind of explanation about him and his behavior, because I can't understand. I find myself very different from him in the ways that I explained to you, but alike in ways that I haven't mentioned. I constantly think of him and the pain that his parents must be feeling . . .

Thank you.

E. G.

Dear E. G.

I'm so sorry that you've had such a tragic event in your life. It's very difficult to say exactly what led your friend to kill himself. It's impossible to imagine what's in a person's mind or to guess what's happening in a person's life. The fact that your friend was taking drugs and drinking tells me that he had some serious problems in his life. People often use drugs and alcohol to try to forget or reduce the pain they're suffering. The fact that he killed himself in his father's dressing room suggests to me that his father must have caused him a great deal of distress. Suicide was for him a way to send a very strong message to his father.

It's a terrible shame that the psychiatrist he was seeing couldn't help him. It seems to me that the real problem may not have been located in your friend at all, but rather in his family situation. If life at home with the parents was unbearable for your friend then psychoanalyzing him isn't going to help a lot.

The feelings of guilt and pain you're having are natural and don't need to be treated as some sort of problem. Please allow yourself the time to grieve for your friend. But also try to keep in mind that when parents are the cause of a young person's distress there's not much other young people can do to help. It took a lot of courage for your friend to kill himself; suicide is not easy. Remember him as a courageous young man who eventually found his own final solution to what must have been for him a terrible life situation. I hope this helps.

Best regards,

Peter

SUBJECT: "CORRECT" CONSOLING

Hi,

Q1. Pondering, how should I console someone whose love ones has passed away (normal and sudden). Is it "correct" to mentioned that our life is so uncertain, and God love us and care for us. This misfortune is a "will of God" and that God's plan for us will eventually be known, but we need to hold on and trust in the Lord always. There is no other way.

Q2. When someone is going to pass away, do we really need to assist them to salvation, even when we have a lot of objection from their close ones. Many a time, I can't bring myself in to challenge them on this.

Q3. When a person keep on justifying for his wrongs. Do we rebuke them for this. I wonder if we should, and if we do it, are we being judgmental on them.

Thanks and God Bless.

M. N.

Dear M. N.,

When trying to console someone it's important to ask yourself what consoling is all about. Is consoling about doing what *you* think ought to be done? Or is consoling giving the other person what *they* believe they need? You see, in consoling someone we try to make them feel a little better. But we won't make them feel better by trying to force our thoughts or ideas on them. If you think of consoling someone as trying to help them then the question you have to ask yourself before you begin is, What can I offer that they may want? And the best way to find out what someone else wants or needs is to ask them, What can I do to help?

But sometimes the person who is suffering doesn't need anyone to do much of anything for them at all except listen and be close. Sometimes the best consolation we can give to someone is to not force on them what we think they ought to accept from us, but to let them know that we are there for them and are willing to give them whatever they may ask of us. Dying and death can be very distressing events in life, and different people deal with it in different ways. What may be comforting for you may not be comforting at all for someone else. That's why it's important to listen and to ask, and to be willing to give whatever is asked without judging that request as either good or bad. Giving comfort is a gift. And a gift will not be appreciated if it is simply forced on others. I hope this helps.

Best regards,

Peter

SUBJECT: A WIFE DEALING WITH HER OWN ANGER

Help please!

My husband and I have been married for seventeen years and for the most it is fairly happy. We just happen to get into these destructive battles where I lose control and say things that I do not mean and then we both start in on each other. Once I get started I cannot stop and it can go on for hours. Most of the arguments are about the long hours that my husband works and he says he does it for the family and I see it as a rejection of me when he is not at home. He wants to change jobs and to earn the same money he says that there might be a lot of travel involved. We have been together since I was 14, married when I was 20 and I do not cope well when he travels. It annoys me that I must stay at home with the kids while he is traveling and having a good time with other people. He is getting really upset about these battles and so am I. I have such strong body language that I do not even have to say something and he can sense that I am really upset and that upsets him. I really want this marriage to work but I do not know how to cope anymore. I probably have issues with my father with whom I do not get along too well (he lives in a different country) and I sometimes think I am punishing my husband for my father's treatment of me. I always think my husband is out to get me when he works late or travels and I know it is ridiculous but at the time it is happening it feels so real.

Hope you can help before it is to late

G.

Dear G.,

Your situation is a difficult one but it's not unusual. As you say, you may have some issues with your father that need to be sorted out, but many women feel bitter about having to stay at home to take care of the kids while the husband is out. Even if he isn't traveling, the husband has other adults to talk with and work with, while the wife must stay home with only the kids and TV for company. A study done in the US found that children increased depression among non-employed wives. In contrast, for employed mothers, if child care was accessible and husbands shared in child care, depression levels were low.[3]

You have already mentioned one possible solution: your husband can get a different job, one that lets him spend more time with you. Another possible solution is for you to arrange for daycare for your kids (maybe only a couple of days each week) and for you to do something with your own life (like working at some job outside the home, volunteering at some service agency, participating in some sport or craft activities, or going to the movies with a girlfriend). By taking some time to enjoy yourself, to develop your own interests, and to connect with other adults, you may feel less bitter towards your husband, who seems to be having such a good time (although I know he's working hard).

Your anger may not be anger at your father or husband at all, but anger about the kind of life you seem forced to live. Maybe the best approach is not to try to change your husband but to change your own life situation, to make your own life more fulfilling and even enjoyable. I hope this helps.

Best regards,

Peter

SUBJECT: THE CHILDISH HUSBAND

hi, i have a question i have been kicking around for a year and need input, even though i believe i have the answer if not the fortitude to do it. i find myself in a four yr relationship, we have been married two of those. i know from living with him he is not your ordinary person. i dont know how much to tell you. he does some strange things. he will almost continually plays with his genitals, walks around most of the time nude, has been known to masterbate on my nightgowns when i have to go out of town. even if just for a couple of days. i have noticed he doesnt do it nearly as often as he used to this past 8mo to a yr. he will tell me sometimes that he is going to the bathroom to masterbate (very weird in my book). he told me he was diagnosed at age 5, in an orphanage as being masochistic w/narrcisstic tendencies. he flies into rages, it used to be several times a week, the last yr it varies now sometimes only once a month. he tells lies about inconsequencial things, like he just wants to get away with something. however if you corner him in a lie get out of the way he flies into a terrifying rage tearing up things tvs vcrs pictures windows, whatever enters his head i guess. i have done some studying and he has all the charcteristics of a narcisstic. the thing is, i have met his family and they all seem to be cut from the same cloth, same charateristics personality traits, which i think is really strange that the whole family is like that. of course they all pretty much grew up on the bad side of town, verbal and some physical abuse. their father got out of prison for burglary and got them out of the foster system. by then he says he wittnessed his two yr old sister be raped by two teens and one raped him for trying to stop them. this at a very early age. i am afraid to leave him, i know i can disappear but i worry about my grown kids as well as my extended family. i am in a fix and dont know what to do. yes he has threatened bodily harm to me and to them. you can see my dilema. he is 34 yrs old. my question i what are my risks of continueing in this relationship. emotioally it is very tireing he needs constant attention. almost like a child, in fact i notice he likes shows that would entertain a 14 yr old. getting this computer has helped a lot with that it seems to get his attention focused on something other than me. he is not mentally impaired in any other way than the ones ive told you, he holds down a job is fairly responsible. its this other stuff that preys on my mind. ive tried counseling with him in the past he gets angry if criticised in the least or told hes doing something wrong. what is your best advice. sometimes i feel like his rages are staged like he just feels like putting on a show or grandstanding or something. when i tell him this he gets very angry. i tell him i can see it his eyes. if you answer this please do so in the am hrs Monday–Thursday so as i can erase it so he doesnt find it. thank you for any insight about him or this situation u can give me. sincerely, G.

Dear G.,

Not all bad behavior is symptomatic of a mental illness. Sometimes a diagnosis just puts a medical-sounding label on what is simply bad behavior. Regardless of what your husband has been diagnosed with, or what you have read about his 'symptoms,' another way of describing him is that he is just being a bully. I have had many clients who were abused as children and are now decent human beings. They have told me their abuse as children doesn't need to affect them now that they are adults. In other words, as an adult we can make choices about how to behave with others. A bad childhood is used by some people as a convenient excuse for their bad behavior.

One of the things at the heart of a good marriage is respect. By masturbating on your nightgowns your husband is being highly disrespectful of you. And it is disrespectful of him to fly into rages, break things, and threaten harm. Rages and threats are a way of controlling (bullying) other people. Sure, we all get angry with our spouses from time to time but using rages and threats creates fear and denies the other person the right to say what they feel or be who they want to be.

You say he lived in an orphanage, and that his whole family has his personality characteristics. This tells me that your husband may not be 'mentally ill.' He simply learned his behavior in the environments he grew up in, both the orphanage and his family. He has learned that he can get what he wants by throwing a temper tantrum. You can put a diagnostic label on it and call it 'narcissism' or whatever you like, but by his being able to live a 'normal' life outside of your home and yet demand constant attention at home it tells me your husband is using his rage and threats as a way to manipulate you and get what he wants. This is why I say he is being a bully.

It's interesting that you say your husband still watches TV shows meant for 14 year olds. This tells me he's happy still living life as a child, that this immature lifestyle brings him comfort. His childish temper tantrums get him whatever he wants, and that's why he's still using them. Most children, as they grow up, learn self-control, and they're taught how to go beyond tantrums and relate to other people in a more empathetic manner. What your husband seems to need is instruction on how to be a grownup. I don't mean this as an insult. I mean that your husband needs help in creating an adult version of himself; he needs to learn self-control; he needs to learn how to relate to others respectfully—especially family members—and resolve issues without resorting to violent tantrums.

I'm worried that one day, during one of his tantrums, your husband will strike out at you or others. That's why I think the best thing would be for your husband to get professional help in changing his interpersonal strategies. You say he refuses to do this. I don't know what to suggest that will not result in harm to you. For example, you could go to your local women's shelter (the police can tell you where to find one). This may bring your husband to see how severely his bad behaviour is affecting you, and it may bring him to agree to go to counseling; but it may also enrage him all the more.

I think you're in a very serious and potentially dangerous situation. My advice is that you don't stay silent about it, but that you tell others about it, and that you find help from a counselor, from a priest or minister, or from the police. I hope this helps.

Regards,
Peter

SUBJECT: SOCIAL ANXIETY DISORDER?

I seem to have a problem that maybe you can help me with. I'm going through what I believe is social anxiety. I've just been promoted in my job to a supervisory position but when I have to train someone I get extremely nervous to the point where my hands start to tremble and it's really hard to hide my nervousness. My boss makes me extremely nervous as well when asked to do something I get really nervous. I only feel this way with my boss, when I'm placed in the spotlight or when I feel I'm being scrutinized. I'm also getting married in three weeks and I don't know how I'm going to face 150 guests at my wedding because of this problem. No one knows what I'm going through. I'm too embarrassed to confide any of my friends with this problem or even my fiancée. I feel like maybe my friends would treat me differently, and I don't want anyone's pity. It's funny because as a child I was always the popular one but now as an adult I hate the spotlight and it's really affecting my life. You're actually the first person I've turned to and maybe you can guide me in the right direction. How can I address this problem?

F. D.

Dear F. D.,

On the one hand, most people are nervous in the situations you mention. Just because you're nervous in front of the boss, in front of a crowd, or in front of a church full of people at your wedding doesn't mean you're suffering from some sort of anti-social mental disorder. A certain amount of nervousness can sharpen your sense, heighten your awareness, and generally make you perform faster and smarter. The term 'social anxiety disorder' is a relatively recent term that was coined by an advertising agency and has come into common usage in the commercial promotion of pharmaceuticals meant to alleviate only the so-called undesirable symptoms. Psychotherapists used to diagnose someone as having 'social phobia' when there was an excessive or unreasonable fear of all social situations, accompanied by panic attacks and avoidance that significantly interfered with a person's normal routine.[4]

So don't let advertising convince you that you're somehow abnormal when you become nervous in situations that would make any normal person nervous.

On the other hand, it's not uncommon for a person to be confident as a child only to have that confidence pounded out of him by classmates and even family members later in life. Your nervousness is based on your imagining that you will fail at what you do. This in turn comes from a lack of self-confidence, and self-confidence is based on what you believe about yourself. It sounds to me like you have been led to believe some negative things about yourself. This is what causes your nervousness when you're around others. In a sense it's your worry that they will see what a terrible or incompetent person you are (as you imagine you are).

You are obviously competent or you would not have been promoted to a supervisory position at your job. You must also be a good person or else your fiancée would not have chosen to be with you. If you focus on positive thoughts like these it will start to help you overcome your worries. Another very good way of building your self-esteem is to discuss your fears with your fiancée. Opening up to her will not result in losing her respect. On the contrary, while men see the expression of feelings as a sign of weakness, women discuss their feelings as a way to bond with each other. I'm certain that discussing your feelings with your fiancée will bring you closer together and strengthen your future relationship together. She will welcome your openness and respect your willingness to discuss your feelings with her. I hope this helps.

All the best in your future married life,

Peter

SUBJECT: BUSINESS ETHICS

Peter

R. G. Collingwood in "An Essay on Philosophical Method" offers a valuable lesson to tax lawyers/academics: the importance of attending to questions of why and how—which I understand in my context as relating to the question of 'what is tax avoidance'. Since 1900 the ground rules have subtly changed—increase in taxes, governmental attempts to introduce a general anti-avoidance provision, media highlighting of tax planning as being negative and the political complicity in this respect. The debates however rely on the nature of the judicial process and the rules of statutory interpretation. Lawyers in particular, tend to reduce the issues of 'tax avoidance' to the canons of construction and focus on matters like 'liberty' and 'property'. Viewed in those terms it deprives us of one potential insight—the evolving concept of citizenship: i.e., is there a duty not to avoid paying taxes? I shall leave you with these thoughts. As I am just embarking on my research, it would be premature to suggest that I have worked the ideas through to the end. I was hoping that your thoughts will quicken the process.

Regards

Joseph

Hi Joseph,

What you're pointing out is a very important distinction to philosophers: the difference between the law and morality. The two often conflict, and the question as to what to do is then left to the individual. While lawyers will argue that the right thing to do is to obey the law, Aristotle would say that the virtuous individual makes every decision in light of moral considerations. The law is, in a sense, meant to force people to be moral. But the law often falls short. A case in point is the law which said at one time that owning a slave was within a man's legal right. Of course morality held that it is wrong to own another person. (The law got around this by defining 'person' as only those having white skin). This law was eventually changed by moral people who thought it was not good enough to simply live life according to secular laws regardless of how those laws are worded.

Lawyers are similar to what in Socrates' day were called Sophists. The reason he hated the Sophists ('Sophist' means teacher) was not, as some people believe, because they charged for teaching others how to argue. Socrates hated them because they were mercenaries; they were willing to teach a person how to win an argument regardless of the consequences of such a win, or the truth of the conclusion to the argument—in other words, devoid of any moral considerations. Lawyers are similarly bound to defend the rights of an individual to do whatever the law allows, regardless of what is morally right or wrong. Recall that in Shakespeare's play 'The Merchant of Venice' Portia talks about "the letter of the law" versus "the spirit of the law." Lawyers generally always work to the letter of the law (for example, they will find 'loopholes' in tax laws that allow wealthy clients to avoid paying taxes), whereas a philosopher will examine the spirit of the law by considering more than simply what the law says but also what the larger intention is behind a law (taxes are needed to fix the roads, build the hospitals and schools that are also used by tax evaders).

You're right, the issue of tax evasion, when looked at philosophically, comes down to the question of, What are taxes for? For Aristotle the question would have been, What would a virtuous person do? For Immanuel Kant and others the question is, What is my moral duty? For lawyers and most business people taxes simply represent an obstacle to the maximization of their own profits. But lawyers and business people are not (for the most part) philosophers. I hope this helps.

Regards,
Peter

SUBJECT: DETERMINISM

Sir,

Myself is S G. having 22year age an Indian doing M.B.A. And from very beginning of my life till now i have done nothing. The autocratic environment made me introvert. The social conditions prevails make me sad. i am not aware of responsibilities because life to me looks like a money web. The expectation of parents from me is very high and it obvious being a youngest son. Rest everything is question mark for me.

S

Dear S,

By having been born into an autocratic environment as the youngest son to parents with high expectations you are in a difficult situation. What you describe in your life is the sort of life that makes young people here in North America sometimes run away from home and become 'street kids'. But the life of a street kid is also very difficult, and street kids are not very happy. What street kids, and you, need is a major change in your life. But it's not always possible to change your life when you are a young person, or when all of society supports the kind of values your parents are forcing you to accept, but which you find make your life miserable.

All I can suggest is that you try to find peace for now with your life as it is. Keep in mind that you have values that are different from your parents' values, but your parents don't see their values as bad, or your values as better. The ancient philosopher Epicurus once said "No one who sees what is bad chooses it, but being lured by it as being good compared to what is even worse than if he is caught in the snare." So try to keep in mind that your parents are trying to do what they believe is good for you and your family, and thank them for it even if what they give you is not what you want for yourself. Try to be at peace with yourself until you are old enough to make the kind of life you would like for yourself, or until you are able to change what is making you unhappy. I hope this helps.

Regards,

Peter

NOTES

1. See chapter 3, "The Characteristics of a Helping Relationship," in Carl R. Rogers' book *On Becoming a Person* (1961). Boston: Houghton Mifflin, 1989. 39–58.

2. Richards, Janet Radcliffe. *The Sceptical Feminist.* 289. Quoted in *A Dictionary of Philosophical Quotations.* Edited by A. J. Ayer and Jane O'Grady. Oxford, U.K.: Blackwell, 1994. 378.

3. Ross, C. E. and J. Mirowsky. "Child Care and Emotional Adjustment to Wives' Employment." *Journal of Health and Social Behavior* 29. 1988. 127–138.

4. Taken from the *Diagnostic and Statistical Manual of Mental Disorders* Fourth Edition (DSM-IV). Quoted in *Caring for the Mind.* Hales, Dianne and Robert E. Hales. New York: Bantam, 1995. 141.

Chapter 7

Sex and Logic

Just because so-called gay rights have been instituted in many countries doesn't mean it has made the life of same-sex oriented men and women any easier. Homosexuality (and I include lesbianism in this term) is still merely tolerated, rather than accepted as part of the norm, in most communities. Fears and biases run deep. "Gay bashing" has slowed not because of an upsurge in compassion but because the legal penalties for it have been stiffened. While, to the casual observer, life on the surface may seem normal, the treatment these individuals receive in their communities and even within their own families can cause an enormous amount of suffering and confusion. Even after having been granted "gay rights" many homosexual individuals have not been able to grant themselves the right to be who they truly are. I've had a number of clients whose sexual orientation has been at the epicenter of a host of personal problems that have brought on everything from serious depression to attempted suicide. Self-doubt, guilt, and self-condemnation are not unusual in both men and women whose sexual orientation was considered a mental illness by healthcare professionals until only a few years ago.

I have found that the approach in philosophical counseling that has helped these clients the most has been an examination of common arguments against homosexuality and the formulation of meaningful responses. But it is not necessary for the philosophical counselor to train the client to respond literally to challenges from homophobics; what most clients want from the philosophical counselor is to gain a perspective that will stop the self-doubt and involuntary shame and bring peace of mind.

A good place to begin is by telling the client that, sadly, homophobia has a very long history. At various times same-sex orientation was condemned as being a great evil that brings disaster to any society that allows it to occur in its midst. In early biblical times homosexuals were routinely stoned to death. As late as 1725, long after the French had given up burning women as witches, they continued to burn people for their sexual orientation. During the Second World War, German concentration camps held homosexuals as well as Jews. Yet in ancient Greece, during one of humankind's greatest periods of enlightenment, same-sex encounters were considered to be a natural part of a young man's education and maturation process. Paradoxically, while accepting same-sex orientation, those enlightened Greeks condoned the decidedly unenlightened practice of owning slaves. It seems that Greek enlightenment had its limits, and it could therefore be argued that their toleration of homosexuality was as misguided and unenlightened as their ownership of slaves. But was it?

The fact that modern North Americans think there is something wrong with owning slaves is not just a matter of our feeling differently about it than the ancient Greeks did. It is a matter of our having come to understand that the arguments in support of slavery, such as that slavery is part of the natural order of things or that it is a right bestowed by God, don't hold up under close scrutiny. Similarly, arguments against same-sex orientation don't hold up under careful scrutiny either.

Many individuals feel that the arguments which say that same-sex relationships are bad, unnatural, evil, sinful, or wrong are somehow not quite right but they don't know why they feel this way. They are unable to put a finger on exactly what is wrong with the various arguments against homosexuality. This is where the philosophical counselor can help by examining the arguments and suggesting philosophical responses. The six most common arguments used against homosexuality are as follows:

1. Homosexuality is not natural, so it is wrong.
2. The Bible says homosexuality is wrong, so it is wrong.
3. Everyone agrees that homosexuality is wrong, therefore it is wrong.
4. Homosexuals are a threat to our children, therefore it is wrong.
5. Homosexuality is a threat to the family and will destroy society as we know it, therefore it is wrong.
6. Homosexuality is caused by making a wrong choice in sex partners. If boys and girls are raised properly they won't grow up making wrong choices. Therefore homosexuals are just poorly raised individuals making wrong choices.

1. HOMOSEXUALITY IS NOT NATURAL, SO IT IS WRONG

This argument is expressed in two main variations: (a) homosexuality in both males and females goes contrary to what is obviously and observably the natural behavior of males and females in human society and is therefore unnatural and wrong; (b) homosexuality does not occur among nonhuman species in nature, therefore human homosexual behavior is unnatural and wrong.

Response

Variation (a) of this argument is a case of what is sometimes called the "naturalistic fallacy." This fallacy or faulty reasoning occurs when it is argued that, since it is observed to be the case that the majority of men and women are heterosexuals, heterosexuality is natural and homosexuality is therefore unnatural. The argument moves from reporting what *is observed to be* the case in most instances to insisting what *ought to be* the case in all instances. It's easy to see the problem with this line of reasoning when we recall that not long ago left handedness was considered to be unnatural. The reasoning that condemned left handed individuals ran the same way: most people are right handed, this makes right handedness natural, therefore left handedness is unnatural. The fear and concern over "sinister" left handedness is no longer a problem today but the flawed logical basis that led to its denouncement remains one of the arguments against homosexuality. Simply put, it is faulty reasoning to believe that a statistical majority in a population automatically makes the majority's behavior right and natural and all others wrong and unnatural.

A second response against the naturalistic fallacy is that, since humans are part of the natural world, anything humans do is in fact a natural part of their being human. Of course there is behavior, such as murder, that is held to be socially unacceptable and morally wrong but this does not mean murder is therefore an unnatural act. Likewise homosexuality may have been socially unacceptable at various times in history but this does not automatically make it an unnatural act.

Variation (b) above, that homosexuality does not occur in nonhuman species and is therefore unnatural, is a case of the fallacy of "improper appeal to observation." This observation is guilty of being contrary to known facts. In his book *Christianity, Social Tolerance, and Homosexuality* John Boswell points out that scientists have observed homosexual behavior in both sexes of a great number and variety of nonhuman creatures.

Homosexual behavior, sometimes involving pair-bonding, has been observed among many animal species in the wild as well as in captivity. Much material has come to light since Wainwright Churchill published his *Homosexual Behavior Among Males: A Cross-Cultural and Cross-Species Investigation* (New York, 1967). . . . For more recent material, see George Hunt and Molly Hunt, "Female-Female Pairing in Western Gulls (Larus occidentalis) in Southern California." (*Science*, 1977. 196)[1]

There are two responses possible to variation (b) above. The first is that the conclusion of variation (b) is just false since it is based on an incorrect assumption or faulty information about the sexual behavior of nonhuman species. Second, even if it were true that nonhuman species in fact never exhibited same-sex orientation, homosexuality in humans would still not necessarily need to be considered unnatural. Reading and writing also do not occur in nonhuman species yet we don't hold literacy as unnatural in humans. The same can be said of human behavior such as shaving, wearing clothes and makeup, or building musical instruments. Animals have never been observed to do any of these things. They are behaviors unique to humans, they are part of what defines human beings, yet we don't condemn them as being unnatural. If we were to hold that animal behavior should be the natural behavior humans are to follow then we would have to give up all those behaviors that make us uniquely human beings. It would also mean we would have to give up long-term monogamous relationships since the majority of nonhuman species are polygamous. For most animals sex is observed as nothing more than a brief and expedient encounter with no emotional component. If we take this to be natural behavior then passionate heterosexual relationships must be defined as unnatural.

This "argument from nature" is a fallacy with a long and varied history. In the sixteenth century Cardinal Robert Bellormine argued that a monarchy is a preferable form of government to a democracy because it is more natural.[2]

More incredible are the authoritative claims that were once made regarding what is natural and unnatural about women. Long before the modern attempt to argue that lesbianism is unnatural, men argued that women in general were abnormal. About 400 years before Christ, in ancient Greece, Aristotle was claiming that females in general are a natural deformity and that women are by nature weaker and colder than men.[3] In the thirteenth century Thomas Aquinas wrote in his highly regarded work, the *Summa Theologiae*, that women are naturally subject to men since men are naturally able to reason better than women. Aquinas argued that a man's seed was in miniature a perfect likeness of the masculine sex, and since a woman is not a perfect likeness of a man she is obviously defective. Aquinas was not unique in holding this view of women. In her book *Women: From the Greeks to the French Revolution* Susan Bell writes that every one of the major Christian writers from the first century through the sixth "assumed the mental and moral frailty of women."[4] Even the nineteenth-century psychotherapist Sigmund Freud was convinced that women were by nature inferior, vice-ridden, and half savage.[5] If these arguments about the abnormality or unnaturalness of all women seem familiar it is because the same sort of arguments are still used today against women (and men) who prefer same-sex relationships.

The fallacious argument from nature was also used at one time to condemn women and men to slavery. In the 30 years before the American Civil War scholars in the southern United States invested a considerable amount of time and energy gathering scriptural and historical proof that keeping blacks as slaves was part of the natural order of things. Some even went so far as to argue that those with a black skin color did not behave naturally like normal human beings but something more like animals. And just as it is sometimes argued today that same-sex desire is some sort of mental disorder, so it was argued by whites that the desires of some black slaves, such as the desire to escape and the desire to disobey the master's orders, were mental disorders as well (diagnosed as drapetomania and dysaethesia, respectively).[6]

In the same way that the argument from nature doesn't hold against left handedness, women, or people with skin colors other than white, it does not hold against individuals with a same-sex orientation.

2. THE BIBLE SAYS HOMOSEXUALITY IS WRONG, SO IT IS WRONG

Opponents of same-sex orientation refer to three main areas of the Bible—Romans 1:18–32, 1 Corinthians 6:9–10, and Genesis 19:1–11—as proof of God's unquestionable condemnation of homosexuality. In July 1992, the Vatican urged its U.S. Roman Catholic leaders to fight legislation that would make it illegal to discriminate against homosexuals. In other words, Catholic leaders were compelled by their church to endorse discrimination against individuals who prefer same-sex relationships. Fundamentalist and right-wing conservative religious groups who hold to a literal interpretation of the Bible see homosexuality as disobedience to a Divine commandment prohibiting same-sex relationships.

Response

The exegesis of biblical texts is a complicated and demanding task. In this chapter it is possible to give only a brief summary of the work that has been done. It should be noted that the examination of scripture does not need to go into theological debate. In other words, it is possible to allow that the Bible is in fact the divinely inspired and inerrant Word of God and still cast serious doubt on the way in which some individuals use portions of it to support their contention that homosexuality is sinful.

Of the many Bible translations of Romans 1:18–32 available today, the *Jerusalem Bible* seems to be one of the most direct in its translation of verses 24 to 28 as a condemnatory statement against homosexuality. In it are found such terms as "filthy enjoyments," "degrading passions," "shameless things," and "perversion." All of this "monstrous behavior" comes as a result of the "irrational ideas" of men and women who have "turned from natural intercourse" and gone against nature to follow "unnatural practices."

Paul is translated as having written in these verses that all homosexuals deserve to die. But this statement loses credibility in light of his statement that all children who are rebellious to their parents also deserve to die (verse 30). If it is the case that Paul's Jewish background led him to denounce homosexuality as an "unnatural" act how should we interpret his declaration in his first letter to the Corinthians that long hair on a man is also "unnatural" (1 Corinthians 11:14–15)?

Historians tell us that no clear idea of "natural law" existed in Paul's time, or for many centuries thereafter. He would therefore not have been referring to homosexuality in the sense of it being a violation of natural law. It seems more plausible that Paul was in fact speaking about either the violation of the social hierarchy of his day or the excess of sexual desires and activities, also condemned by Judaism and Stoicism, because they distract from "correct worship." His use of the Greek term *para phusin*, rather than meaning homosexual acts which are "*against* nature" or "unnatural," may be more accurately interpreted as sexual acts in general which are "*more* than what is natural" or "excessive." Even if we grant that Paul was writing specifically about homosexuality, the most compelling conclusion is that Paul's reference to same-sex activity is simply a mundane analogy to the theological sin of forgetting God due to the distractions of sex; it is clearly not the crux of his argument. Once the point has been made, the subject of same-sex activity is quickly dropped and the major argument concerning the correct form of worship is resumed.[7] If we see Paul's words as a warning against the evils of idolatry and infidelity to the true God, it is possible to perceive a number of other terms in this passage differently. For example, rather than as referring to homosexuality, the Greek words translated into "unnatural intercourse" can be read as meaning intercourse that is not meant for the purpose of conceiving offspring—that is, sex for pleasure which distracts the mind from thoughts of God; and the "shameless acts" that men committed with men could be seen as men taking part in acts of false worship with their fellow men. Even Paul's reference to men being "consumed with passion for one another" can be read as a denouncement not of men's passion toward each other per se, but because they should instead be spending their time cultivating their passion for God.

To argue that 1 Corinthians and Genesis 1 are proof of the evilness of homosexuality is to fall victim to the fallacy of "improper appeal to authority," because the authorities on scriptural hermeneutics disagree as to their correct interpretation. For example, it is not unanimously accepted that the correct interpretation of the passage at 1 Corinthians 6:9–10 refers to "homosexual perverts." Some Bible scholars believe it refers to "lust, promiscuity and other behaviors destructive to healthy love" and that it is a warning to all followers of Christ to act in a morally upright manner, regardless of sexual orientation or marital status. Others say the meaning of the Greek words *malakos* and *arsenokoites*, which have been translated as "homosexual" in some editions of the Bible, are more correctly translated as "morally weak" or "lacking in self-control."[8]

Rather than dwelling on the disagreements about the translation of ancient Greek a different response to this fallacy is that if we accept 1 Corinthians 6:9–10 as a literal condemnation of homosexuality we must also literally accept and obey the scripture at 1 Corinthians 14:34–35 which says, "Women should be silent in churches. They are not permitted to speak, but should be subordinate . . . for it is shameful for a woman to speak in church."[9] We must also allow slavery since the Bible says at Leviticus 25:44–46 that it is acceptable to own slaves. There was a time when these scriptures were taken literally. Today most churches no longer teach that it is shameful for women to speak in church, or that owning a slave is acceptable, yet many still teach that homosexuality is sinful. If we only accept the first scripture as literally applying to us and condemn homosexuality but refuse the second and third by allowing women to speak in church and condemning slavery then we are then guilty of the fallacy of "inconsistency."

A third fallacy occurs when we examine the stance taken by some fundamentalist Christians who insist that, since homosexuality is a sin, in order to become good Christians homosexuals must either become heterosexual in their behavior or remain celibate. A homosexuality information newsletter published in the early 1990s by a British Columbia–based Christian fundamentalist church refers to "healing for the homosexual," and infers that homosexuality is irresponsible sex. The newsletter also suggests that a reasonable alternative to sexual desire for same-sex partners is celibacy. But this is like suggesting that a reasonable alternative to hunger is not eating. By demanding that same-sex oriented individuals stifle their desires and become something different than what they are, critics of homosexuality are committing the fallacy of "contradiction," since this demand is contrary to what the Bible says. The scripture at 1 Corinthians 7:24 commands Christians, "In whatever condition you were called, brothers and sisters, there remain with God." This clearly infers that if an individual is same-sex oriented he or she should remain in this condition and not try to change his or her God-given sexual orientation.

The account at Genesis 19 regarding Lot and the destruction of the city of Sodom, which is often (mistakenly) interpreted as God's sweeping condemnation of same-sex orientation, holds no direct reference to homosexuality. Some Bible scholars believe that the sin of Sodom was in fact not homosexuality at all but "a failure to live up to charity, hospitality, and the imperative that guests be welcome and free from fear."[10] The fact that some religious leaders still use this Scriptural passage to condemn same-sex orientation is an interesting case of "selective focus." Lot's unbelievably cruel and cowardly behavior in Genesis 19, as well as similar behavior by another man of God at Judges 19, is consistently ignored by most Christians. At Genesis 19 Lot offers his two virgin daughters to the riotous mob of men outside his door, while at Judges 19 the Levite Gibeah offers his virgin daughter and his concubine to mob rape in exchange for the safety of the men of God in their homes. If the scripture at Genesis 19 is read as a condemnation of homosexuality as immoral behavior then logical consistency requires the condemnation of Lot and Gibeah's immoral behavior as well—the very men the Bible holds in high regard.

If, for the sake of argument, we were to agree that Christians have the right to condemn same-sex relationships, because the Bible says it is wrong, then, in order for Christians to be consistent in their application of scripture and their obedience to it, they must also stop praying in public places of worship and pray in their rooms with their doors shut (Matthew 6:6), they must cut off the parts of their own bodies that cause them to sin (Matthew 5:32), and they must be as perfect in their behavior as God (Matthew 5:48). Furthermore they must obey the Hebrew scriptures at Leviticus 20:13 which are interpreted as saying that homosexual men must be put to death; they must obey Leviticus 20:12 which says that if a man forces himself on his daughter-in-law not only must he be put to death but his daughter-in-law must be killed as well; and they must accept the Greek scriptures at Romans 1:29–31 which say that anyone who feels envy, anyone who debates, whispers, feels pride, boasts, or is disobedient to his or her parents deserves to be killed.

An interesting side note to biblical interpretation on the question of homosexuality is that, historically, the Bible was interpreted as saying that *all* sex is sinful. The references by Paul at Colossians 3:5 and 1 Thessalonians 4:5 regarding fornication, lustful passion, and evil desire were interpreted by many of the early Christian leaders as Paul's way of saying any and *all* sex is bad.

It was Augustine who epitomized a general feeling among Church Fathers that the act of intercourse was fundamentally disgusting. Arnobius called it filthy and degrading. Methodius unseemly, Jerome unclean, Tertullian shameful, Ambrose a defilement. In fact there was an unstated consensus that God ought to have invented a better way of dealing with the problem of procreation.[11]

It's not inconceivable that the modern-day condemnation of same-sex orientation is partly the result of leftover puritanical attitudes toward sex in general which hold that *all* sex is ugly, sinful, and dirty, attitudes that were sown by the early church Fathers at the inception of Christianity and blossomed during the Victorian era.

3. EVERYONE AGREES THAT HOMOSEXUALITY IS WRONG, THEREFORE IT IS WRONG

The argument goes as follows: because everyone agrees that homosexuality is bad, and since that many people can't be wrong, it must be the case that everyone is right and homosexuality is bad. In other words, the side of the argument with the greatest number of people on it is right; the other side is wrong.

Response

This line of argument suffers from the "popularity" fallacy also sometimes called the "band wagon" fallacy. There are two ways to respond to this fallacy. The first is to point out that within this fallacy of popularity lurks the fallacy of "improper appeal to observation" because the observation "*everyone* agrees that homosexuality is bad" is simply incorrect. The U.S. *Economist* reports that in the United States some 40% of heterosexual Americans do not personally disapprove of same-sex relationships, and some 80% believe homosexuals should not face discrimination when applying for employment.[12] A 1992 Gallup poll conducted in the United States found that 41% of respondents held homosexuality to be an acceptable alternative lifestyle, while 58% said they approved of legally sanctioning homosexual marriages.[13] A more recent Canadian survey found that 75% of Canadians feel that homosexuals deserve the same legal rights as heterosexuals when it comes to spousal entitlements such as retirement pensions, life insurance claims, and so on.[14] These surveys clearly show that not everyone agrees that being same-sex oriented is unequivocally wrong or bad.

A second response is that popular opinion can sometimes be badly mistaken. For example, most people at one time thought that left handedness was evil. Later it was seen as either a neurobiological disorder or pathological behavior that needed to be corrected. Most people at one time also believed that what is now called "mental illness" was demon possession. Besides being factually wrong, majority opinion can also be morally wrong. The ancient Greeks and the majority of white people in the southern United States at one time considered slavery morally acceptable. But this majority opinion did not in fact make slavery morally acceptable. In the case of homosexuality, even if every heterosexual person in North America were of the opinion that homosexuality should be condemned it does not make same-sex orientation deserving of condemnation.

4. HOMOSEXUALS ARE A THREAT TO OUR CHILDREN, THEREFORE IT IS WRONG

When the city council of Portland, Maine passed an ordinance barring antigay discrimination in housing, employment, and credit in 1992, several antigay groups gathered their forces to rally against it. To encourage citizens to sign an *anti*-ordinance petition which was being circulated, warnings went out that the ordinance was going to result in gay promiscuity, an increase in the spread of AIDS, and sex with children (pedophilia).[15] In the 1950s similar warnings were published by the Ku Klux Klan to prevent blacks from being granted their civil rights. Whites were informed that blacks were "a breeding ground for syphilis, and little white girls would be highly susceptible to contracting syphilis" from blacks if drinking fountains, books, towels, and gym clothes were integrated.[16]

The argument that homosexuals are a threat to children is more like an outright warning than an argument. The innocent young are very vulnerable. It claims that if we don't believe homosexuals pose a threat to us, we will let our guard down and they will harm the fragile bodies and innocent minds of our children.

Response

Parents can't help but worry about their children. The human desire to safeguard our young runs so deeply in us that it seems to be part of our fundamental genetic programming. The argument that homosexuals are a threat to our children is an attempt to use this programming against us. Like the racist warnings of the Ku Klux Klan that blacks are a danger to little white girls, the warning that same-sex oriented people pose a threat to children is nothing but a scare tactic meant to stir up panic and hostility.

It is interesting to note that at one time Jews were believed to pose the same kind of threat to Christian children as homosexuals are today. Yale professor of history John Boswell sees the fate of gay people as being almost identical to that of Jews, from early Christian hostility toward them to their extermination in concentration camps in the 1940s. The same countries that made it illegal to be a Jew imposed majority standards of sexual conduct that made it illegal to be same-sex oriented. Same-sex oriented individuals were not only seen as evil in themselves, they were also said to pose a threat to the children of heterosexuals. "The same methods of propaganda were used against Jews and gay people—picturing them as animals bent on the destruction of the children of the majority."[17]

The belief that homosexual men are a threat to young boys may be connected with the historical incidence of pederasty. In ancient Greece older upper-class men often took young men under their wings to educate them not only in the fine arts but also in the art of loving. This was considered a natural step in their education and prevented early unwanted pregnancies among the young girls in upper-class families. Not unlike our modern laws, Greek laws forbade sexual intimacy with prepubescent individuals. It was always only practiced between consenting individuals with the blessings of the young man's parents. Pederasty made a comeback in the Victorian and Edwardian eras, especially in England.[18]

Modern-day homosexual men are not accused of pederasty but something much more insidious, namely having intercourse with sexually naïve young boys. This accusation does not merely say that there have been homosexual men who have been accused of the crime of pedophilia, but rather that *all* gay men are either guilty of having committed this crime or are likely to commit it in the future. It infers that if a man is same-sex oriented he is certain to sexually assault young boys. This assumption suffers from the fallacy of "guilt by association." The structure of this flaw in reasoning can easily be seen in the statement, There have been heterosexual men who robbed banks, therefore all heterosexual men are bank robbers.

A second variation of the above argument is that lesbian mothers are a negative influence on their own children. It is not clear in this argument what the negative influence might be, except that it infers lesbians might try to influence their daughters to become lesbians. There are two responses to this claim: first, research has shown that children cannot be swayed into any particular sexual orientation by parents or anyone else; and second, professor of psychology Janet Hyde points out that in a study which had lesbian mothers and heterosexual mothers rate their concept of the ideal child, lesbian mothers did not necessarily wish their children to be same-sex oriented. "There were no significant differences between the lesbian and heterosexual women in their rating of the ideal child. This evidence indicates that lesbians are not 'abnormal' mothers, and that they have views similar to those of heterosexual women concerning what children should be like."[19]

A third variation of the argument that homosexuals are a danger to our children is based on the assumption that a person became same-sex oriented because of some sort of same-sex encounter, and the fear that they will in turn influence the children of heterosexuals to become same-sex oriented. But there is no evidence to justify this fear. In fact research shows that "homosexuals were not more likely than heterosexuals to have had negative experiences such as rape . . . nor were they more likely to have been seduced by an older person."[20] Same-sex orientation is not caused by a difference in family experiences between homosexuals and heterosexuals.

A fourth variation says that homosexual women and men are simply bad role models for our children. This is not based on the fear that children will witness and imitate a particular type of sex act but that they will copy the homosexual "affectations," that is, the stereotypical behavior associated with homosexuality, namely the limp-wristed "swishiness" in men and the tough "butch" attitude in women. In other words, it will bring out the feminine in a young man and the masculine in a young woman, confusing their so-called normal sex roles in heterosexual society.[21] But those who argue that homosexual men are not men because they take on women's roles or homosexual women are not women because they take the place of men in same-sex relationships are again guilty of imprecise observation. Research has shown that the stereotypical image held by many individuals who imagine that one of the women in a homosexual couple is a "butch" while the other is a "femme" is false for the majority of lesbian couples.[22] In her book *Half the Human Experience*, Janet Hyde observes that "most lesbians have a female identification—that is, they are quite definitely women; they dress and behave like women; but they simply choose to direct emotional, sexual love toward other women."[23] The same can be said of same-sex oriented men. Personal appearance and manner can no more be used to determine an individual's sexual preferences than these can be used to determine whether they prefer to eat apples or oranges. This means that those heterosexual individuals who claim they can pick out the homosexual women and men in a crowd are simply deluding themselves.

The argument that homosexuals are a threat to our children, in any of the variations above, is either a blatantly calculated fear tactic or simply a mistake based on assumptions, prejudices, and fear.

5. HOMOSEXUALITY IS A THREAT TO THE FAMILY AND WILL DESTROY SOCIETY AS WE KNOW IT, THEREFORE IT IS WRONG

This is almost a continuation of the above argument, that is, if same-sex orientation is a threat to our children then it is a threat to the entire structure and stability of our society. A *Newsweek* poll found that although 78% of respondents felt discrimination against gays in employment is wrong, 45% said they felt gay rights are a threat to American family values.[24]

While in some ancient societies it was believed that same-sex orientation posed an immediate threat to society in the form of famines, earthquakes, and diseases from God, today it is seen as more of a long-range threat. There are three forms of this argument. The first says that (a) since a homosexual union cannot result in offspring, homosexuals pose a threat to the natural procreative process which enables a society's population to grow or at least remain stable. The second variation is a more far-reaching prediction which says that (b) homosexuality threatens the very continuance of the human species as we know it. Again, because homosexuals can't reproduce, the human species will disappear from this planet. The third variation offered by some fundamentalist religious organizations is that (c) procreation is a divine command. The production of children is a requirement if an adult couple hopes to gain spiritual rewards and security both on the present mortal plane and later in the spiritual realm. Same-sex couples who don't produce children are therefore automatically damned to be punished by God, not necessarily for committing a prohibited sexual act but for disobeying the divine command to produce offspring. A fourth, rather odd, variation says (d) if our society allows homosexuality to continue unhindered then humankind will eventually become exclusively homosexual.

Response

The main argument above, that homosexuality will lead to the end of society as we know it, suffers from the fallacy called "false dichotomy," also known as the "either-or fallacy." This error in reasoning states that all humans must be heterosexual or else society will be destroyed. The argument allows for no middle ground, no combination or range of sexual preferences within a society that still enables it to thrive. It assumes there is only one way to avoid doom, through the elimination of all homosexuality. This argument is also guilty of the fallacy known as "specter" because it seems to predict a terrible future as a consequence of homosexuality without offering any evidence why this gloomy future is inevitable.

The fourth variation (d) of the argument above assumes that the preference for same-sex relationships is somehow contagious, that, given enough homosexuals on the planet, the remaining heterosexuals will be unable to resist becoming homosexuals themselves. First of all, this variation of the main argument fails to take into consideration the wide range of desires and preferences in other areas of human life that have so far failed to cause everyone's desires and preferences to merge into one. For example, the many individuals who enjoy Western classical music have so far been unable to convince the rest of humanity to enjoy Western classical music. Second, no current scientific data regarding the origins or reasons for same-sex orientation in a society suggest that if a society tolerates same-sex orientation its incidence will steadily increase. Boswell notes that "Even purely biological theories uniformly assume that it would be a minority preference under any conditions, no matter how favorable."[25]

It is easy to imagine, however, that since our North American culture is becoming increasingly more tolerant toward homosexuality its incidence would be on the rise. There are fears among some members of the heterosexual community that homosexuality has increased to a staggering 10% of the population. But a recent University of Chicago study shows that between 1989 and 1992 the population of homosexuals in the United States remained constant at 2.5% among women and 2.8% among men. In her book *Kinsey, Sex and Fraud*, researcher Judith Reisman argues that homosexuals typically constitute as little as 1% of the population.[26] These findings seem to indicate that tolerance or permissiveness toward same-sex orientation in a society does not necessarily increase the rate of homosexuality.

The first and second variations (a) and (b) of this argument focus on the absence of procreation within same-sex relationships. These arguments assume, first of all, that heterosexual desire is necessary for human reproduction, and second that homosexual individuals have no desire to, and therefore don't, reproduce. Both of these assumptions are false. There is no evidence to support the claim that homosexuality induces nonreproductivity in individuals or population groups. A significant proportion of homosexual men do in fact marry women and father children. Many lesbians desire children and wish to experience the joys of motherhood but they are often kept from doing so by various discriminatory civil laws.[27] An August 9, 1993 CTV newscast reported that more than half the artificial insemination clinics in Canada at that time were discriminating against lesbians by refusing to take them as patients, yet it was estimated that in the United States alone there were already some 10,000 children being raised by lesbians who conceived them through artificial insemination.[28] It seems reasonable to speculate that it is the antihomosexual stance of modern societies, not the mindset of homosexuals, that keeps homosexuals from reproducing and forming family groups.[29]

If we assume that sexual activity in same-sex oriented couples is nonprocreative and is therefore a threat to society, then we must also hold that all other human sexual activity that does not lead directly to conception and procreation is a threat to society as well. This would include intercourse when the woman is not fertile, the use of birth control devices, masturbation, and the practice of voluntary celibacy. To push the point *ad absurdum*, any individual who does not begin an attempt to procreate when they reached puberty should similarly be considered a threat to society. Paradoxically, the practice of intercourse during infertile times in a woman's cycle, the use of birth control devices, the acceptance of masturbation as natural, and the practice of voluntary celibacy by some members of society seem so far to have had no detrimental effects on the survival of any society on earth nor on the evolutionary success of the human species as a whole.

Variation (c) of this argument, that it is essential for adults to produce children for the spiritual well being of the parents, requires a response of a different type. This is not a case of an informal logical fallacy in argument but rather a case of questionable moral reasoning. When children are born to adults who view their existence only as an offering to God, one which will elicit His favor or secure *the parents* a place in the afterlife, these children are being used by their parents as barter in the pursuit of their own immortality. They are merely a means to an end. This argument, that same-sex orientation is bad because it does not lead to the birth of children who will procure for their parents favor from God, is simply morally reprehensible.

One other modern-day argument offered to show that same-sex orientation is bad for society is the claim that in order to have a cohesive, stable society, relationships must last. Since homosexual relationships don't last, the argument goes, they therefore hinder the maintenance of a stable society. A simple response to this argument is that many heterosexual relationships don't last very long either. The present divorce rate among heterosexual married couples is somewhere around 50%. While research has shown that lesbian relationships can range from one month to 25 years, it was found that almost 100 percent of gay women interviewed said they prefer stable, long-term relationships. It was also found that a lesbian appears to emphasize emotional intimacy in her relationship more than a gay man does.[30] These findings concerning emotional intimacy in the relationships of gay couples are not very surprising, since they reflect similar differences between men and women in heterosexual relationships. Another response to this charge is that many individuals who admit to being same-sex oriented and who enjoy same-sex relationships are, at the same time, partners in stable heterosexual marriages.[31] The point is that not all individuals who admit to having a preference for same-sex encounters engage in nontraditional roles within their community or exert a negative, and nonprocreative, influence on their society.

6. HOMOSEXUALITY IS CAUSED BY MAKING A WRONG CHOICE IN SEX PARTNERS. IF BOYS AND GIRLS ARE RAISED PROPERLY THEY WON'T GROW UP MAKING WRONG CHOICES. THEREFORE HOMOSEXUALS ARE JUST POORLY RAISED INDIVIDUALS MAKING WRONG CHOICES

This argument harks back to early psychoanalytic theories about the causes of homosexuality phrased something like this: "If there is defensive detachment from the father or male figure then the deficit creates a deep and wide chasm, a confused difference of feelings that only another man can fulfill. Homosexuality comes not from relationship problems with the opposite sex parent but with the same sex parent."[32]

Response

This argument is guilty of a number of fallacies. First is the fallacy known as "false cause" or *post hoc ergo propter hoc* (in English: after this therefore on account of this). The argument implies that because a homosexual individual chooses a same-sex partner the act of choosing a same-sex partner turns an individual into a homosexual.

Second, the terms "wrong choice," "raised properly," and "poorly raised individuals" are ambiguous, and third, they beg the question: Is same-sex orientation a "wrong choice"? Does a person's sexual orientation reflect how they were raised? and, Is same-sex orientation caused by a child being "raised poorly"? Fourth, the statement is both a faulty assumption and a hasty conclusion since there is no evidence to support the claims being made.

Over the years there has been much speculation and many theories have been advanced in an attempt to explain what causes same-sex orientation. The factors that have been held to cause lesbianism have over the years included fear of growing up and assuming adult responsibilities; fear of dominance and destruction; fear of rejection; fear of the opposite sex; fear of castration and of the penis; the desire to conquer and possess the mother; neurotic dependency; heterosexual trauma (including rape); seduction in adolescence by an older female; first sexual experience with someone of the same sex and finding it pleasurable; tomboy behavior in early childhood; prolonged absence of the mother; masturbation with a resulting clitoral fixation; social factors (such as heterosexual taboos and unisexual, all female, groups); and physical factors (genetic, constitutional, and endocrine abnormalities).[33]

A list could also be compiled of similarly negative speculations as to what causes male homosexuality. For a long time it was believed that a boy raised without a father in the home was more likely to take on the feminine traits of his mother and more likely to develop a same-sex orientation. But a major meta-analysis of 67 studies on the effects of father absence on boys found little or no harmful effects. There was also a decided lack of effect on girls. In fact it was discovered that there was a slight tendency for older father-absent boys to be more stereotypically male than father-present boys.[34] If it were true that a father's absence will cause the son to become same-sex oriented there ought to be a far higher incidence of homosexuality in U.S. inner-city ghettos where the absentee rate for fathers is many times higher than the national average.

The theory that the lack of a father or mother can cause children to become male or female homosexuals carries with it the implication that young women and men become same-sex oriented because they have weak or unstable personalities. In her book *The Second Sex* Simone de Beauvoir writes from the perspective of existentialism—a philosophy that holds, among other things, that everyone is responsible for the course of his or her own life. Beauvoir sees lesbianism (this may also apply to male homosexuality) as a conscious choice, a lifestyle that is freely adopted from the position of acting authentically.[35] This takes homosexuality out of the hands of fate, against which an individual is powerless, and places the control over one's sexual life squarely back into the hands of the individual. But it suggests as well that homosexual women and men must also have an abnormally strong sense of self and a powerful determination since they choose to take on a lifestyle they know will make them victims of discrimination, social and familial ostracism, fear, criticism, and open hostility. While it makes homosexuality seem rather gallant, Beauvoir's theory does not hold for the many same-sex oriented individuals who feel they have not in fact chosen the sexual desires they feel. If it is indeed the case that a homosexual orientation is a choice made by an individual then it must also be the case that heterosexuality is chosen. An examination of one's own sexual urges will easily reveal that to assume one's sexual orientation is a choice is clearly a faulty assumption.

Occasionally it is also argued that homosexuality must be abnormal because biologists and geneticists are searching for its cause. This is an interesting argument that leads logically to the question, What is it that causes heterosexual desire? And when biologists and geneticists begin searching for the cause of heterosexual desire will it mean that heterosexual desire is also abnormal?

CONCLUSION

It should by now be fairly evident that these six most popular arguments condemning same-sex orientation prove to be neither morally relevant, logically consistent, nor forcefully convincing (cogent). In fact, and in general, most antihomosexual arguments are based on fear, false assumptions, faulty biblical interpretations, and other mistakes in reasoning and research. The client who is helped to understand the structure of these arguments and the errors in reasoning on which they are based will find it easier to deal with the day-to-day homophobia still prevalent in most societies. But while differences between heterosexual and homosexual men and women are not as pronounced as might be expected, there is in fact a significant difference between the way men and women, regardless of their sexual orientation, tend to communicate. Understanding this difference is vital to effective philosophical counseling.

NOTES

1. Boswell, John. *Christianity, Social Tolerance, and Homosexuality.* Chicago: University of Chicago Press, 1980. 12 fn.

2. Shea, William R. "Galileo and the Church." In *God and Nature.* David C. Lindberg and Ronald L. Numbers, eds. Berkeley: University of California Press, 1986. 116.

3. See, for example, Aristotle's *De Generatione Animalium.*

4. Bell, Susan Groag. *Women: From the Greeks to French Revolution.* Belmont, Calif.: Wadsworth, 1973. 89.

5. Millet, Kate. *Sexual Politics.* New York: Doubleday, 1970.

6. Wade, Wyn Craig. *The Fiery Cross.* New York: Simon and Schuster, 1987. 10, 11, 114.

7. Boswell, 108–109.

8. Dench, Brian. *Homosexuality: Is It Wrong?* Toronto: The Unit on Human Rights, Anglican Church of Canada, 1992. 5.

9. Metzger, Bruce M. and Roland E. Murphy, eds. *The New Oxford Annotated Bible.* New York: Oxford University Press, 1989.

10. Ibid., 5.

11. Tannahill, Reay. *Sex in History.* New York: Stein and Day, 1982. 141.

12. *Economist.* February 6, 1993.

13. *Newsweek.* August 27, 1992.

14. The Vancouver *Province.* July 16, 2001. A3.

15. *Newsweek.* September 14, 1992.

16. Wade, 299.

17. Boswell, 16.

18. Tannahill, 85–93, 375–381.

19. Hyde, 292.

20. Ibid., 298–299.

21. *Newsweek.* March 12, 1990. 27.

22. Peplau, Letitia Anne. "Research on Homosexual Couples: An Overview." *The Journal of Homosexuality*, 8 (2) 1982. 3–8.

23. Hyde, 287.

24. *Newsweek.* September 14, 1992. 5.

25. Boswell, 9.

26. *Newsweek.* February 15, 1993. 46.

27. Hyde, 287.

28. *Newsweek.* September 14, 1992.

29. Boswell, 9–10.

30. Hyde, 288, 299.

31. Ibid., 287.

32. From an information newsletter titled *Homosexuality—A Christian Response* published by the Burnaby Christian Fellowship in British Columbia. No publication date cited.

33. Hyde, 298.

34. Ibid., 379.

35. Beauvoir, Simone de. *The Second Sex.* New York: Knopf, 1952. 398.

Chapter 8

Speaking Like a
Woman/Listening Like a Man*

The vast majority of published philosophy has been written by men. Most of those men wrote as though the human race consisted exclusively of males. To avoid this obvious mistake much of the published material available today in the field of philosophical counseling talks of the client in generic terms. The client has become a "he or she," a "he/she," a "s/he," or simply a genderless "client." This makes it seem as though the writers of material on philosophical counseling are working under the assumption that the person who comes to see the philosophical counselor has a neutral psychology that is neither male nor female in orientation.[1] Advice to philosophical counselors concerning how the counselor ought to relate to the client is therefore almost always put in generic and universal terms, as though it doesn't matter whether the client or the counselor is male or female. In their attempt to avoid male bias, writers give the impression that what will work for men will work for women and vice versa. Implicit in this "politically correct" style of gender-neutral publishing is the erroneous assumption that to achieve political *equality* between the sexes a presupposition of gender *sameness* is required. This may be leading philosophical counselors to assume that there does not need to be any difference between how they ought to relate to a male client and how they ought to relate to a female client. But even an informal survey of the information consumption habits of women and men—print media, movies, radio, television, and the Internet—shows that there is a substantial difference between women and men in what they find humorous, what they consider entertaining, and what is taken seriously. Despite attempts to find a foundation of absolute equality between

*An earlier version of this chapter was presented at the Helene Stöcker Gesellschaft e.V. conference. Berlin, Germany. November 10–12, 2000

the sexes, communicative actions are offered and received differently by and between men and women. Research done in North America in the social sciences has shown that "men and women come from different sociolinguistic subcultures, having learned to do different things with words in a conversation, so that when they attempt to carry on conversations with one another, even if both parties are attempting to treat one another as equals, cultural miscommunication results."[2]

In other words, men and women have different discursive styles: they speak differently and they hear each other differently. Men don't talk about things in the same way that women do, and they don't talk about these things in the same way with women as they do with other men. Women generally understand other women better than they understand men and vice versa. The research of ethicist Carol Gilligan indicates that men and women may assume they're speaking the same language, but they are in fact "using similar words to encode disparate experiences of self and social relationships." Their words "contain a propensity for systematic mistranslation, creating misunderstandings which impede communication and limit the potential for cooperation and care in relationships."[3] It is often exactly because of this problem of mutual misunderstanding that a man or a woman will consult a philosophical counselor and become a client in the first place.

This talk about differences in communicative interaction is not at all meant to suggest that one style is better than another. It simply means that there are different ways of conceptualizing, articulating, and dealing with issues and problems, all of which are considered legitimate by those who use them. The difference between men and women was already recognized several thousand years ago. In ancient Greece Philodemus said that the women of his day offered more resistance to Epicurean arguments than men did since they disliked receiving the sort of "frank criticism" of belief that, according to Philodemus, was the approach used by Epicurus and his followers.[4]

I received a very clear example of the kind of miscommunication that can happen between a man and a woman when Karl and Hilda came to see me in my capacity as a philosophical counselor. Karl was a client of mine for almost a year. He was good looking, physically fit, outgoing, active in sports, and the executive head of a very successful company. Hilda, on the other hand, had spent the past 15 years raising their children. She had been a fashion model many years earlier but had given up her "life in the fast lane" to focus all her energies on providing a safe, comfortable, and supportive home for her family. Karl found it difficult to settle down to the extent that Hilda had. He saw his role in the family as the one who had to compel the children to accomplish as much as possible and to strive for perfection. When Hilda and the children no longer joined Karl in his quest for challenge, excitement, and adventure—including participating in a number of dangerous sports—Karl found himself attracted to other women. After several affairs, Karl came to realize something was wrong with the life he was living. He came to me without Hilda at first and asked me to help him deal with his feelings of guilt and shame over having had these extramarital affairs and to save his marriage. It was only after about eight months of working with Karl on the problems he was having with himself that he felt ready to invite Hilda into our discussions.

As you can imagine, Hilda was upset with Karl for the way he had betrayed her. But she also felt a sense of relief that he was coming to see me. She said she was beginning to see a change in him, and appreciated the fact that Karl had been spending so much time trying to mend his ways. The session seemed to be going smoothly. Karl expressed his regret to Hilda and asked her forgiveness; Hilda expressed her anger at Karl but agreed to try to forgive him. But it was at this point that Karl almost ruined everything, not out of spite but because neither Karl nor Hilda could see how differently they were speaking and hearing each other.

Karl said, "I'm so sorry about all this, Hilda. How can I make it up to you?"
Hilda nodded and said, "By having patience."
Karl asked again, "But what can I do? Tell me what to do."
Hilda answered, "Just be there for me, Karl. Listen to me. Give me time."
Karl tried again, "Sure. But I need to know what you want me to do in the meantime. What do you want me to do for you, Hilda? Ask me anything you like."
Hilda tried again, "I don't know. It's OK."
Karl persisted, "But I want to make it up to you. I'm really sorry and I want to undo the wrong I've done. Can't you tell me what I can do for you?"

By now tears of frustration were beginning to well up in Hilda's eyes. Karl was becoming more and more agitated because the harder he tried to make things better the worse things got. Without being aware of it, Hilda and Karl had run headlong into a major difference between men and women. This is the very same difference that can also cause enormous problems between two academic philosophers and between philosophical counselors and their clients. But this difference isn't something that appears ready-made in adulthood; in fact it isn't experienced exclusively by adults. It begins in early childhood.

ORIGINS

The important differences between men and women, when it comes to the relationships between them, are not biologically given sexual differences but those of gender, that is, differences that are culture and epoch specific, that are learned by each generation and transmitted to the next, and that must be maintained within each culture and generation by means of continuous effort. Research in sociology and anthropology has shown that in general women and men are not innately different, but they must learn to follow different rules when engaging in conversation, and they must learn different ways to interpret the same information within any given conversation because of their dissimilar early childhood experiences.[5] In other words, while every child is clearly born with unique and innate personality traits, social behavior always must be (and is) learned.

Girls tend to play with other girls of similar age, in small groups and in private or semiprivate settings that require participants to be invited in. Their play is often gentle and cooperative, and they learn to exchange information and confidences to create and maintain relationships of closeness. Best friends share secrets with each other to strengthen their friendship, and if they want to end a friendship they share formerly exclusive secrets with others. They argue with each other without becoming overly aggressive, focusing on maintaining equality among the participants of their discussion. Girls also learn to hide the source of their own criticism, presenting it as though it is coming from someone else, or simply forwarding it through a third party. Because girls express conflict indirectly, they must learn to read the subtleties of relationships and situations sensitively. Girls learn to seek the approval and protection of others, and their social survival and success depend on interpreting all the abstruse discursive and relational nuances correctly.

Boys, on the other hand, typically play in larger, more hierarchically organized groups. The intention behind boys' games and discussions is not so much closeness as toughness. Games are frequently rough and usually competitive, and are often meant to challenge each other's status within the group and to produce a leader whose ideas may be played out. To gain membership into a group a boy cannot wait for it to be offered to him; he must win it for himself. Boys therefore learn at an early age how to assert themselves and how to maintain their place in the group by presenting their opinions confidently, and by dealing effectively with challenges from other boys. Discussion among boys is often assertive and aggressive, and while the rules of a game may change frequently they are clearly and openly stated.

These differences can already create misunderstandings and confusion at an early age whenever the activities of girls and boys overlap. For example, when a girl wishes to join a boy's group she may find herself waiting indefinitely on the sidelines because she has assumed the boys will invite her in. Instead they pay her no attention, expecting that she will simply make her own way in when she's ready. And when a boy is invited to join a girl's group he may find it difficult and confusing when trying to determine what his role is in a group where there is no clear leader giving him orders to be followed.

For adolescent boys growing up is seen as requiring a movement toward toughness, self-assertion, individuation, and an unwillingness to be dictated to. There is a reluctance to simply adopt what society defines as good behavior. The North American ideal for a young man is for him to be strong, independent, and comfortable with defiance. For girls, on the other hand, the rebelliousness of youth is left behind and they see themselves as settling down into the interconnected life of family, school, and society. Growing up is seen by them as striving to fit in with their community and its expectations.[6]

The sociolinguistic characteristics developed throughout childhood and adolescence therefore produce different assumptions in young men and women as to what is important in life. Aristotle's claim that "to a certain extent all men attempt to discuss statements and to maintain them, to defend themselves and to attack others,"[7] Friedrich Nietzsche's assertion that humankind's ultimate drive is 'the will to power'[8] and Michel Foucault's well-known dictum that all discourse is an attempt to exercise power over others[9] are clearly male perspectives on interpersonal relationships that do not necessarily agree with the way many young women see the world and their place in it. Carol Gilligan's empirical research in the field of moral psychology revealed that males are characteristically concerned with substantive moral matters of justice, rights, autonomy, and individuation. In their moral reasonings they tend to rely on abstract principles and to seek universality of scope. Women, by contrast, are more often concerned with substantive moral matters of care, personal relationships, and avoiding hurt to others. They tend to avoid abstract principles and universalist pretensions and to focus instead on contextual detail and interpersonal emotional responsiveness.[10]

Gender differences have their beginnings in childhood but are perpetuated by sex role stereotypes, different normative expectations, differential social opportunities, and differences in access to power. The question this leaves us with is, Which differences between adult men and women should be taken into account in both the discourse of academic philosophy and philosophical counseling?

AN OVERVIEW OF DIFFERENCES

Viewpoint

A review of the literature of sociology, psychology, and anthropology that deals with the differences between men and women suggests that the feminine outlook is typically holistic, simultaneous, synthetic, and concrete whereas the masculine view is more linear, sequential, reductionist, and abstract.[11] Women more often believe they cannot and should not act alone. This can be problematic when a quick and decisive decision is called for. But for men, the conviction that they must act independently and always find their way without help from anyone can be problematic when the situation calls for the input of more information or alternate points of view before a good decision is possible. While men may see life in terms of a contest or struggle against nature and other men, women see it more in terms of a struggle to maintain their connection with their community.[12] Women are said to see the world in terms of connectedness and are threatened by isolation, while men see the world in terms of autonomy and are threatened by the perceived dependent nature of intimacy.[13] Men tend to place importance on individual achievement, independence, external evaluation of themselves, and future time orientation while women are said to value group identity, duty and loyalty to kin, harmony with the world, and present time orientation.[14]

Relationships

Men are said to conceive of relationships as being either one-up or one-down. In other words, when two people come together or encounter each other, the male assumption is that one of them must be superior and the other must be inferior. Men do not necessarily need to be one-up; they just don't want to be one-down. This concern with one-upmanship is also central to a man's choice of a female life partner. Men are often accused of typically preferring female partners who are less intelligent than they are (the "dumb blonde" syndrome). But in light of what has been said regarding men's preoccupation with competition, clearly it's not so much a case of men preferring women who are less intelligent than they are as it is a case of men preferring women who will not compete with them the way other men do.

Women are said to conceive of their relationships as peer until proven otherwise. A woman is therefore more likely than a man to assume that in each new encounter there is a condition of equality even when there is not.[15] Women find it more natural to consult with their partners at every turn, while men take it upon themselves to make even the most difficult decisions without consulting their partners.[16] A woman will also at times have made up her mind about an issue or problem and yet proceed to discuss it at length with others in her peer group in an attempt to gain affirmation from the group for a decision she has made independently and to solidify her connection with the group through consensus.

A woman is more likely to want to connect on an emotional level with her dialogue partner; she will tune in to the emotional element of what is being said. A man is more often content to connect on an intellectual or factual level; he will focus his attention primarily on the informational content. Women have also been found to be more prone to reveal their emotions in facial expressions, while men are more prone to internalize their feelings. Women are far more likely to smile than men whether or not they are actually happy or amused. A smile is used to cover up uneasiness or nervousness, to meet the social expectation that women ought to smile and look pretty, to soften or mitigate critical statements they are making about others, or to show submission to someone in a position of power.[17]

Women continually focus on each other's faces during conversations, glancing away only occasionally, while men will look elsewhere in the room, glancing at each other only occasionally. A likely explanation for this is that men believe looking directly at another man would seem like a threat, while looking directly at a woman might seem like flirting. Women and men therefore tend to be indirect about different things. Women tend to be more indirect with criticism—thus safeguarding their connection with others. They will often resort to "telling it slant" (softening the truth) to avoid the risk of hurting their discussion partner.[18] Men may translate this as lying, deceitfulness, or manipulation, rather than caring. Men tend to be more direct in the statements they make, and more indirect in verbally expressing feelings or personal problems, in order to avoid the loss of status inherent in such admissions.[19]

Friendships

Females are more self-disclosing to same-sex friends,[20] and in particular about intimate topics.[21] In adulthood, close female friends converse more frequently about personal and family problems, intimate relationships, doubts and fears, daily activities, hobbies, and shared activities. Male friends, on the other hand, discuss events or achievements in sports or at work more frequently.[22]

The major contrast, then, between male friendships and female friendships appears to be located in their different orientations toward close relationships. Male friendships will more often involve communication about abstract matters external to the self; they engage more in sociability than in intimacy.[23] Female friendships encompass personal identities, intimacy, and the immediacy of daily life, paying less attention to abstract issues.

Discursive Styles

In a man's world conversations are often negotiations in which people try to achieve and maintain the upper hand if they can, and protect themselves from others' attempts to put them down and push them around. Life is a contest, a struggle to preserve independence, avoid failure, and maintain status. A woman is more likely to see herself as an individual within a network of connections. In her world conversations are negotiations for closeness in which people try to seek and give confirmation and support, and to reach consensus. Life is a community, but also a struggle to preserve the intimacy of relationships and avoid isolation.[24]

Both women and men desire to avoid conflict, but the strategies they prefer for doing so are different. Women choose to voice objections, seek compromises, and talk out a problem. These are behaviors consistent with what researchers have labeled "collaborative conflict-avoidance" strategies. To men this strategy can seem like women are intentionally confrontational and argumentative, and as though they are maliciously refusing to just drop a bad situation and forget about it. Men choose what researchers have labeled "unilateral conflict-avoidance" strategies as exemplified by their desires to withdraw, to have those around them be less emotional, and to generally avoid sensitive topics of discussion altogether.[25] To women a strategy of avoidance can make men seem callous and uncaring because they read it as indicating that they are not interested in making a bad situation better.

In less confrontational situations men will freely offer suggestions and solutions to problems without waiting to be invited to do so. Men will understand a question to be a request for information, whereas a woman will often ask a question simply to gain the listener's support. Women will allow others to state their problem without offering a solution. For women, not only is providing solutions to minor problems beside the point, but it also cuts short the conversation and the intention behind it, namely, intimacy through discussion.

For a man it can seem like a complete mystery why, after he has struggled hard to come up with a solution to a problem, a woman will immediately find another problem and keep the conversation going. While the endless discussions that women value as a sign of intimacy can seem like a monotonous and pointless parading of hopeless dilemmas to a man, women become frustrated by a man's turning his attempt to solve a problem into a long-winded "expert" lecture. To her talk is for interaction; listening is a way to show interest and caring; telling things is a way to show involvement with others and to ease the burden on oneself. To him, talk is for offering solutions to a problem or at least for exchanging useful information. A crucial difference, then, between men and women is that for him talking at length about a problem without aiming at a solution brings only a feeling of helplessness and frustration. But to her, talk brings relief.

One of the reasons men's talk with women frequently turns into lecturing is because women listen attentively and do not interrupt with challenges, sidetracks, or matching information the way men do. Men often find themselves in the role of lecturer, and women often find themselves in the role of audience, not because either one of them purposely chooses that role. It is not something that men "do to" women, neither is it something that women "ask for." The imbalance is created by the difference between women's and men's habitual discussion styles. Men are more likely to speak up spontaneously and continue speaking unless interrupted. Women tend to speak up only when a pause in the conversation or a direct question invites them to do so. This can give men the impression that women are hesitant and indecisive, that they are insecure, that they have no opinion, or that they are unwilling to speak up; and it can give women the impression that men are aggressive and domineering know-it-alls. Women expect their conversational partners to encourage them to join in. Men do not typically encourage quieter others to speak up; they assume that anyone who has something to say will simply say it.[26]

Men and women also have different ways of showing they're listening. Women are more inclined to ask questions. They give more listening responses. Nodding or sounds like *mhm, uh-uh*, and words like "yeah" sprinkled throughout someone else's talk provide continuous feedback to the speaker. And they respond more positively and enthusiastically, for example by agreeing and laughing. Men listen more quietly, making statements rather than asking questions, and challenging and testing rather than agreeing. Women also use "yeah" to mean "I'm with you; I follow what you're saying," whereas men tend to say "yeah" only when they agree.[27] Men are also more likely to use forms like "I think" and "you know" to express uncertainty, while women use these forms more frequently to convey certainty and to give emphasis and weight to their propositions.[28]

With these general differences in mind it may now be easier to understand why problems may arise in academic philosophy and philosophical counseling sessions when discussion crosses the gender line. Although it would require writing a book to examine all the possible problems that may arise, articulating at least a few of them here may be useful so that they may be avoided in the future.

THE DIFFERENCES IN COUNSELING

Research suggests that men place greater emphasis on displays of dominance and hierarchy in interaction with men than with women. It is not that men are inexpressive and nondisclosing, but rather that our culture's normative expectations discourage men from being self-disclosing with other men. This means that the more competitive nature of male interactions may make the expression of personal vulnerabilities more difficult for some men in their relationships with other men and with a male counselor.[29] This would explain why women typically seek mental health services more than men.[30] This means also that a woman is more likely to have had previous experience with counseling prior to visiting a philosophical counselor, and that she is therefore more likely than a man to accept a slower pace and a more introspective process. And because seeking help is anathema to the male sex-role stereotype, those males who do come to counseling are often in more serious difficulty than females.[31] That the values of therapy and counseling are those more commonly associated with women's ways of relating to each other than with men's might explain why studies have shown that among inexperienced counselors, women do better than men—although over time and with experience this gender difference disappears.[32]

Women

At one time a majority of women sought male therapists, perhaps with the latent or manifest belief that they represented professional authority. Today more women preferentially seek women counselors for a number of reasons: they fear that the discussion with a male counselor will be based on sexist values; they believe that it is too easy and too tempting to deceive a male counselor into avoiding discussion of the most serious problems; they wish to avoid the possibility of sexual overtones and thoughts during discussion; and a woman seeking help in resolving personal problems often wants to have a strong, competent woman as a role model.[33]

For a woman, telling her philosophical counselor about a problem may simply be a way of getting a problem off her chest—or "venting"—without it being a request for a solution. It may also be a bid for an expression of understanding ("I know how you feel") or a similar complaint ("I felt the same way when something similar happened to me"). In other words, "troubles talk" is intended to reinforce rapport by sending the metamessage "We're the same; you're not alone." Women are frustrated when they not only don't get this reinforcement but, quite the opposite, feel distanced by offers of advice, which seem to send the metamessage "We're not the same. You have the problems; I have the solutions."[34] I actually experienced this difference firsthand in counseling by e-mail. After a woman had sent me a long and detailed message about all that was wrong in her life I responded with several suggestions. She sent a message back complaining that my trying to tell her how to solve her problems was paternalistic and insensitive of me. After giving the situation further thought I sent a message explaining that I felt I understood her problems better now, that I had suffered from similar problems myself, and that I could imagine how she must feel. I was careful to be empathetic without offering any more solutions to her problems. She sent back a very short message that simply said, "Thank you. You are a real friend."

A woman can also become frustrated when, for example, she tells her counselor about a physical ailment and he recommends a good medical doctor for her to visit. The difference here is that he is trying to be helpful whereas she may prefer to simply hear an expression of sympathy. When the situation is reversed a man can also become frustrated. He may tell his counselor of a physical ailment hoping that she will make some suggestions as to what to do about it, but she offers only what she believes to be a comforting nod.

A woman may come to a male philosophical counselor with the problem that she feels she is not being listened to or taken seriously in conversation by the men in her life. So sometimes, rather than as an attempt to discover a solution to the problem, a woman's visit to a philosophical counselor may be her attempt to simply make a connection with a man who openly accepts her as a capable intellectual discussion partner. His respectfully listening to her then becomes the solution.

Men

It is often very difficult for a man to go to counseling and tell another man about his failures. It is even more stressful for a male to enter therapy and abdicate power to a woman with whom he is usually expected to be dominant. Asking for help in our culture often leads men to feel weak and inadequate. Not only is it unacceptable to have problems, but it is also "unmanly" to ask for help from anyone, and especially from other men. A male client working with a male counselor may feel ashamed and embarrassed; he may be hesitant or downright resistant to reveal his inner thoughts and especially his feelings. That is why it is not uncommon for men to seek female counselors. Men see women as not in competition with them, and thereby more able to be nurturing. A male entering a counseling relationship with a female counselor will often feel better if he is given early assurances of his competence and worth.

While working with a female counselor can give a male client valuable insights into women's ways, working with a male counselor gives the client the opportunity to observe his counselor as a role model of interpersonal skills such as owning and expressing a range of feelings. For a man, to be understood by another man can be validating and highly therapeutic. But this intimacy may be confused by the client with sexuality because intimacy and sexuality are often interrelated for men. For the client to feel psychologically close to another man (the counselor) may lead to a range of homophobic reactions. To counteract the possibility of unwanted sexual feelings toward the counselor, the counselor, whether male or female, is better off reflecting the feelings of camaraderie rather than intimacy—the sense of partnership and belonging that men in particular have learned to value through team sports and male-oriented institutions such as fraternities and the military.[35]

Counselors

A man (and therefore a male counselor) is more likely to try to argue a man or woman out of the way he or she is feeling. This is an attempt to make the other feel better by showing that the problem expressed is not as serious as it may appear. Since women expect to have their feelings validated by a discussion partner, however, the men's approach makes them feel as though the counselor doesn't care, or worse, that their feelings are being dismissed. On most occasions it is better if the counselor simply sits back and listens to a female client rather than confront her or make suggestions. Women get enough confrontation and suggestions from other men in their lives. And while most counselors are generally careful not to offer advice or suggestions this is, unfortunately, the very thing that most male clients are listening for in discussions with their counselors.

Research has shown that people who are believed to be less competent are treated with more dominance. To the extent that gender stereotypes depict women as less competent than men, a male philosophical counselor must be careful not to treat his women clients as less competent than men.[36] Counseling will not help solve problems if all it does is reinforce cultural biases, if the male counselor sets himself up as an authority figure who tells the client (either directly or implicitly) what is wrong with her and what she should be thinking, feeling, or doing.[37] For example, if the client says she feels powerless and frustrated with her situation at work the first thing she wants is an acknowledgment of the legitimacy and importance of those feelings. If instead her counselor tells her that in fact she does have power, that she has the right to stand up for herself, and that therefore she should not feel frustrated she will see this as her feelings being discounted, as though what she is feeling really doesn't matter because she is just another problem the counselor wants to solve. She will see it as yet one more situation in which she must conform to the nonemotional perspective of a male authority figure.[38] She may therefore have serious doubts about trusting the counselor with her story. This can be a very difficult point for male counselors to grasp. But I have learned from personal experience that this sort of disregard from a counselor for the expression of feelings from a female client can easily lead the client to terminate the counseling relationship.

Furthermore, what may at first seem like a woman's personal or internally oriented problem of feeling underappreciated at home or at work may in fact turn out to be a political problem, that is, an externally and socially situated problem of a woman's actual powerlessness in a male-dominated home or work environment. Counselors must be sensitive to issues of power differentials, especially in the lives of women, and help their clients determine the best way to approach changing the problems located in their external, sociocultural reality.[39]

Since a female philosophical counselor will not have had much opportunity to participate in male/male interactions in her formative years, it may be difficult for her to understand male competition, male bonding, and male friendship. It is therefore advisable for her to spend time learning from her clients what that experience is like without judging it.[40]

Counselor self-disclosure during a discussion of troubles is more likely to get a positive response from a female client than from a male client. When a discussion partner says, "I know what you mean. I had the same experience," a woman will see this as empathy and connection while a man is more likely to interpret it as shift of focus from him to the speaker, or as a competitive comparison of coping abilities and problem-solving strategies. Women generally expect their expression of troubles to be met with a matching expression of troubles from their discussion partner, whereas when a man expresses troubles he expects to be offered a variety of possible solutions.[41]

The female counselor may think that when her male client uses expressions like "I think" and "you know" he is expressing certainty when in fact the exact opposite is true. The male client sitting opposite a female counselor who has been saying "yes, yes" while he was speaking may assume she has been agreeing with him.

When she then turns out not to agree, he may conclude that she has been insincere, or that she was merely agreeing politely without really listening. A female client whose male counselor is listening quietly and does not give enough listening responses may assume he is not interested or just not listening. Conversely when a female counselor is confronted with a male client who does not say "yes," or much of anything else, she may conclude that he hasn't been listening or that he is disinterested whereas he may simply be waiting intently for her to offer a suggestion. In fact a strong directive approach may be more suitable to men clients than to women clients, while a nondirective approach may be more appropriate for women clients.

Male and female counselors also need to understand that, for a woman, talking can be a way of diffusing problematic emotional states rather than as a request for assistance in problem solving. That is, the emotional state aroused by a situation may be the very issue a female client may wish to deal with rather than the issue itself. For example, a woman may be explaining her distress at nearly hitting a careless pedestrian with her car on the way to the counseling session. The very act of focusing on her feelings of shock, panic, and anger diminishes the intensity of those affective states. She may become frustrated—and for good reason—if the listener shifts the focus from her feelings to other topics such as her driving style, the pedestrian's carelessness, the lack of crosswalks in the area, and so on. She will interpret this as a sign that the listener is not interested in how she feels or that the listener is intentionally taking control of the discussion, and dictating to her the direction in which it should go. Yet if a man were to offer his counselor a similar story of nearly hitting a pedestrian with his car it is likely he would not want to dwell for very long on his feelings but would instead prefer to talk about what he did to avoid a more serious situation or what he could do to avoid a similar situation in the future. This is not to suggest that a counselor ought to routinely lead female clients into a discussion of their feelings about such an event and male clients into a discussion of the details of the event. Quite the contrary, each individual is different and it is therefore imperative that a counselor take careful note with each client exactly where that client wishes to focus his or her attention in the counseling dialogue.

Furthermore, for a woman, crying is a form of expression. Crying allows her to show her feelings of sadness, joy, frustration, anger, and so on. For a man, crying is typically a sign of utter despair and hopelessness; it is all that remains to be done when everything else has failed. That is why when a man sees a woman crying he immediately fears the worst, and when a woman tells a man that he should feel free to cry more often he has no idea why he should do that. A woman may also be very reluctant to express her anger or rage other than by crying. She may believe that doing so will lead to her being abandoned by the significant men and women in her life. And while men do occasionally cry in a counseling situation they are more likely to show anger. There is some truth to the adage, "Women cry; men get angry." To understand a male client better it might be instructive for a counselor to imagine the man as crying whenever he gets angry. But in many cases men are simply unable to explain what emotional state they are feeling if asked to do so by the counselor.

CONCLUSION

To assume that the sex of two speakers engaged in a discussion makes no difference in how that discussion unfolds or that the sex of the counselor and the client in a counseling situation is unimportant to the efficacy of the counseling encounter is to miss a very important element of human interaction. We are always aware of the sex of those whom we encounter, and knowledge of their sex leads us to form different assumptions about them, for the traits they will possess, for their expectations of us, and for the type of thinking, speaking, and behavior styles they will display. But our perceptions are not always accurate representations of reality. Research clearly reveals that we may perceive a man or a woman differently even if they display identical behavior because we have socioculturally developed models for the behaviors we expect of men and women and for the traits they will possess. If the other's speech does not conform to the stereotype we hold, we may simply overlook the discrepancies between our mental model and the actual behavior of the other.[42] And this is where misunderstandings originate.

Psychotherapist Barbara G. Deutsch believes gender should not be overlooked by counselors, because an awareness of differences in intergender communication can positively affect a counseling relationship. "I think that an assertion that issues regarding gender can be neutralized in a well-conducted psychotherapy is questionable. It denies the rich nuances that careful attention to the subtleties of gender can bring to the treatment situation."[43] Asking the question whether gender *can* be neutralized in a therapeutic situation is, in a sense, focusing on the wrong question. Better to focus on the normative question: *Should* there be an attempt to neutralize it? If an understanding of the subtleties of gender can enrich therapy or counseling then the attempt by the counselor to actively try to neutralize or simply disregard gender would clearly be counterproductive to the entire process. Furthermore, part of the goal of counseling is to help individuals improve their relationships by helping them to develop successful interpersonal skills. An understanding of gender differences in communicative styles is a fundamental part of such skills. Therefore, a philosophical counselor not only should be aware of gender influences in the way he or she relates to clients. A philosophical counselor also can teach both women and men that their lives may be improved and that they can avoid many of the problems they have been encountering if they make themselves more familiar with each other's styles. Women could be taught to accept from men some competition, conflict, and difference without seeing it as a threat to intimacy, and men could be taught to accept interdependence with women without seeing it as a threat to their status and freedom.

The important point in all of this is that men and women have different communicative styles, neither of which is superior to the other in all situations. While men and women are clearly political equals this equality should not be misconstrued as meaning that men and women are exactly alike in every respect. It is not a matter of women learning to be more like men or men learning to be more like women; it is a case of both women and men becoming aware of their differences and then taking those differences into account during discussions so that neither will fall victim to unintentional misinterpretations.

So what could a philosophical counselor do for Karl and Hilda if that counselor were aware of these gender differences? Recall that their conversation went like this:

> Karl said, "I'm so sorry about all this, Hilda. How can I make it up to you?"
> Hilda nodded and said, "By having patience."
> Karl asked again, "But what can I do? Tell me what to do."
> Hilda answered, "Just be there for me, Karl. Listen to me. Give me time."
> Karl tried again, "Sure. But I need to know what you want me to do in the meantime. What do you want me to do for you, Hilda? Ask me anything you like."
> Hilda tried again, "I don't know. It's OK."
> Karl persisted, "But I want to make it up to you. I'm really sorry and I want to undo the wrong I've done. Can't you tell me what I can do for you?"

If Hilda and Karl had been more aware of their different communicative styles, then Hilda would have understood that Karl was doing his best—the way that a man learns to do it—by actively trying to fix the problem between them. It was not that Karl was not listening to what Hilda was saying, it was that Karl was being a typical male. If Karl had understood Hilda's womanly ways better he would have understood that she was not expecting him to do anything other than to be intimately connected with her in conversation. He would have seen that by wanting to *do* something, rather than just being there and listening to her, he was leading Hilda to believe he was not interested in giving her what she needed most: his understanding.

Some Differences in Discursive Styles

Women

1. In a group situation, women generally don't offer their opinions as readily as men do; they tend to wait to be invited into a discussion before speaking, or they wait for a pause in the discussion before speaking up.
2. Women display a greater tendency to ask questions of their discussion partners.
3. Women attempt to achieve solidarity, closeness, or connection and may therefore be less critical of erroneous or contentious statements made by their discussion partners.
4. Women will continue discussing a problem to diffuse its emotional content even after a solution has been agreed upon.
5. Women tend to aim for compromise and consensus and will therefore often postpone definitive decision making when there is no unanimity.
6. Women are more likely to draw out positive responses from their discussion partners with "tag questions" such as "you know?" "isn't it?" "don't you think?" and to use

high-rising terminal inflection (making a statement sound like a question) in order to gain the support of others.

7. Women show a greater tendency to interject nonverbal responses, especially "mm hmm," throughout the stream of a fellow speaker's talk, not as agreement but to indicate support.

8. Women are often more attentive to what a person's words reveal about how they are feeling than to the information they are conveying.

9. Women are less likely to freely offer suggestions or advice, often waiting instead until asked for it directly.

10. Women tend to use pronouns such as "we" and "you" more often, thereby converting general or universal issues into the specific and personal.

Men

1. Men are more likely to enter a discussion spontaneously and assume others will do the same.

2. Men are more attentive to the information or issue that is being conveyed by a speaker's words than to what the words are conveying about how the speaker is feeling.

3. Men attempt to find solutions to problems presented and expect the same of others. They see this problem-solving ability as a reflection of their competence as a discussion partner.

4. Men will tend to put a problem out of mind once a solution has been decided on.

5. Men make more direct declarations of fact or opinion, and are more likely to offer more detailed explanations.

6. Men are more likely to give suggestions or advice freely, without waiting to first be asked for it.

7. Men have a greater tendency to offer their own thoughts during the utterances of their discussion partners.

8. Men are more likely to shift a discussion to their own area of competency either by developing the current topic along more familiar lines or by introducing a new topic.

9. Men display a greater tendency to challenge what their discussion partner has said in order to test their partner's conviction.

10. Men are more likely to discuss issues in general and universal terms than in the specific and personal.

NOTES

1. After I presented this paper in Berlin it was pointed out to me that gender difference is a very serious obstacle for women and women philosophers in Germany. Nouns are always gender neutral in English (indicated by "the") whereas in German nouns are always gendered (indicated by *der, die*, or *das*). So while it is unfortunate that English speakers will often *think* of a man when they use the term "the philosopher" German speakers have in fact, until very recently, had only the masculine term *der Philosoph* to designate a philosopher. This meant that, in speaking or writing, the masculine term was all that was available to the speaker or writer, regardless of the actual sex of the individual to whom the term was

being applied. The recently coined female term *die Philosophin* and its plural *die Philosophinnen* are considered awkward and unwieldy by most German-speaking male philosophers (their complaint is similar to the one made by English-speaking males about having to use terms like Ms, he/she, or s/he, etc., when writing philosophy in the English language), and is still used primarily by women writers. The German words for "client" and "counselor" are also always either masculine or feminine so, to some extent, the point about the neutrality of the term "client" in the earlier part of this presentation was a puzzle to those participants at the conference who had read only the German text in which "philosophical counselor" had been translated only into the masculine *der Philosoph* and "client" had been translated only into the masculine *der Klient*. To add to the confusion, the German language does not differentiate between "gender" and "sex." Although the difference was readily understood in conversation by conference participants, the German language has only the word *Geschlecht* to indicate both biological sex and sociological gender.

2. Maltz, Daniel N. and Ruth A. Borker. "A Cultural Approach to Male–Female Miscommunication." *Language and Gender*. Jennifer Coats, ed. Malden, Mass.: Blackwell, 1998. 420. See also *Sex Differences in Human Communication* by Barbara Westbrook Eakins and R. Gene Eakins. Boston: Houghton Mifflin, 1978. 78.

3. Gilligan, Carol. *In a Different Voice*. Cambridge, Mass.: Harvard University Press, 1982. 173.

4. Nussbaum, Martha. *The Therapy of Desire*. Princeton, N.J.: Princeton University Press, 1994. 118.

5. Maltz. 417–434. See also *Constructing Women and Men: Gender Socialization* by Marlene Mackie. Toronto: Holt, Rinehart, and Winston. 1987.

6. Eisikovits, Edina. "Girl-talk/Boy-talk: Sex Differences in Adolescent Speech." *Language and Gender*. Jennifer Coats, ed. Malden, Mass.: Blackwell, 1998. 48.

7. Aristotle. *Rhetoric and on Poetics*. Philadelphia: The Franklin Library, 1981.

8. Nietzsche, Friedrich. *Will to Power*. Originally published in 1930 as Kroner's *Taschenausgabe*, vol. 78.

9. Foucault, Michel. *Power/Knowledge: Selected Interviews and Other Writings*. Colin Gordon, ed. New York: Routledge, 1980.

10. As discussed in the essay "Feminism in Ethics: Conceptions of Autonomy" by Marilyn Freedman. *The Cambridge Companion to Feminism in Philosophy*. Miranda Fricker and Jennifer Hornsby, eds. Cambridge, U.K.: Cambridge University Press, 2000. 206.

11. Shlain, Leonard. *The Alphabet Versus the Goddess*. New York: Viking, 1998.

12. Tannen, Deborah. *You Just Don't Understand*. New York: Ballantine, 1990. 178.

13. Gilligan, Carol. *In a Different Voice*. Cambridge, Mass.: Harvard University Press, 1982.

14. Eakins, Barbara Westbrook and R. Gene Eakins. *Sex Differences in Human Communication*. Boston: Houghton Mifflin, 1978. 19.

15. Schaef, Anne Wilson. *Women's Reality*. San Francisco: Harper & Row, 1985. 104–105.

16. Tannen, 27.

17. Eakins, 155–156.

18. For a good discussion of "telling it slant" see Gillian Michell's essay, "Women and Lying: A Pragmatic and Semantic Analysis of 'Telling it Slant.' " *Hypatia Reborn*. Azizah Y. Al-Hibri and Margaret A. Simons, eds. Indianapolis: Indiana University Press, 1990. 175–191.

19. Tannen, 1990. 269.

20. Jourard, Sydney. *Disclosure: An Experimental Analysis of the Transparent Self.* New York: Wiley, 1971. See also Gloria A. Mulcahy, "Sex Differences in Patterns of Self-disclosure among Adolescents: A Developmental Perspective." *Journal of Youth and Adolescence* 2. 1973. 343–356.

21. Morgan, Brian S. "Intimacy of Self-disclosure Topics and Sex Differences in Self-disclosure." *Sex Roles* 2. 1976. 161–166.

22. Aires, Elizabeth J. and Fern L. Johnson. "Close Friendship in Adulthood: Conversational Conduct Between Same-Sex Friends." *Sex Roles* 9. 1983 (12): 1, 183–196.

23. Pleck, Joseph H. "Man to Man: Is Brotherhood Possible?" *Old Family, New Family.* Nona Glazer-Malbin, ed. 229–244. New York: Van Nostrand, 1975.

24. Tannen, 24–25.

25. Belk et al. "Avoidance Strategy Use in Intimate Relationships of Women and Men from Mexico and the United States." *Psychology of Women Quarterly* 12. 165–174.

26. Tannen, 81, 94–95, 125, 129, 133, 138, 142, 144, 145–146, 159–160.

27. Ibid., 142.

28. Aires, 91, 94, 122.

29. Ibid., 160.

30. Hepper, Paul P. and Daniel S. Gonzales. "Men Counseling Men." *Handbook of Counseling and Psychotherapy with Men.* Murray Scher, Mark Stevens, Glenn Good, and Gregg A. Eichenfield, eds. London: Sage, 1987.

31. Kirschner, L. A. "Effects of Gender on Psychotherapy." *Comprehensive Psychiatry* 19. 1978. 79–82.

32. Tannen, 121.

33. Person, E. "Women in Therapy: Therapist Gender as a Variable." *Between Analyst and Patient.* Helen Meyers, ed. Hillsdale, N.J.: Analytic Press, 1986. 195.

34. Tannen, 53.

35. Hepper, 34, 36.

36. Aires, 188.

37. Schaef, Anne Wilson. *Women's Reality.* San Francisco: Harper & Row, 1985. 9.

38. Ibid., 96.

39. For a discussion of feminist approaches to philosophical counseling see the section entitled "Feminism in Philosophical Counseling" in chapter 4 of my book *Philosophical Counseling: Theory and Practice.* Westport, Conn.: Praeger, 2001.

40. Carlson, Nancy L. "Woman Therapist: Male Client." *Handbook of Counseling and Psychotherapy with Men.* Murray Scher, Mark Stevens, Glenn Good, and Gregg A. Eichenfield, eds. London: Sage, 1987. 48.

41. Tannen, 293.

42. Aires, 169, 186.

43. Deutsch, Barbara G. "Women in Psychotherapy." *Psychotherapy: The Analytic Approach.* Morton J. Aronson and Melvin A. Scharfman, eds. Northvale, N.J.: Jason Aronson, 1992. 183–184.

Chapter 9

Rational Passions*

Again BW is close to tears.

"I don't know why I feel like crying whenever someone is just being friendly with me. It's so embarrassing and it makes no sense. Am I being completely irrational, or maybe crazy? It's very frustrating, but I can't help it. I've come to the point where I'm just about ready to give up."

It is not uncommon for a psychoanalyst or psychotherapist to encounter a scenario similar to the one above in which the patient presents an uncontrollable emotional experience for which there seems to be no apparent cause. The patient approaches the therapist with the expectation that the therapist will eventually find the cause, whether physiological or psychological, and will then arrange a suitable treatment.

The philosophical counselor, on the other hand, might be faced with a similarly emotionally distraught client who, rather than expecting a remedy, will apologize to the counselor for presenting an emotional problem which the client supposes is inappropriate in a philosophical counseling situation. So-called folk wisdom typically conceives of emotion as the absolute antithesis to rationality, and since philosophers are believed to be functioning at the pinnacle of rationality the client therefore assumes that an emotional problem is beyond the competency of a philo-

*An earlier version of this chapter under the title "Passionate Judgements in Philosophical Counseling" was first published in *Practical Philosopher: Journal of the Society of Consultant Philosophers*. Vol. 3, No. 3. November 2000. I am grateful to the two anonymous referees whose suggestions improved the earlier version of this chapter.

sophical counselor. But this assumption is based on a fairly common and problematic preconception about the relationship between the emotions and rationality.

Throughout most of recorded history the emotions have not only been described as different in kind from rationality but the emotions and rationality have also been attributed to different segments of the population, with the emotions being portrayed as belonging primarily to women and children, and rationality to men.[1] While readers of this chapter will no doubt say, "I don't believe in the separation of rationality and emotion between men and women," it is very likely that most readers will in fact assume that the person referred to as "BW" at the beginning of this chapter is probably female. Two things should be noted: First, the assumption that BW is female is very likely based on the *feeling* that this is the case since there is no factual evidence indicating it. This illustrates how easily feelings or emotions can interfere with reasoning. This raises the question, Which comes first: the emotion or the reasoning?

Some philosophers and psychologists see the emotions not as simply interfering with thinking but rather as important in leading the way in good thinking. For example, eighteenth-century English philosopher David Hume asserts that reason "is and ought only to be the slave of the passions (emotions), and can never pretend to any other office than to serve and obey them."[2] Ernest Hartmann, professor of psychiatry, claims that an emotion is

the force that guides or drives our minds; it is the guiding force that gets us moving and moves us in a particular direction. . . . Our emotions tell us rapidly and powerfully whether something is "good" or "bad" or something to be approached, explored, or avoided. Emotions are needed to lend value to our thoughts and enable us to make decisions. . . . Our emotions always colour the world for us.[3]

While it seems reasonable to agree with these authors that the emotions at times precede reasoning, it still leaves unanswered the question, Where do the emotions that precede reasoning come from? What are these emotions based on?

Second, while it is reasonable to *think* of the above quote as not necessarily belonging to either a man or a woman the usual *feeling* that BW is not a man occurs because of the reference to tears, crying, feelings, making no sense, irrationality, frustration, and giving up. These are not commonly held to be characteristic of a man. It is women's personalities that are believed to be interlaced with the affective (emotional) domain; men are supposed to be solidly welded to the intellect and rationality.[4] But the corollary of this dichotomy is that women, by virtue of their supposed greater emotionality, are therefore often deemed to be predominantly irrational. This raises the questions, Are the emotions irrational? And is an emotional problem an irrational problem? The answers to these questions have important ramifications for a number of approaches in psychotherapy and for the entire field of philosophical counseling.

Therapists and counselors are well aware of the fact that for a young person the experience of an emotion may simply be the result of raging hormones. Teenagers are prone to irrational fits of crying, euphoria, and anger for which no explanations will be found in an examination of life events. Such emotions are physiological in origin and can be understood only in terms of causal explanations. Therapists and counselors also know that not all teenage emotions are irrational, that most individuals eventually outgrow the irrationality of their youth, and that troubling emotions experienced by an adult are more likely to be philosophical or conceptual in nature than biological. But if the mature emotions associated with adult philosophical or cognitive problems are not biological in origin, then how are they to be explained? Interestingly, the ongoing empirical research that has been done in the social sciences—particularly cognitive science and psychology—has generated the most intriguing theories of the emotions.

EMOTIONS EXPLAINED

There have been three stages in recent attempts to understand emotions: emotions have been characterized as simple physical arousal, as physical arousal plus interpretation, and finally as "thought full."[5]

In the nineteenth century, American philosopher and psychologist William James proposed that an emotion is simply the perception of a visceral or gut reaction to a stimulus. James' conception was in line with theories of the emotions held much earlier by early modern French philosopher René Descartes[6] and German philosopher Immanuel Kant.[7] At about the same time that James was writing, a Danish psychologist named Carl Lange developed a similar theory but maintained that an emotion was the experience of vascular changes, that is, changes in blood pressure throughout the body. But in 1929 psychologist Walter B. Cannon countered the James-Lange theory by pointing out that when the viscera was surgically separated from the central nervous system it did not alter the emotional behavior of the individual. Cannon argued that emotions, rather than being felt viscerally, were in fact the thalamus causing a discharge of the autonomic nervous system which caused the feelings associated with the concomitant increased heart rate, faster breathing, perspiration, and other physiological changes. These theories stressed physical arousal as both the cause and the defining characteristic of all emotions. This exclusively physical model of the emotions was the standard for more than 70 years.

But in the early 1960s Stanley Schachter, psychologist at the University of Minnesota, proposed a "two-factor attribution theory of the emotions." Schachter maintained that emotions depend both on a change in somatic arousal and on some sort of cognitive interpretation. Schachter held not only that an emotion is an individual's perception of the activation of personal physiological changes but also that this perception is combined with an individual's causal interpretation which she imagines will explain her own experiences and her own and others' behavior. In other words, if asked, a person would respond with a description of her feelings as well as a conjectural cause of those feelings. Unfortunately, carefully controlled psychology experiments proceeded to demonstrate how inaccurate the reasoning of an individual actually is when attempting to explain the cause of an emotion.

During this same time period Magda Arnold, a psychologist at Loyola University in Chicago, conducted a scholarly review of the major psychological theories of her day concerning the emotions. In her published report Arnold hypothesized that, while most of the prevailing theories postulated that bodily changes simply *are* emotions or that bodily changes *cause* emotions, it may be the case that neither is actually true, but rather that both bodily changes and emotions are the effects of something else entirely. Arnold analyzed what had been described by other theorists as the constituent events in the experience of an emotion and discovered that these events form a fairly consistent sequence. The first step is the actual *perception* (or the imagining) of a person, object, or event. The second, and perhaps most important, step is the *appraisal* of what is perceived; only then come the emotion as such and the accompanying bodily changes. Finally there may be an intention to act and a subsequent action. In effect what Arnold did—which many philosophers agree with[8]—is identify the reasoning behind the emotions. That is, Arnold's theory of emotion described a continuous process of reaction and appraisal. Arnold argued that emotional behavior is "thought full" in contraposition to the prevailing physical model in which an emotion was said to be merely a corporeal response or a purely visceral reaction. The conclusion Arnold reached was that her meta-analysis of scientific research data strongly suggested that emotions are undeniably rational.[9]

In 1965, research conducted at the University of California at Berkeley led Richard Lazarus to come to a similar strong conclusion. Lazarus wrote,

Cognitive activity is a necessary precondition of emotion because to experience an emotion, people must comprehend—whether in the form of primitive evaluative perception or a highly differentiated symbolic process—that their well-being is implicated in a transaction, for better or worse. A creature that is oblivious to the significance of what is happening for its well-being does not react with an emotion.[10]

But it could be argued that if the emotions fall within any definition of rationality then rationality must have been too broadly construed. This raises the question, Can there be an acceptable description of rationality that would include, for example, the emotional distress experienced by BW?

WHAT DOES IT MEAN TO BE RATIONAL?

Rationality may be said to be a normative account of reasoning.[11] That is, reasoning is rational when it conforms to some defined set of criteria. Philosopher and cognitive research scientist Alvin Goldman suggests that the criteria on which rationality is based should include at least the following three conditions: first, a person's judgments should conform to the principles of *probability*. That is, a person is thinking rationally when she considers the probable likelihood of various scenarios, prioritizes them, and then gives greater weight to those at the top of the list. Second, a person is rational when her belief is well supported by the total *evidence* she has at that time. And third, a person is rational when her beliefs have an internal *consistency*; her beliefs must be logically noncontradictory.[12]

Unfortunately there are many problems with this list. For example, research in cognitive science has demonstrated that human beings are generally notoriously bad at correctly evaluating probability.[13] Does this mean that human beings are therefore generally irrational? Furthermore, the total evidence a person has at a given time may include information that has been forgotten but is still located in the memory. Is a person irrational when he fails to consider vital information that he would have included if he had been reminded of it? And finally, it has been demonstrated that the condition of internal consistency is extremely difficult for human beings to meet.[14] In fact it is not uncommon for individuals to live happy lives despite the fact that a rigorous examination of their beliefs would show evidence of multiple inconsistencies. But despite these problems, employing the criteria of probability, evidence, and consistency is at least a fairly serviceable method in determining whether someone's reasoning may be considered rational.

Goldman also warns that when it comes to reasoning about ourselves, we all have tendencies toward epistemic irrationality. That is, our ideas about ourselves don't necessarily conform to the objective truth of the matter.[15] For example, a woman may believe that her ability to play golf is far greater than her actual game scores indicate, or a man may believe that he is more honest than common opinion within his community would have it. Goldman points out that this sort of self-deception is completely rational from a prudential or pragmatic perspective. Fooling ourselves into thinking we are better athletes or better moral agents than we are helps us to cope with a challenging world. In other words, our subjective beliefs don't always have to match objective facts in order to be rational. The philosophical counselor who has BW for a client would therefore have to ask herself, In evaluating whether BW's emotions are rational should I use an objective or a subjective measure as the standard?

If the philosophical counselor chooses to evaluate rationality by objective standards she will then be faced with a significant additional problem. In requiring the condition of consistency as one of the criteria for rationality the counselor must consider not only the *internal* consistency of the client's beliefs but also the relationship between the client's beliefs and the external world. External consistency—and therefore rationality—is defined not only by a simple one-to-one correspondence between the client's beliefs and the existence of external objects but also by the relationship between the client's own beliefs and such factors as his sociocultural milieu, the prevailing religious belief system, commonly accepted family values, the contemporary *Zeit Geist*, and even his sex.

For example, it would have been completely irrational for a medieval European peasant to believe he could one day become the owner of an estate if he simply worked hard enough, and yet today it is considered rational for a man to believe that if he works hard enough he may one day become the president of the United States of America. It seems that for a goal to be rational it must be achievable within the sociocultural limitations of the specific time period during which the goal is pursued. Therefore, the peasant's goal of becoming a landowner seems far less rational than the U.S. citizen's goal to become president because the sociocultural limitations on a peasant living in medieval times were far greater than they are for a person living in the United States today. In fact the peasant would have been so conditioned to simply accept the rigid hierarchical structure of his medieval culture that the thought of becoming a landlord would probably never even have crossed his mind in the first place. Furthermore, a goal that is only achievable in principle seems less rational as a personal goal than a goal that is achievable in actuality. This means that a black, female citizen's goal of becoming president of the United States, although achievable in principle, clearly seems less rational than if her goal were merely to become president of a local service club. But does it even make sense to use terms like *more* rational and *less* rational?

Anyone who has ever practiced philosophical counseling will know that with every client suffering from emotional distress the counselor is put into the position of having to determine not only whether or not that client's emotions are rational, but also to what degree they are reasonable. For example, anger may be a perfectly rational emotion in a particular situation, but the *level* of anger experienced by a client in that situation may be unreasonable given an accurate assessment of the circumstances. Philosophical counseling helps individuals assess their circumstances and determine the reasonableness of an emotion. The process on which this determination is based is hermeneutic.

HERMENEUTICS OF EMOTIONS

Philosophical counseling is in large part hermeneutic.[16] That is, not only does the philosophical counselor try to interpret the intended meaning of the "text" of what the client says, but also the counselor and client attempt to develop a mutual understanding of the significance of the client's experiences as those experiences relate to the problem at hand. This interpretation is not particularly based on how closely it matches some kind of objective truth but rather, as psychotherapists Jerome and Julia Frank explain, "[Most important is] the interpretation's fruitfulness—its beneficial consequences for the patient's ability to function and for the patient's sense of well-being."[17]

This instrumental approach to the interpretation of the client's experiences, and the one that seems to be most appropriate to emotional distress in a philosophical counseling situation, is the "transformation of a puzzling, indeterminate situation into one that is sufficiently unified to enable warranted assertion or coherent action."[18] But in order for BW to develop a sense of well-being it is necessary that a hermeneutic interpretation of his concerns includes coming to a conclusion regarding the rationality of the emotions expressed. For most clients the decision as to whether their emotions are rational or irrational is a judgment call that has already been made by that client himself. It is the belief in the irrationality of his emotions that motivates a client to seek counseling in the first place.

Recall that BW wonders aloud whether the counselor believes his emotion in a particular situation is irrational. During the course of counseling BW might reveal the following: BW was adopted into a family at a young age. The adoptive parents clearly favored their several biological offspring over BW. As a child this gave BW a sense that he was not as good or deserving of attention as the other children, and this feeling of unworthiness has persisted into adulthood. Yet at the same time BW believes that he was a good child and that he has led a decent life. He cannot think of what he might have done that led his adoptive parents to hold him in such low regard. Now whenever anyone shows the slightest interest in him, or offers him the simplest kindness, BW finds himself immediately moved to tears. An appropriate place for a philosophical counselor to begin work on the puzzle of BW's seemingly irrational emotions is to help him develop a better understanding of his life's events with a hermeneutic inquiry. After this has been completed BW's emotions may be examined in light of the criteria of rationality presented earlier.

The criterion of *probability* might say that BW's feeling that he is probably unworthy as an adult is indeed a rational judgment *if* it is based purely on how his adoptive parents treated him. But this is a monumental "if." The *evidence* criterion will demonstrate that BW's low self-esteem is based on reasonable evidence, namely the evaluation of highly respected authority figures (the adoptive parents) which indicates that he is worth less than other children. The problem is that this evidence is some 20 years old. Basing his self-evaluation on this evidence does not necessarily make BW's conclusions about his worthiness irrational but it clearly makes them outdated. The adoptive parents' obsolete evaluation of him is in all likelihood contradictory to the current evaluation of him by his spouse, his friends, and his coworkers. In that case his present beliefs about himself violate the *consistency* criterion and, by definition, his emotions are therefore irrational.

But there seems to be something wrong with saying that an adult who still suffers from the emotional neglect or abuse he received as a child is just being irrational. It may in a sense be analytically correct to say so, but it also seems absolutely reasonable and certainly understandable that BW feels strong emotions whenever a situation comes up which confronts his mixed up self-image. The crucial point is that an emotion is only irrational if one of two conditions exists: (1) if the emotion is inconsistent with the perceptions and appraisals it is based on, or (2) if the beliefs with which an emotion is associated are also irrational. David Hume made this point more than two centuries ago when he said, "A passion must be accompanied with some false judgment in order to its being unreasonable; and even then it is not the passion, properly speaking which is unreasonable, but the judgment."[19] This philosophical assertion has now been corroborated with data from research done in psychology.[20]

In BW's case it can be said that his emotions are in fact completely rational since they are consistent with his confused beliefs about himself and with the anguish he feels when others acknowledge his worthiness contrary to the negative messages about himself from his adoptive parents. It is his confused belief of low self-worth that is irrational since the most probable state of affairs (that he is indeed worthy) is prioritized too low on his hypothetical list of probabilities, the initial evidence of his low worth is outdated, the available evidence indicating his worthiness is ignored (his family, friends, and coworkers say he is worthy), and his belief about his unworthiness is inconsistent with his own feeling that he is in fact worthy (internal, self-defensive) and with the affirmations of his significant others (external).

CONCLUSION

An emotion is not necessarily irrational. This means that even if women were indeed more emotional than men it would not lead to the conclusion that they are therefore more irrational. Cognitive science and psychology have proposed a number of theories of the emotions. Currently the most widely accepted theory among both social scientists and philosophers is that mature emotions (those not simply caused by hormonal activity) are precipitated by beliefs that are in turn based on perceptions and their appraisal. Both psychologists and philosophers commonly hold that affective processes are actually also cognitive in nature, that there is a unity of affect and cognition, of feelings and ideas. To determine whether an emotion is in fact rational it is necessary to first define rationality. One serviceable method is to define a belief as rational when it meets the criteria of probability, evidence, and consistency, despite the problems inherent in each. The determination of the extent of an emotion's rationality can be aided by means of a careful hermeneutic. Since an emotion is based on an underlying belief, the rationality of an emotion is thereby determined not only by its consistency with that belief but with the primary rationality of that belief. Furthermore, the interpretation of the rationality of an individual's emotions must also take into consideration external factors such as the sociocultural milieu of the day, prevailing religious beliefs and values, the contemporary *Zeit Geist*, and so on, as well as the emotion's instrumental value.

Clearly, then, in philosophical counseling the answer to the question of whether an emotion is rational—and, concomitantly, whether the distressed client is being irrational—cannot be based solely on an analytic scrutiny of the connection between the client's emotions and his beliefs, or on the rationality of the underlying beliefs in isolation. Philosophical counseling calls for an empathetic alliance between the counselor and the client in which a respectful yet heuristic atmosphere is developed that will facilitate both a thoughtful and care-full "therapy of the soul."[21] After all, philosophical counseling is not simply the academic analysis of a hypothetical dilemma; philosophical counseling is an attempt to both understand and alleviate the suffering of a fellow human being.

NOTES

1. Hannah, a Polish-Canadian friend of mine, told me that in her country of origin men are considered to be both more emotional and more irrational than women. This is based, she said, on the fact that men are known to be incredibly irrational when trying to prove their honor and bravery, especially in times of war. There is a legendary Polish war hero who, it is said, in the height of passion, ran up to an enemy cannon to thrust his arm into it. Of course, said Hannah, both he and his arm were blown to bits. And although he is admired as one of that country's greatest heroes, many Polish women consider his act to have been both irrationally self-destructive and typical of the behavior of their men when they are caught up in

the heat of the moment. It is the rationality of Polish women, Hannah told me, that has repeatedly helped her war-ravaged homeland to recover and rebuild.

2. Hume, David. *A Treatise of Human Nature* (1739). New York: Prometheus, 1992.

3. Hartmann, Ernest. *Dreams and Nightmares.* Cambridge, Mass.: Perseus, 2001. 68, 69.

4. See, for example, Jean Grimshaw, *Philosophy and Feminist Thinking.* Minneapolis: University of Minnesota Press, 1986. 195–204. See also Ross Poole, "Morality, Masculinity and the Market." *Radical Philosophy.* No. 39, Spring 1985.

5. The following account is condensed from *Psychology Today: An Introduction.* Arlyne Lazerson, ed. New York: Random House, 1975. 339–345.

6. Descartes, René. "Treatise on the Passions of the Soul." In *The Philosophical Works of Descartes.* E. Haladane and G.R.T. Ross, trans. Cambridge, U.K.: Cambridge University Press, 1948.

7. See *The Encyclopedia of Philosophy.* New York: Macmillan, 1967. Vol. 1, p. 480.

8. Some examples are Plato, Epictetus, Aristotle, Thomas Aquinas, Thomas Hobbes, John Locke, Jean-Paul Sartre, and Robert Solomon.

9. For an in-depth discussion of the interaction between cognition and neurobiology in emotions see Antonio R. Damasio's book *Descartes' Error* (New York: G. P. Putnam's Sons, 1994), especially chapter 7, "Emotions and Feelings."

10. Lazarus, Richard S., E. M. Opton, et al. "The Principle of Short-Circuiting the Threat: Further Evidence." *Psychology Bulletin,* 49. 293–317. As quoted in Hunt, Morton. *The Story of Psychology.* New York: Anchor, 1993. 506.

11. For a good discussion of counseling and rationality see William O'Donohue and Jason S. Vass, "What Is an Irrational Belief?" *The Philosophy of Psychology.* William O'Donohue and Richard F. Kitchener, eds. London: Sage, 1996. 304–316.

12. Adapted from Alvin Goldman, *Philosophical Applications of Cognitive Science.* Boulder, Colo.: Westview Press, 1993. 9–32.

13. Ibid., 30.

14. Cherniak, Christopher. *Minimal Rationality.* Cambridge, Mass.: MIT Press/Bradford Books, 1986.

15. Goldman, 16.

16. For a discussion of the importance of hermeneutics in philosophical counseling see my book *Philosophical Counseling: Theory and Practice.* Westport, Conn.: Praeger, 2001.

17. Frank, Jerome D. and Julia B. Frank. *Persuasion and Healing.* Baltimore: Johns Hopkins University Press, 1991. 72.

18. *The Oxford Companion to Philosophy.* Ted Honderich, ed. Oxford, U.K.: Oxford University Press, 1995. 197. See also William James. *Pragmatism* (1907). New York: Dover Publications, 1995. 23.

19. Hume, David. "A Treatise of Human Nature" (1739). *Hume Moral and Political Philosophy.* Henry D. Aiken, ed. New York: Hafner Press, 1975. 26.

20. See for example *The Rationality of Emotion* by Ronald de Sousa (Cambridge, Mass.: MIT Press, 1987), and "Typical Emotions" by Aaron Ben-Ze'ev in *The Philosophy of Psychology*, edited by William O'Donohue and Richard F. Kitchener (London: Sage, 1996. 227–242).

21. Pierre Hadot discusses the fact that the Stoics and Epicureans considered philosophy to be therapy for the soul in his *Philosophy as a Way of Life* (Oxford, U.K.: Blackwell, 1995. 82–84).

Chapter 10

All Seriousness Aside

"The answer to the Great Question . . . of Life, the Universe and Everything is forty-two," said Deep Thought, with infinite majesty and calm.

"Forty-two!" yelled Loonquawl. "Is that all you've got to show for seven and a half million years' work?"

"I checked it very thoroughly," said the computer, "and that quite definitely is the answer. I think the problem, to be quite honest with you, is that you've never actually known what the question is."[1]

If it's true that we all see the world differently, why aren't there more people bumping into each other?[2]

An individual or couple will typically search out a counselor when the problems of life become too serious to simply ignore and too difficult to handle. But as psychologist Gerald Corey points out, while counseling is a responsible matter, it need not be deadly serious.[3] Humor can help a client to appreciate the lighter side of a predicament, regain a sense of perspective, and learn to take himself or herself less seriously. In any counseling situation genuine laughter can work wonders. It can relieve unnecessary tension, deepen trust, and strengthen the working relationship between the client and counselor.[4]

But philosophical counseling has two strikes against it when it comes to the use of humor. First, the experiences many clients have had of academic philosophy has led them to believe that philosophy consists of trying to comprehend the difficult, abstract, and convoluted writings of, in common parlance, "dead white guys" (DWG's). Their personal brush with academic philosophy, or what they have heard about it, has led them to assume that the philosophical counseling encounter must consist of the kind of dour discourse found in places of higher learning. The common belief is that philosophy ought to be serious business. The response to this, as every laughable philosopher knows, is, Who says?

Second, humorous passages are almost completely nonexistent in standard philosophy texts. Some passages, such as a few in Plato's writings, that seem as though they may have been written with tongue stuck firmly in cheek are simply approached with too much reverence and awe to allow for any giggling or guffaws (Yes, you can find hero worship among philosophers too). Philosophers have certainly written _about_ humor but their writings have been completely humorless. And there are a few undergraduate texts available in such areas as informal logic that dare to include the odd cartoon or two. And there are some educators who attempt to lighten up the darkness. For example, one professor told his class, "Hobbes wrote that in a state of nature _men_ were solitary, poor, nasty, brutish, and short." (in fact Hobbes said _life_ was solitary, and so on). But for the most part it is impossible to find a "phunny" bone in philosophy. Ludwig Wittgenstein is said to have said that "a serious and good philosophical work could be written that would consist entirely of jokes."[5] Of course, as a serious philosopher, Wittgenstein never seriously considered writing such a work himself.

While the famous philosophers have written overwhelmingly in straight-faced prose (and much of it is indeed overwhelming), there are other writers, nonacademic ones, whose works are clearly philosophical and at the same time very funny. These authors aren't discussed in any essays or books on philosophical counseling, nor are they mentioned in any encyclopedias of philosophy. To find their work you would have to search your library's entertainment section. What you would find there are the philosophical works of such great men as Marx (Groucho not Karl), Milton (Berle not John), George (Burns not Berkeley), and Woody (Allen not Woodpecker). Philosophical counselors may find that quoting even a single joke written by one of these profoundly profane philosophers may prove to be far more therapeutic for their clients than hours spent quoting the crypticisms of a Heidegger, a Kant, or a Ristotle.

For example, when a client's immediate problems have been mostly mitigated it's not uncommon for him to ask the counselor something about what it is that makes a philosopher. Is a philosopher simply someone who can quote recondite maxims, such as "Life is like a tree"? The counselor can respond with the following story by comedian Milton Berle:

> Two old friends were sitting on a park bench looking at the beautiful trees.
> One man said, "You know, Joe, life is like a tree."
> The other said, "Why is life like a tree?"
> "How should I know? I'm not a philosopher!"[6]

This joke could be used to make the serious point that there's more to philosophy than spouting (or is it sprouting?) profundities about trees. For Berle philosophy is "finding out how many things there are in the world that you can't have if you want them, and don't want if you can have them." This may be a slightly simplistic view of philosophy but it is also an insightful perspective on life not found in any introductory philosophy texts.

Speaking of life, certainly the question of the meaning of life often comes up in philosophical counseling sessions. Berle relates the following story.

A young man wanted to know the meaning of life. Hearing that a swami in Nepal knew the answer, the young man sold off all of his property and went off to Nepal. He traveled through the harshest land, eating the most basic foods and sleeping on the bare ground. He arrived at the foot of the high mountain atop which the swami lived. The young man climbed the mountain. His feet were blistered and bloody, but he kept going. He reached the top and approached the swami. He asked, "Swami, what is the meaning of life?"

The swami said, "Life is a bowl of fruit."

"And?"

"No 'and,' my son. Life is a bowl of fruit."

The young man said, "Swami, I sold my worldly possessions, I traveled through all kinds of terrain, I suffered, and all you can say is, 'Life is a bowl of fruit?' "

The swami said, "All right. Life is *not* a bowl of fruit!"

Is this a lesson in existentialism? A critical comment on Eastern philosophy? A meta-metaphysical inquiry into the contingent ontic state of bowls and fruit? No. It's just a laugh at how seriously we sometimes take our desire to have some authority figure spell everything out for us.

While comedian and filmmaker Woody Allen sees life as pretty serious he has the remarkably frenetic ability of helping people laugh at it. For example, in the movie *Annie Hall* his character says, "I feel that life is divided up into the horrible and the miserable. Those are the two categories. The horrible would be terminal cases and blind people, crippled. I don't know how they get through life. It's amazing to me. And the miserable is everyone else. That's all. So when you go through life you should be thankful that you're miserable, because you're very lucky to be miserable."[7]

At another time Allen says, "There's an old joke. Two elderly women are at a Catskills mountain resort, and one of them says: 'Boy, the food at this place is really terrible.' The other one says, 'Yeah, I know, and such small portions.' Well, that's essentially how I feel about life. Full of loneliness and misery and suffering and unhappiness, and it's all over much too quickly." This is one of those exceptional philosophical stories that makes you laugh and nod in agreement at the same time.

On the other hand, a counselor may want to offer her client a response to the kind of negative attitude toward life Allen manifests by once again quoting Berle: "Considering the alternative, life isn't such a bad deal!" "Life may not be all you want, but it's all you have." And finally, "I like to count my blessings, but I wish I was better at fractions!"

There is no better philosopher to turn to than George Burns when it comes to the lighter side of what most people consider to be a very distressing but unavoidable element of life: old age. If a client complains half-seriously that he or she is getting old, it may help to quote the expert himself when he says, "You'll know you're old when everything hurts, and what doesn't hurt, doesn't work; when you feel like the night after and you haven't been anywhere; when you get winded playing chess; when your favorite part of the newspaper is '25 Years Ago Today'; when you're still chasing women, but can't remember why; when you stoop to tie your shoe-laces and ask yourself, 'What else can I do while I'm down here?'; when every-body goes to your birthday party and stands around the cake just to get warm."[8] If George can laugh at old age, why should the rest of us take it so seriously?

When it comes to deadly serious philosophical topics there is no subject matter more serious, and certainly no more deadly, than death itself. And yet a Woody Allen quote has the potential to make a client smile about even this dire discussion topic. Allen says, "The thing to remember is that each time of life has its appropri-ate rewards, whereas when you're dead it's hard to find the light switch. The chief problem about death, incidentally, is the fear that there may be no afterlife—a de-pressing thought, particularly for those who have bothered to shave. Also, there is the fear that there is an afterlife but no one will know where it's being held. On the plus side, death is one of the few things that can be done as easily as lying down." This is truly philosophical insight into death. I would add to this that while death is no laughing matter we should keep in mind that life is fatal, and all of us come with an expiry date (although maybe some people should come with a 'Best Before' date). But a word of caution: this sort of philosophy may be considered dangerous, not because of its weird logic and obvious irreverence, but because of the risk that your client may die laughing.

And speaking of logic, sometimes the best laugh comes from the worst logic. Berle asks, "Do you realize that very few people die after a hundred years of age?" He also points out that when he looked at the obituary page one day he realized that everybody dies in alphabetical order. Other (in)famous twisted logic statements made by philosophers such as Marx (again, Groucho not Karl) can be adapted to fit a client's own situation and raise not only an awareness but a guffaw. For example, his famous existentialism: "I would never belong to a club that would have me as a member" can be used as the ratiocinative starting point of a client's examination into low self-esteem.

Ronald de Sousa, professor of philosophy at the University of Toronto, points out that laughter is an "avenue to knowledge" that has the advantage over serious-ness in the search for truth in that it is always seeking a fresh perspective.[9] It is this fresh perspective, the unexpected incongruity of humor, which can sometimes res-cue a counseling session from the detrimental downward spiral of serious discus-sion. But Sousa warns that, given our limited capacity for attention, humor may distract us from those things that ought to be taken seriously. This warning has been given by men of serious countenance (more commonly referred to as prune-faced) for centuries. For example, in Book 3 of his *Republic* Plato warns that, in order to do their jobs properly in his utopian state, Guardians should not be prone to laughter, because "when one abandons himself to violent laughter his condition provokes a violent reaction."[10] Please note: serious scholars disagree whether Plato means by this that *he* would be provoked to a violent reaction against such a laughing Guardian, or that violent laughter will lead a Guardian to blow up. In any event, he clearly means that, as far as he's concerned, a laughing Guardian is no laughing matter.

But what really matters is the question of who is to say how much seriousness is appropriate in philosophical counseling, or what may be laughed at and what may not. Sousa says that the charge that some people are just having too much fun to attend properly to the serious and important business of life raises the question of authority. It makes one ask, Who is to judge which things are more important and therefore ought to only be taken seriously and which things may be attended to with a bit of merriment? "If we place mirth in competition with other things to which it is more appropriately compared—serious but useless things like love, art, philosophy, or religious meditation—who is to say that laughing is not intrinsically more important?"[11] Of course, the practice of philosophical counseling takes philosophy out of the realm of completely "useless things," although, granted, it does not eliminate all of seriously useless philosophy nor every uselessly serious philosopher.

Whether a counselor needs to challenge a client's logic, ethical reasoning, conception of death, or philosophy of life, or to simply laugh at himself, a humorous approach may at times do more good than harm. There is a lot to be said for "phunny" philosophy. After all, what can you say funny about algebra that hasn't already been said?

While it's been said that laughter is the best medicine, you can overdo a good thing. And when laughter comes too easily you risk being diagnosed as mentally ill and needing to be medicated. There is nothing funny about that. The next two chapters examine the decidedly unfunny controversy surrounding the use of drugs to change a person's mind.

NOTES

1. Stolen from Douglas Adams, author of *The Hitchhiker's Guide to the Galaxy* (London: Pan Books, 1978).

2. Not stolen from anyone.

3. Corey, Gerald. *Theory and Practice of Counseling and Psychotherapy*. Pacific Grove, Calif.: Brooks/Cole Publishing. 1996.

4. This is endnote number four which actually serves no purpose whatsoever.

5. Quoted in *I Think Therefore I Laugh* by John Allen Paulos. New York: Vintage Books, 1990. 5.

6. From his book *Milton Berle's Private Joke File*. New York: Random House, 1989.

7. Quoted in *The Metaphysics of Death*. John Martin Fischer, ed. Stanford, Calif.: Stanford University Press, 1993. 31.

8. From his book *Dear George*. Minneapolis, Minn.: Routledge, 1985.

9. Sousa, Ronald de. *The Rationality of Emotion*. Cambridge, Mass.: MIT Press, 1987. 295.

10. Plato. *Republic*. Book 3, Sec. 388d. But then what does he know?

11. Sousa, *The Rationality of Emotion*, 295.

Chapter 11

Medicating the Mind

Many of the feelings that help define us as human beings, and help us to cope with human affairs, are now being diagnosed as classifiable ailments and diseases that need to be corrected with psychotropic drugs. In fact a quick flip through a recent popular magazine reveals advertisements offering pharmaceutical products claiming to combat everything from feeling uncomfortable in a crowd (dubbed "Social-Affective Disorder") to excessive worry (called "Adjustment Disorder" or "Depressive Disorder"—which may mean a man *still* feeling low even though it's been six months since his wife left him). The advertising copy literally says swallowing their pills will end your worries.

Some professional therapists are insisting that sadness, anger, depression, and even the inability to finish a task have nothing to do with a person's character, self-esteem, or internal belief system. These are said to be "hidden psychological disorders" or "shadow syndromes."[1] Therapists see these syndromes as simply inherent in the structure and the chemistry of the individual brain. The recommended treatment for a "shadow syndrome" is a regimen of powerful medication along with some counseling. In the six years between 1990 to 1996 prescriptions in the United States for the antidepressant fluoxetine (sold under the brand name Prozac) rose from 136,000 to 2.5 million. The total number of prescriptions for all similar medications written in 1996 alone was 5.4 million. Independent researchers are now also beginning to compile alarming statistics on the number of powerful and controversial neuroleptic drugs being routinely prescribed to North American children.[2] It is estimated that in the year 2001 there were some 8 million U.S. children on the drug Ritalin alone.

While the use of medicines to correct an organic malfunction in cerebral bio-chemistry seems legitimate and justified, the use of psychopharmaceuticals to con-trol emotional distress, confusion, or depression, or what has been called the rise in "behavioral medicine as a new paradigm,"[3] is for many philosophical counselors a highly contentious issue. This is because the use of drugs to alter feelings or thoughts seems to be based on the faulty assumption that because drugs can be used to change the brain's chemistry and thereby alleviate feelings of distress therefore those feelings of distress originated in a chemical imbalance in the brain. Elliot Valenstein, professor emeritus of psychology and neuroscience at the Uni-versity of Michigan, cautions that causes and treatment effects are easily confused when it comes to attributing a so-called mental illness to brain abnormalities.

There is no reason to assume that any biochemical, anatomical, or functional difference found in the brains of mental patients is the cause of their disorder. It is well established that the drugs used to treat a mental disorder, for example, may induce long-lasting biochemical and even structural changes [in the brain], which in the past were claimed to be the cause of the disorder, but may actually be an effect of treatment.[4]

In other words a condition like a chemical imbalance or a structural abnormality in the brain, which is cited as the cause of a particular patient's mental problems, may in fact be iatrogenic, that is, the consequent side-effects of the very medica-tion prescribed as the treatment.[5] There is an odd sort of faulty logic inherent in claiming that the cause of a disease is proved by the effectiveness of a drug used to treat it. It is something like saying because water can be used to extinguish a house on fire therefore the cause of a house fire is an absence of water in the house. In a philosophical café I facilitated on the topic of suicide one participant explained how she had suffered from suicidal thoughts when she was younger. She was con-vinced by her doctor that her suicidal thoughts were being caused by a chemical imbalance in her brain. Her home life had caused her to suffer from depression and chronic fatigue for a number of years and even to have suicidal thoughts, but she explained that when her doctor prescribed Prozac for her the drug cured her of these unwanted thoughts. Her argument was that because she believed it was the Prozac that ended her suicidal thoughts this proved that her suicidal thoughts were in fact caused by a chemical imbalance in her brain. Other participants at the café were quick to point out that her argument contained a very odd implication: that while she was having suicidal thoughts she must have been suffering from a "Prozac deficiency." It is faulty reasoning at its worst to claim that the remedy to a problem always indicates the nature of its cause.[6]

The belief that suffering and distress are proven to be caused by a chemical im-balance in the brain because of the effects of the treatment administered not only confuses causes with treatment effects but can also lead to a diagnosis of mental illness where there is no illness at all. Emotional distress, confusion, and depres-sion, rather than being the symptoms of a mental illness, may in fact be the scars left behind by what has been called "psychiatric injury."[7] A person examined ac-cording to the hypotheses of natural science and diagnosed as having a neurobiological disorder may actually be suffering from the aftereffects of a physical, emotional, spiritual, or intellectual attack inflicted on her by some other person. Conditions with labels such as Post Traumatic Stress Disorder (PTSD) and Prolonged Duress Stress Disorder (PDSD) are not necessarily mental illnesses but rather natural self-defensive reactions to deeply disturbing experiences. Some psychotherapists argue that even schizophrenia, which most health care practitioners today believe to be a clear-cut endogenous organic illness—that is, the result of an internal process—is at least partly the result of psychiatric injuries sustained by the patient in his relationship with significant others.[8] There are a number of distinct differences between a mental illness and a mental injury. For example, while the cause of a mental illness often eludes identification, the cause of a mental injury can easily be identified but is often denied by those legally and morally responsible; the clinical depression of mental illness is said to be irrational and endogenous while the depression suffered by a person who has sustained a mental injury is reactive—that is, it is a rational response to an injury received; and the person suffering from a mental illness is often despondent and ready to give up, while the person who has been attacked and mentally injured is often willing to work hard to overcome her injuries. Clearly, when a person struggling with the aftermath of a mental injury is diagnosed as having a mental illness—that is, when she is dealt with as though her mental state is either a neurobiological pathology or an intrapsychic problem caused by her unconscious, and then treated with medication—she is being doubly victimized.

This is not to say that there are never physiological or biochemical problems in the brain caused by congenital defects, disease, or environmental toxins (such as mercury, lead, or pesticides), similar to the kind of pathology that may be experienced in any other organ of the body. But problems arise when the mind is held to be equal to the brain, when thinking and feeling are claimed to be *merely* the mechanistic activity of a biological organ, when an understanding of the biochemistry of a person's brain is held to be the same as an understanding of that person,[9] and when the pharmacological suppression of a person's feelings is claimed to have ended that person's problems.

At our present scientifically oriented time in history the mind is often compared to a computer.[10] The brain is said to be the hardware and the mind the software. In this way, it is argued, the mind is clearly a mechanical, chemical, and/or electrical entity and not something distinct from the physical reality of the machinery. The problem with this metaphor is that it overlooks a very important element present in my own computer and in many others. My computer consists of both hardware and programming software but it also has essays (life narratives) within it. These essays contain elements such as arguments, reasoning, conclusions, points of view, beliefs, biases, concerns, values, hopes, the expressions of emotion, and much more. And all are continually edited and updated to a greater or lesser extent depending on what is happening in my life.

From this perspective it is easy to see why it is a mistake to believe that by mechanically/chemically altering the organism—that is, by medicating the brain—that person's problems are also fixed. My computer repair man has the tools to fix both the hardware and the software of my computer but his tools are not effective in altering the reasoning contained within the many essays in my computer. His most sensitive Ohm meter will not show him axiological contradictions in my essays; none of his antivirus programs can fix my essays if the arguments within them are logically flawed or morally misguided; and no new processing chip will rid my essays of their biases or faulty assumptions. And yet my computer repair man can do things to my hardware and software that can make it very difficult, if not impossible, for me to properly access my essays in the future. In fact, if he is not careful, he can do things to the hardware and software that will erase, scramble, or otherwise damage my essays beyond repair. Both prescription and illicit drug use can easily do this sort of harm.

Psychotropic drugs work on the hardware and software that are brain while philosophical counseling works on the contents of "the essays that are mind." Unfortunately, many mental healthcare professionals defend the validity of the computer model which holds that the mind simply *is* the physical brain, and that when the content of those essays are problematic it is because the hardware or software is defective. For example, Paul Mohl, director of psychotherapy services at the University of Texas, San Antonio, has argued forcefully in support of the mechanistic/biological perspective of mind.

Psychotherapy is a biological treatment that acts through biological mechanisms on biological problems. . . . Medication, dream interpretations, and empathy become simply different ways to alter different neurotransmitters. . . . Modern developments in basic neuroscience are uncovering the underlying medical nature of psychotherapy.[11]

Mohl, in attempting to advance the scientific stature of psychotherapy, is arguing that medication, dream interpretation, and empathy in psychotherapy are effective in changing the mind because they each alter the biochemistry of the brain. This is a mechanistic perspective of human beings which reduces the intentional act of changing one's mind (editing essays) to an event that is *caused* by alterations in cerebral neurotransmitters (the software or hardware). Of course this raises the question, What caused those alterations in cerebral neurotransmitters? The question, Does a chemical imbalance in the brain cause depression or does depression cause a chemical imbalance in the brain? is a chicken-and-egg problem. Research has shown that while the chemical activity within the brain generates thoughts, thinking causes a change in the chemistry within the brain. In other words, the relationship between brain chemistry and thinking is clearly reciprocal.[12] This reciprocity is what causes concern among philosophical counselors when medication is used to treat a client's problems. Concern about medication is found not only among philosophical counselors but within the psychotherapeutic community itself. Kay Redfield Jamison, professor of psychiatry at the Johns Hopkins University School of Medicine, writes that drugs work well at first in grappling with anxiety, distress, depression, and psychosis. But, to the extent that they work,

they do so by altering the fine tuning of the brain and muffling consciousness. As such, they are blunt agents that, with prolonged use, alter or damage the brain's delicate chemistry. In doing so, they work huge damage in the relationships, jobs, health, and pride of those who are dependent on or addicted to them.[13]

When medical doctors and psychiatrists prescribe psychotropic drugs to control a patient's symptoms, they affirm their eliminativist materialist assumption that causality rests in brain chemistry. This sort of thinking relegates the existential *reasons* a person has for low self-esteem, emotional distress, and ethical uncertainty to a place of lesser importance behind cerebral anatomy and neurochemistry. And yet, as mentioned above, there is no convincing evidence that those individuals who are labeled "mental patients" or are said to be suffering from a "mental illness" always have more cerebral malformations or a greater chemical imbalance in their brains than the general population of so-called normal individuals.[14] The resultant predicament this causes can be illustrated with the following case based on a true story.

"Stan" gets average marks in his college courses, but he is a member of the university league's winning basketball team. He came to see me for philosophical counseling with the consent of his psychiatrist. He was taking both antidepressant and antipsychotic medication to combat what he described as profound sadness, confused feelings, and anger that could erupt seemingly for no reason. Stan explained how distressed he had been lately at his having become unreasonably angry with his friend "Karl." During the course of discussion with me the story emerged of how Stan considered Karl to be a far better basketball player than himself, how Karl never had any problems getting girls and always had several girlfriends at the same time, and how Karl had recently charmed Stan's girlfriend away from him, supposedly as a harmless joke. Stan said he could understand why his girlfriend had left him and gone with Karl. He wondered if he was even worthy of a girlfriend considering how poorly he played basketball compared to Karl. But through all this he insisted Karl was a good friend, and that "all's fair in love and war," even between friends. When asked to define what a friend is, Stan responded that it is someone you respect but are inferior to.

Over the weeks that followed Stan told of how his mother had remarried when he was young, how he had several younger step siblings, and how his stepfather treated "his own flesh and blood" with more love and respect than he felt Stan deserved. His stepfather was quick to point out his faults, and never offered to help Stan correct his mistakes. His stepfather taught Stan to develop a negative view of the world, the people in it, and himself. Stan remembered asking his stepfather questions that were judged by him to be bad questions that a good boy would not have asked. Stan said his stepfather was never a friend to him and that he had convinced Stan he could never do anything right. When I asked if he could perhaps think of one thing he had gotten right since then, Stan could not answer. When I asked him about the fact that he was a player on a winning basketball team, Stan said his ability to concentrate and focus on the game had deteriorated dramatically over the past month and he was considering quitting the team.

The sessions continued in this vein. Stan revealed that he expected only perfection from himself. When he failed to reach this goal on the basketball court Stan saw it as a confirmation of his own and his stepfather's low opinion of him. He re-called all his failures—every missed basket—in vivid detail but could not think of a single instance of success. He was even worried that he was failing to do what I expected of him in the counseling sessions. But by the end of the fourth session I was already beginning to see some improvement in Stan's self-confidence. Stan was clearly enjoying the opportunity to speak freely and to ask questions without the fear that his questions would be judged good or bad. Stan and I came to agree that Stan had a serious case of low self-esteem and that he would probably benefit from an exploration of a number of issues such as what he believed about himself and why, what friendship is all about, and what success means when you're part of a team.

When Stan arrived for his fifth session he was smiling broadly. He began by an-nouncing that he had discovered the meaning of life. His conclusion was that "the purpose of life is movement." This puzzled me, so I asked him to explain. Stan said when he looked around him it was as if he could see movement in everything. This explained where his problems had come from. He said that when he now comes up against a problem with a girl he simply tells himself "everything is movement" and the problem goes away. In this way, he assured me, he could now solve any problem he might encounter.

"In fact," he told me, "I feel invincible."

I had a strong sense that something was not right. I asked Stan if he'd been drinking. He said he had not. I then asked if his medication had been changed. Stan replied that he had gone to see his medical doctor and the doctor had doubled the dosage of his antidepressants. I cautioned him that his euphoric state may just be the result of the increased medication, and not because all of his problems had been resolved. Stan agreed this might be the case but said it simply didn't matter as long as all his problems were gone. I explained that the antidepressants were like taking a painkiller for a broken leg: It will alleviate the pain but it doesn't fix the leg. But Stan was confident that my services were no longer required. Finally I warned him that just like his medication had been increased as his body had adapted to the orig-inal dosage, his body would probably adapt to this higher dosage as well.

"When that happens," I told him, "you're likely to be faced with the reasons for your depression and anger again. Are you simply going to have your doctor in-crease the dosage again?"

But Stan was adamant. He did not return after the fifth session.

What I had seen in Stan as existential axiological issues, that is, issues of nega-tive self-evaluation and low self-esteem, had instead been diagnosed by Stan's medical doctor as organic brain dysfunction requiring only symptom suppression by means of biochemical alterations in his cerebral machinery. Stan's case is a classic example of the medical approach to mental suffering which centers on the individual's biochemistry while underplaying or completely ignoring social cir-cumstances. This medical model approach to confusion and distress is based on the belief that medication "can help restore a therapeutic alliance, along with the patient's ability and motivation for self-reflection, by alleviating serious regres-sion, severe affective disturbance, overwhelming anxiety, and cognitive disorganization. It can encourage the use of verbal expression by enhancing memory, by reducing vegetative disturbance, and distractibility, and by limiting impulsive action."[15] Unfortunately, rather than motivating Stan toward greater self-reflection, an increase in medication led him to *end* the therapeutic alliance we had established. In essence the increase in his drug dosage induced in Stan the iatrogenic symptom of mistakenly believing he had solved all of his problems without any of his problems actually having been resolved at all. Furthermore, Stan had come to counseling with a desire: he had wanted to regain his joy of life. The medical approach to Stan was to get rid of this desire because it was ostensibly causing him distress. But notice with the logic of this approach the ideal medication would be a drug that eliminates all unfulfilled desires.

Psychotropic medication alone may be appropriate in a small number of severe cases (see Figure 2.1), but in most cases a drug's effects on the brain can seriously undermine therapy by relieving the negative symptoms (including desires) that motivated a patient to undertake the work of self-scrutiny and the evaluation of his social context.[16] This work is essential if the existential problems (difficult interpersonal relationships, value conflicts, low self-esteem, etc.) which created the need for medication in the first place are to be resolved. But drugs are difficult to resist because they often cost less than counseling and they can at times work very quickly. How can the long hours of hard work and often painful emotions encountered in counseling compete with that!

Philosopher Hans-Georg Gadamer argues that modern psychiatric drugs seem to have "instrumentalized" the human body. Gadamer finds it worrisome that through psychiatric drugs "doctors are now able not only to eliminate and deaden various organic disturbances, but also to take away from a person their own deepest distress and confusion." Gadamer's point is that using drugs in psychotherapy is often simply the act of taking away the symptoms rather than helping the person to resolve, readapt, and reintegrate into society.[17]

What Gadamer's argument suggests is that just as physical pain indicates a causal factor, so mental or psychological pain denotes the presence of a reason for that pain. If it is clearly a mistake to believe that in taking an aspirin tablet to take away the physical indicator (the pain) of an infected splinter in the finger we have eliminated the cause of the pain (the actual splinter in the finger), then it is likewise clearly a mistake to believe that in taking a psychoactive drug to eliminate a mental or psychological pain we have eliminated the reason for that pain.

But despite cases like Stan's above, and Gadamer's persuasive argument, philosophical counselors are not utterly condemning the use of psychotropic drug therapy. Some argue that if one of the most important goals in philosophical counseling is helping to make the client feel better then why not allow this goal to be reached by means of drugs? And if swallowing a pill can bring symptomatic relief almost overnight, why bother with counseling at all? Others warn that making a person feel better is not all a drug does. Many side effects are often accepted as a reasonable price to pay for the relief of mental anguish. But when one undesirable symptom is merely replaced by four or five others (the side effects), is the price too high for the limited peace of mind attained?

The following is the relevant portion of an e-mail that was one of many received after this chapter was posted as an essay on the Internet. It is reprinted here with the permission of the sender.

Subject: RE: Your Article
Date: Sun, 18 Jun 2000 22:02:38 -0400
From: XYZ
To: "Dr. Peter B. Raabe" <raabe@interchange.ubc.ca>

Dear Dr. Raabe

When I read your article and the story of Stan, it struck a chord in me. I am going through a similar situation. I've always had low self esteem, but last year, when I got married (which is supposed to be the happiest point of people's lives), I became increasingly depressed and self destructive. I began having panic attacks that grew in frequency and intensity until I lived in fear of the next one. I finally went to a psychiatrist, and was diagnosed with Panic Disorder, and put on Zoloft. Over the course of the first month, my dosage was increased three times. I was also (and still am) using Xanax, between .25 and .5 mg, daily. I've now decided that it's time for me to come off the medication, which I've been tapering off slowly for the last three months. I'm finding that I'm more prone to attacks again, but I seem to be able to handle them better than I did originally. However, I believe the underlying issues that caused me to develop them to begin with are still present, and that I need to return to sessions with a psychologist to work them out. It's just so hard for me to find someone that I feel comfortable enough to spill out my guts to.

Regards,
XYZ.

NOTES

1. Ratey, John J. and Catherine Johnson. *Shadow Syndromes*. New York: Pantheon, 1997.

2. While the medical establishment in Canada has recently reported that the prescription of psychotropic drugs in Canada is quite low, and therefore acceptable, independent research conducted by the Vancouver *Province* newspaper has shown that the report is based on faulty methodology and interpretation of statistics, and that the figures are significantly higher, well beyond the level the medical establishment itself deems acceptable. This raises two important issues: the reliability of information *about* the medical establishment offered *by* the medical establishment itself, and the alarmingly high rate of psychopharmaceuticals prescribed to children and deemed "acceptable." For a discussion about these issues see the special section on children and drugs in the Vancouver *Province* of December 21, 2000.

3. Kächele, Horst and Rainer Richter. "Germany and Austria." In *The Challenge to Psychoanalysis and Psychotherapy*. London: Jessica Kingsley Publishers, 1999. 50.

4. Valenstein, Elliot S. *Blaming the Brain: The Truth about Drugs and Mental Health*. New York: Free Press, 1998. 126.

5. On November 11, 2001 CNN reported that researchers have found Ritalin (used to treat children with attention deficit hyperactivity disorder [ADHD]) to have the same harmful long-term effects on the brains of laboratory rats as amphetamines and cocaine.

6. As a relevant side note, the recent "genetic gold rush" has also led to some incredibly faulty reasoning concerning the causes of certain mental problems. For example, it is argued

that because schizophrenia tends to run in families it surely must have a genetic cause. Since this is the case, the argument goes, we simply need to find the schizophrenic gene and fix it. But this is like saying because child abuse and wife battering tend to run in families they must have genetic causes and we simply need to find the child abuse gene and wife battering gene and fix them.

7. For an online discussion of this topic go to http://www.successunlimited.co.uk/PTSD/#Definition.

8. Some psychotherapists argue that schizophrenia is at least partly the result of a dysfunctional family environment. See, for example, the essay by Gregory Bateson et al., "Toward a Theory of Schizophrenia" in *Behavioral Sciences,* 1956, 1. 251–264. See also "Researching the Family Theories of Schizophrenia: An Exercise in Epistemological Confusion" by Paul F. Dell in *Family Process* Vol. 19, no. 4, 1980. 321–335. And see *Abnormal Psychology in a Changing World* by J. S. Nevid, S. A. Rathus, and B. Greene. Englewood Cliffs, N.J.: Prentice-Hall, 1994.

9. Or when we depersonalize the brain to the extent that its owner is lost.

10. In the past the brain has been compared to a telephone switchboard, a telegraph system, hydraulic and electromagnetic systems, a mill, and a catapult. See John Searle's *Minds, Brains, and Science*. Cambridge, Mass.: Harvard University Press, 1984. 44.

11. Valenstein, 152.

12. Ibid., 125–163.

13. Jamison, Kay Redfield. *Night Falls Fast: Understanding Suicide*. New York: Vintage, 1999. 127.

14. Valenstein, 125–163.

15. Kessler, Richard J. "Medication and Psychotherapy." *Psychotherapy: The Analytic Approach*. Morton J. Aronson and Melvin A. Scharfman, eds. Northvale, N.J.: Jason Aronson, 1992. 165.

16. Jerome D. and Julia B. Frank make this point in their book *Persuasion and Healing*. Baltimore: Johns Hopkins University Press, 1991.

17. Gadamer, Hans-Georg. *The Enigma of Health*. Stanford, Calif.: Stanford University Press, 1996.

Chapter 12

Medicating the Mind:
A Second Dose

An information leaflet from the National Parkinson's Foundation in Gainesville, Florida explains that more than 40% of people with Parkinson's disease (a degenerative neurological disorder) develop depression. The leaflet says that this depression "should be evaluated, treated, and monitored on an ongoing basis by a physician." By implying that the depression can be treated by a *physician*, the leaflet leaves the reader with the impression that the depression has an organic cause. The reader is thereby led to the conclusion that medication is called for. What is wrong with this picture?

Most psychotherapists agree that depression is a symptom of something. What they can't agree on is whether depression and other so-called mental disorders are symptomatic of a chemical imbalance in the brain or of an irrational thought process in the mind. Some philosophical counselors are now even proposing the hypothesis that depression, rather than being an illness caused by a chemical imbalance or irrational thoughts, is a perfectly reasonable reaction to certain seemingly hopeless situations in life. But if depression is sometimes reasonable then why use drugs to get rid of it?

In the 1980s seratonin-based drugs flooded the marketplace and became the cure-all of choice for most physicians treating depression. When risks of their use started to be made public in the early 1990s, there was a brief but widespread rejection of the practice of taking a pill to reduce depression. The view that depression was the result of social rather than chemical factors was once again dominant within the helping profession. In 1995 only 20% of psychiatrists felt that depressed individuals should be treated with drugs. But since then the next generation of so-called more reliable and safe drugs have been developed and aggressively promoted by pharmaceutical corporations,[1] and, not surprisingly, drug use has increased correspondingly. Physicians are increasingly pressured by pharmaceutical manufacturers to approach their patients exclusively in terms consistent with the hypotheses of natural science and to prescribe chemical treatments for even the slightest deviation from the norm. Discursive therapies are therefore once again being perceived as only adjunctive treatments to maximally implemented drug therapy.

Canadian psychiatrist Dr. Heinz Lehman was one of the early pioneers of what is sometimes called "biologic psychiatry" or drug therapy for mental illness. But Lehman was a reluctant pioneer. In an interview broadcast in February 2000 on CBC television Lehman said he and his colleagues working at a Montreal psychiatric hospital in the 1950s had discovered that empathetic discussions were very effective therapy for the majority of their patients. But they were forced to abandon such discussions, and compelled to give their patients psychoactive drugs, when hospital administrators deemed therapy sessions too expensive in comparison to the cost of newly developed medications. In other words, their treatment of choice was a therapeutic dialogue but this was almost entirely abandoned in favor of the administration of psychotropic drugs because it was deemed more cost effective.

Studies indicate that, at best, medication alone helps only to a very limited degree;[2] drug treatment provides significant help in only about 50% of schizophrenic patients, and that up to 40% of manic-depressives are not helped sufficiently by lithium or any of the other common mood stabilizers, such as valproate and carbamazepine.[3] Research has also shown that the type of improvement following antidepressant medication is indistinguishable from the improvement following cognitive therapy.

In one multicenter study, a comparison of treatment modalities conducted by Irene Elkin and her associates demonstrated the value of both interpersonally oriented and cognitively based therapies in treating depression. These psychological treatments were found to be as effective as antidepressant medication on eighteen-month follow-up.[4]

Research has also shown that two-thirds of all psychotherapy patients put on drug treatments for depression do as well as or better with a placebo than those treated with what the medical establishment believes to be active chemical ingredients.[5] Researchers have theorized from this that the positive "chemistry" between the patient and the doctor may be far more important to the improvement in most patients than the chemical formula in the medication. The technique which is used is now generally considered less important than the personality and experience of the therapist, and some psychotherapists believe that "the relationship with the therapist is a necessary, and perhaps often a sufficient, condition for improvement in any kind of therapy."[6]

Not only is the necessity of pharmacological treatment questionable in many cases, but the consumer who takes a psychoactive drug also has a steep price to pay. Every medication, from simple aspirin to the most potent psychoactive drug, causes effects in the consumer other than the relief of targeted symptoms. Pharmaceutical products simply aren't as well aimed as their manufacturers would have consumers believe. For example, common side effects of antidepressant medications are nervousness, restlessness, sleep disturbances, nausea, tremors, constipation, bladder problems, blurred vision, dizziness, and drowsiness. Antipsychotic drugs produce tardive dyskinesia (uncontrollable facial tics, tongue tremors, and jaw movements), pharmacological depression (depression brought on by the medication itself), and neuroleptic dysphoria (an emotional state characterized by anxiety, depression, and restlessness).[7] It is not uncommon for a patient who is already taking psychotropic medication to be prescribed additional medication to combat these and other debilitating side effects. This means that the symptoms of a so-called mental illness may at times merely be replaced by four or five other symptoms. In his autobiographical book—an account of his own battle with severe depression—writer William Styron warns his readers about the horrifying side effects of a tranquilizer he was prescribed meant to combat the insomnia caused by his depression. He writes,

I'm convinced that this tranquilizer [Halcion] is responsible for at least exaggerating to an intolerable point the suicidal ideas that had possessed me before entering hospital. . . . Much evidence has accumulated recently that indicts Halcion (whose chemical name is triazolam) as a causative factor in producing suicidal obsession and other aberrations of thought in susceptible individuals. Because of this Halcion has been categorically banned in the Netherlands and it should be at least monitored more carefully here [in the United States].[8]

Taking a drug to relieve depression may also result in a chemical dependency, not only because of the intrinsically addictive nature of some drugs but because of the body's natural adaptation to a prescribed dosage which must be increased to maintain the drug's perceived level of effect. This may result in the unfortunate consequence of a patient ending up with the dual diagnosis of a mental illness and a drug addiction.

Psychiatric researcher and professor of psychiatry Stanislav Grof points out another serious problem with the use of medication. Grof writes, "it is generally understood that in psychiatry drugs do not solve the problem, but control the symptoms."[9] Grof means by this that taking a medication for a so-called mental illness will often eliminate the outward display of distress, and may even assuage the patient's subjective experience of suffering, but it will never eliminate the initial, and often ongoing, reasons for that suffering such as a poor home environment, problematic beliefs, or misguided values. What is even more troubling is that the very nature of drug use itself has recently undergone a significant change. While drugs were at one time employed as a means of treating extant illnesses, the marketing strategy of today's pharmaceutical industry includes promoting their products as essential *preventive* agents for adults and children even where no clear medical problem exists.[10] This means an individual may come to depend on a drug in his effort to supposedly prevent what would never have occurred. To make sense of this, it must be remembered that pharmaceutical companies are not caregivers, they are in the business of maximizing their profits, and as such they are concerned not only with developing primarily those drugs that will bring significant financial returns, but also with creating a market demand for a drug they are already producing for which there is too little demand. They create that market demand by persuading consumers that what the company produces is what the consumer needs if they wish to function normally.

Ironically, additional problems may be created when a doctor recommends that the patient discontinue the use of a particular drug. For example, anxiety or panic attacks can set in when antidepressants such as fluoxetine (Prozac), bupropion (Wellbutrin), or desipramine (Norpramin, Pertofrane) are no longer taken.[11]

If taking a drug is often no more effective than a therapeutic discussion, if it leaves the client vulnerable to a variety of side effects, if it requires increased dosages to maintain perceived effects, if it only eliminates the symptoms of distress caused by some problem but not the problem itself, and if the cessation of drug use causes additional problems, why would anyone want to take a drug in the first place? There are a number of possible answers. It may be because taking medication is more private. That is, it does not require an individual to divulge sensitive information and argue about painful or embarrassing personal material with an often judgmental authority figure. It may also be because a person who is suffering typically goes first to his medical doctor. Since most physicians are primarily trained in disease diagnosis and the prescription of biophysiochemical remedies the issue of counseling may simply never come up. Furthermore, many patients and their families prefer a diagnosis of a physiological disease whose treatment calls for the prescription of medications because there is less of a stigma and less blame attached to a medical infirmity than is commonly associated with the diagnosis of a psychological problem or mental illness. What's more, pills are often less of a financial drain than long-term psychotherapy or counseling. This is especially relevant in countries that do not have government-funded healthcare systems. Even where healthcare is paid for with tax dollars, some government agencies will only pay for visits to a medical doctor and the medication she prescribes but not for visits to a counselor. Also, according to Dr. Stefan de Schill, director of research at the American Mental Health Foundation, people often feel forced to turn to drugs to alleviate their pain because of the incompetence of their psychotherapists.[12] Furthermore, our fast-food society has conditioned people to unrealistically expect a quick fix for whatever ails them. This expectation is forcing doctors to prescribe pills rather than counseling so as to give their patients what they want. Prescription medications are powerfully seductive for a variety of reasons, and the aggressive promotional campaigns by pharmaceutical corporations can make the use of drugs almost irresistible.

Unfortunately, today many physicians and psychotherapists see emotional distress as having mostly a neurobiological or chemical origin. The problem with this is that the act of prescribing medication can convince a patient that his problem is beyond voluntary control, even when the origin of his problem lies within his familial or societal environment. By adopting a reductionist scientific model, and defining the range of subjective human experiences and emotions largely in terms of degrees of mental illness, psychotherapy has, until very recently, championed a mechanistic conception of human thinking and conduct linked more closely with biophysiochemical reactions than with subjective reasons, intentions, and desires.[13] The problem with this conception is that the administering of psychotropic drugs is not at all an exact science. Science is concerned with the discovery of facts which allow accurate predictions to be made. The "facts" concerning psychoactive medication in relation to the treatment of so-called mental illness do not at all have the same predictive power we have come to expect of any truly scientific endeavor, especially when it comes to the effects of long-term usage.

Philosophical counseling does not claim to be a science, and it sees the importance of not dealing exclusively with brain chemistry but in addressing the very human concerns of everyday life. Jon Mills, philosophical counselor and professor of psychology and philosophy in Toronto, points out that "there is a presumptive bias in the medical, psychiatric, and behavioral sciences that views the mind from a reductive ontology. The standard mentality is to give a pill for any psychological ailment and wait for the results." From his own experience Mills has found that medication may ameliorate the severity of a patient's symptoms, but that it has little effect on eliminating the source of that person's malaise. Even when medication works, he says, there are often many needs and conflicts that a pill could never address.[14]

In an e-mail message to me, philosophical practitioner and professor Wanda Dawe agrees. "If the client originally presented with some one or more philosophically interesting problems with which he was struggling, no medication can possibly provide the solution."

Michael Russell says that he is not at all opposed to medication because he does not see an inherent conflict or incompatibility between human affect seen as choice and seen as a physiological matter subject to helpful chemical intervention. Russell, who is professor of philosophy and human services at California State University, research psychoanalyst and philosophical counselor, says, "There are plenty of people who are extremely miserable, dangerous, etc., without medication, and in a reasonable position to make good use of one form of counseling or another with it." Russell asks rhetorically why it should be considered "an inauthentic path" to take when a person uses a drug to treat a distressing mood if that mood could not be alleviated by means of philosophical counseling.

The vice president of the American Philosophical Practitioners Association (APPA), Paul Sharkey, says that he has had clients "who, after beginning a course of medication, were much more, rather than less, inclined to engage in philosophical reflection. Most of them recognized that even when their biological conditions were stabilized (and sometimes even because of it) they still had a lot to do to resolve the various kinds of issues confronting them (issues of ethical responsibility, meaning, purpose, etc.) which they were simply incapable of addressing while not taking medication."

One of the pioneers of philosophical counseling in the Netherlands, Eite Veening, says the practice of prescribing antidepressants is not as frequent in the Netherlands as it is in the United States. Veening suggests that the issue of whether medication should or should not be prescribed is a question of who is in charge; it concerns the issue of what the client wants from the philosophical counselor. Veening sees the client as being allowed to make his own decisions regarding what kind of treatment he wants. While the counselor may explain and discuss the impact of medication on thinking with a client who is perhaps taking an antidepressant, his primary role, according to Veening, is to deal with the client's philosophical beliefs and opinions. Veening holds that a client's emotional issues are psychological and therefore "his feelings will be *his* concern, not mine."

Jon Mills says in his own practice he has seen drugs work in a number of ways: they can relieve his patient's symptoms without removing the desire to talk; they can help his patient cope and manage therapy better; they can aid his patients to distance themselves from examining other problems; or they can mask the original issue or underlying problem. Wanda Dawe cautions that when medication screens a problem, "the client moves from a position of restricted or unrealized liberty to a position of still greater unfreedom." This leads Dawe to think that "in any discussion of patient/client substance dependency, the issue of the individual's liberty and capacity for self-governance would be raised." For Dawe the question is, "if one is to be held up/together by some strings, however gossamer, who will be the puppeteer?"

Along a similar line of argument, Maria Colavito, president of the Biocultural Research Institute in Florida, psychologist, and philosophical counselor, takes a different stance on the issue. Colavito maintains that, according to the scientific model, the environment selects for appropriate mental and emotional development in each individual's ecosystem. In that case, Colavito asks, "who are we to alter it pharmacologically?" Colavito argues that if emotions outside the accepted curve of so-called normalcy are in fact the way some individuals adapt to their environment, then medicating them to force their emotions back into that acceptable range of normalcy is nothing less than new millennial eugenics. Colavito's position raises the important issue of the relationship between what is in fact abnormal and what is merely socially unacceptable.

While philosophical counselors are divided as to the advisability of altering a client's thoughts and emotions with medication, consumers of psychotropic medication can similarly have mixed feelings about taking them. The following message was received by e-mail and is reprinted here with the permission of the sender:

Subject: RE: Medication
Date: Fri, 15 Dec 2000 22:02:38 -0400
From: ABC
To:"Dr. Peter B. Raabe" <raabe@interchange.ubc.ca>

I have received psychological counseling on-and off for many years, and have taken many 'rounds' of different psychotropic drugs to relieve depression. The drugs are not all they are cracked up to be. . . . For me, the drugs can alleviate the worst, blackest end of the depression, allowing me to at least care enough to make the effort to get counseling. Without the drugs, I wouldn't have been able to believe that psychological counseling could help me, and would probably not be here today. I agree that the relationship between mind and brain is a highly reciprocal one. I think [drugs] work best for people to whom depression is a

real disability, but I do believe that they are over-prescribed.
    Sincerely,
    ABC

The question about the need for psychotropic medication is often asked in conjunction with the question of whether it is worth it for a client to endure the noxious side-effects of such drugs in his effort to get back to normal. But the real question that ought to be asked by individuals who have been diagnosed as suffering from mental illness and by philosophical counselors as well is, What does it take to be considered normal in the first place?

NOTES

1. In the United States alone pharmaceutical companies spend about $12.3 billion a year on advertising and marketing, including promotions that are aimed at influencing the prescribing habits of physicians. See "Why Do American Drug Companies Spend More Than $12 Billion a Year Pushing Drugs?" by S. M. Wolfe in the *Journal of General Internal Medicine* 11, 1996. 637–639.

2. This point is made emphatically by Dr. Stefan de Schill, director of research of the American Mental Health Foundation in New York and vice president of the International Institute for Mental Health Research in Geneva, and author of the book *Crucial Choices—Crucial Changes.* Amherst, N.Y.: Prometheus Books, 2000. 284, 289.

3. Valenstein, Elliot S. *Blaming the Brain: The Truth about Drugs and Mental Health.* New York: Free Press, 1998. 213.

4. Imber et al. in the *Journal of Consulting Clinical Psychologists* 58. 1990. 352–359. Elkin, I., M. T. Shea, J. T. Watkins, et al. "National Institute of Mental Health Treatment of Depression Collaborative Research Program: General Effectiveness of Treatments." *Archives of General Psychiatry*, 46. Quoted in Galanter, Marc. *Network Therapy for Alcohol and Drug Abuse.* New York: Basic Books, 1993. 971–982.

5. Greenberg and Fisher. *The Limits of Biological Treatments for Psychological Distress.* Hillsdale, N.J.: Lawrence Erlbaum Associates, 1989. 1–37.

6. See "France" by Serge Lebovici, and also "Psychotherapies: A Different Perspective" by Jerome D. Frank in *The Challenge to Psychoanalysis and Psychotherapy.* Stefan De Schill and Serge Lebovici, eds. London: Jessica Kingsley Publishers, 1999. 31, 134, 137. See also chapter 3, "The Characteristics of a Helping Relationship," in Carl R. Rogers' book *On Becoming a Person* (1961). Boston: Houghton Mifflin, 1989. 39–58.

7. Ibid.

8. Styron, William. *Darkness Visible.* New York: Random House, 1990.

9. Grof, Stanislav. *Beyond the Brain.* New York: State University of New York Press, 1985.

10. Valenstein, 171.

11. Hales, Dianne and Robert E. Hales. *Caring for the Mind.* New York: Bantam, 1995. 152.

12. Schill, 370.

13. Freud toyed with the concept of psychoanalysis as a kind of technology when he wrote, "Psychoanalysis neither has, nor can have, a philosophical standpoint. In reality psy-

choanalysis is a method of investigation, an impartial instrument like, say, infinitesimal calculus." Freud, Sigmund. *The Future of an Illusion* (1928). New York: Liveright, 1949. 64.

14. Dr. Mills' comments and those following were received by personal correspondence.

Chapter 13

Getting to Normal

Early in the twentieth century psychoanalyst Carl G. Jung wrote, "The normal man is a fiction."[1] There are many more books now than in Jung's day that claim to tell us what constitutes a mentally abnormal person. Perhaps the best known in North America is the series of volumes referred to as the *Diagnostic and Statistical Manual of Mental Disorders* (the American Psychiatric Association's diagnostic manual, generally referred to as the *DSM*) compiled and continually updated by a task force of prominent American mental healthcare professionals.[2] Rather than focusing on the *whys* of mental illness, the *DSM* is said to emphasize the *whats*—that is, its focus is on the specific signs and symptoms said to characterize the various disorders that justify labeling a person as abnormal or mentally ill, and guide mental health professionals in making treatment decisions. But while the descriptive phenomenology of the *DSM* is considered useful by many mental health care professionals it has often been criticized for failing to help make those clear diagnostic distinctions between normal and abnormal most crucial to clinical practice.[3] Nancy Miller, clinical professor and head of the Clinical Research Program at the National Institute of Mental Health in Maryland, points out that there are many problems in the *DSM*'s classifications, even just in the personality disorders alone.

Despite the search for "infallible indicators" meant to yield definitive determination of the presence or absence of a particular disorder, marked variability still remains, in terms of number of underlying dimensions; degree of inference required; level of criterion specificity; number of criteria needed to reach threshold; temporal stability of criteria; and differing base-rates, both among criteria and among disorders. At the same time, the marked absence of agreement regarding core theoretic constructs has been repeatedly demonstrated, for instance, by virtue of the considerable variation found among clinicians regarding which personality disorder they assume a particular symptom reflects.[4]

Variability aside, the phenomenological approach of the *DSM* puts the concept of normalcy into the rather peculiar position of being negatively defined, or defined by omission. In other words, "normal" ends up being whatever is left over, any behavior or feeling which is not included in the *DSM* as a classifiable symptom of some abnormality. But this doesn't tell us much about normal. It's like your parent or employer having a list, which is constantly revised, that includes every behavior they consider wrong without ever explaining what you need to do to get it right.

Paradoxically, the *DSM*'s professional definition of abnormal is so broad and so ambiguous that almost all behavior can be recognized somewhere in its pages. In fact the *DSM* has appropriated many normal human experiences, such as, for example, depression, by defining its typical presentation as abnormal and then medicalizing it by calling it *clinical* depression. What does it do to the definition of normal when virtually all behavior may potentially be interpreted as clinical or abnormal? Where can we find an epistemic norm regarding normality? What would constitute adequate criteria or good grounds for a theory of normalcy?

One of the problems with attempting to define normal is that the term "normal" is often confused with "socially acceptable." A person may consider herself normal at the same time that her family or her neighbors find her abnormal because either her manner of being in the world or her interpersonal behavior does not meet their parochial standard of acceptability. French historian and philosopher Michel Foucault makes the point that a few hundred years ago a person might have been defined as abnormal, or even insane, and therefore locked away indefinitely just because her manner of behavior was considered scandalous, a dishonor to the family, or simply an embarrassment.[5] In defining a person as normal do we therefore wish to say that her manner of being in the world as well as her behavior toward others must be nonembarrassing and acceptable to everyone, or at least a majority of individuals in her neighborhood or the society in which she lives?

Sometimes what is considered normal is nothing more than what is already typical, common, or conventional within a given society because the typical, common, and conventional are defined according to the traditions held by that particular society as a whole, and in line with what is considered best for both its individual members and that society. The modernist perspective has it that normalcy and mental health are defined by means of the accuracy, rationality, or correspondence between a person's cognitions and so-called objective reality. But postmodernists today hold that the entire notion of a definition of normalcy that is reliant on the notion of an objective reality is flawed. They hold that what *passes* for objective reality is in fact largely a system of socially held beliefs (social relativism) into which a so-called normal individual's cognitions must fit. Being normal means, according to postmodernism, an individual's validation by a society when that individual's thinking corresponds to the social consensus. For example, professor of political science Pauline Marie Rosenau points out that courses offered in the early

1990s in a Boulder, Colorado community college included channeling techniques, a crystal workshop, synchronicity, I Ching, transpersonal dimensions of astrology, and alchemy, and that Eastern meditation was taught in elementary schools. In light of this unusual curriculum, and the fact that many members of the community considered themselves "New Agers," it could be argued that this entire community was quite abnormal. Yet Rosenau explains that the adherents to New Age movements "come from the ranks of the American middle class. Their members are not viewed as eccentric or deviant *within those communities* where they are heavily concentrated such as in Boulder."[6] In a sense there is strength in numbers: if enough people do the abnormal then the abnormal becomes the new norm. The health care professionals responsible for compiling the *DSM* acknowledge that what may seem like a mental disorder may not be diagnosed as such if the symptoms are simply too prevalent within a given population. They caution that "Beliefs or experiences of members of religious or other cultural groups may be difficult to distinguish from delusions or hallucinations. When such experiences are shared and accepted by a cultural group, they should not be considered evidence of psychosis."[7] Clearly then "psychosis" is not at all a scientifically and objectively identifiable condition; it is only a "mental illness" if contrary to specific religious or cultural norms. The concept of what is normal can also be seriously skewed when the dominant cultural value is not the welfare of the individual but that individual's usefulness to that society's institutions. In his book *Schizophrenia and Human Value*[8] Peter Barham points out that abnormality has at times been largely determined by the economic ideology of those who hold the most wealth and power within a society: the ruling elite. In the late nineteenth century, the medical establishment was called on to endorse the medicalization of individuals who complained that their vitality was depleted by the harsh demands of the workplace. The ailment came to be known as "constitutional weakness," and it was diagnosed in individuals who were believed to be unduly suffering from what was considered the normal level of misery within an industrialized society. It then fell to psychiatry to forge an authoritative account of the chronic tendencies inherent in both women and men for whom, for example, the repetitious drudgery of factory work or the suffocating exertion of coal mine labor led to physical and emotional distress.

In effect, the demands of industrialized society for a servile workforce (and "warforce") led to the labeling of an individual's inability to cope with wretched living and working conditions and the resultant psychological suffering as the disease of madness or mental illness. The disease model was an effective way of individualizing *social* problems as *personal* illnesses, diverting attention away from the political understanding of those problems, and placing the blame on the victim.[9] The concepts of normal and abnormal were generated and strictly controlled by the economic impetus for the maximization of profit which demanded maximal human productivity. Although founded on values that emerged during the Industrial Revolution, this economy-based model has had substantial impact on the nineteenth, twentieth, and twenty-first centuries. It has included in its list of mental illnesses a black slave's desire to escape slavery (diagnosed as "drapetomania"), a woman's rejection of her supposed innate childbearing nature (diagnosed as "hysteria"), a young man disobeying military orders (diagnosed as "dysaethesia"), and anyone openly critical of the political, economic, or religious ideology of their state (diagnosed as "reform-seeking schizophrenia").

Closely aligned with an economy-based model of normalcy is normalcy as defined in relation to a society's desire for order and discipline in its younger generations. Order and discipline are considered to be important elements of most present-day classrooms. This has led to the designation of "normal" being given only to stereotypically quiet and well-mannered children because this personality type (or at least this type of behavior) is more in line with the behavioral requirements of the structured classroom environment. For centuries girls have generally been socialized to be more cooperative and less rambunctious. Unfortunately, the more frenetic and less disciplined personality that was at one time at least tolerated in energetic boys is today being diagnosed as a mental illness needing pharmaceutical intervention. For example, the presumed childhood abnormality of attention-deficit hyperactivity disorder (ADHD) is listed in the *DSM* as having among its symptoms failing to pay attention and making mistakes in schoolwork, excessive talking, and blurting out answers to questions.[10] It is important to note that the child who is supposedly suffering from ADHD is not *suffering* from anything at all, but is only diagnosed as such by a professional adult. On close examination many of the so-called symptoms of ADHD "suffered" by the allegedly abnormal child have, until very recently, been considered to simply be the manifestations of childhood energy which is more of an irritation to adults, especially in the discipline of a structured classroom environment, than it is an abnormality from which the child is suffering.[11] Not surprisingly, among school-aged children boys are three times more likely than girls to be diagnosed as having these "abnormalities," and to be treated with what are professionally termed "behavioral medicines"[12] such as Prozac and Ritalin.[13]

It has at times been suggested that normal ought to be based on evolutionary biology, or even social Darwinism, that is, letting so-called natural selection weed out the abnormal. Normal is then simply that which survives. Unfortunately what has survived human evolution is not a rigidly defined closed set of properties based on natural law but rather a fluid range of behaviors based on human values and intentions. Research in psychology has shown that concepts of what is normal vary widely by social class, ethnic group, geographical region, historical period, and religious community. For example, while communicating with an invisible being is defined as schizoid behavior in one community, in another community it is called prayer, and not only is it accepted but it is expected as a routine daily demonstration of spiritual normalcy. Take the case of the man who had read in a religious book that everyone has a guardian angel. On the following night he believed he was surrounded by a choir of angels, and he heard celestial music and received revelations from God. This could be the story of the mystical ecstasies experienced by any one of a hundred fundamentalist religious media celebrities in liberal present-day North America whose claims to such visionary experiences have gained them a huge following of believers and allowed them to maintain incredibly profitable religious organizations. But Foucault presented this case from eighteenth-century France as a report of the abnormal hallucinations previously suffered by "a recently cured madman."[14]

Not only has the description of symptoms (semiology) of a number of "mental illnesses," such as schizophrenia, changed dramatically over the years, but also some so-called mental disorders—such as homosexuality and masturbation—have recently been dropped from the list altogether. This means that some particulars of human lifestyles and behaviors that were once deemed abnormalities requiring professional treatment and even pharmacological intervention are now simply ignored. The history of insanity continues thereby to be rewritten on an almost daily basis.[15] Meanwhile, any number of personal experiences that used to be accepted as normal—such as shyness, nervousness, and untidiness—have recently been added to the list of abnormalities with medical-sounding appellations.

It has been argued that when something like shyness is diagnosed as a mental illness (called "social anxiety disorder") in some individuals it is always because the shyness is deemed to be *excessive* in those individuals. Saying that any and all activities, behaviors, or cognitions may be classified as abnormal, the argument goes, is only true to the extent that these activities, behaviors, or cognitions are found to be *excessive* in any one person. But the problem inherent in this argument is fairly obvious: who determines what is excessive? Who has the right to have the final word on whether a person's level of shyness, nervousness, or untidiness fits the criteria of what is held to be abnormal and requiring drug therapy or even institutional confinement?

Normalcy also tends to correlate with measures of status such as age, race, income, and education. Behavior that is regarded as whimsically eccentric in one person (for example, a wealthy young white male drunk on expensive champagne dancing in the street in his underwear) may be defined as disagreeably demented in another (an impoverished old black female intoxicated by the priceless wine of life dancing in the street in her underwear).

One of my clients, I'll call him "Norm," was treated by two different psychotherapists for Post Traumatic Stress Disorder (PTSD) because of the distress he felt after having been brutally attacked by a gang of young men. Norm was a wonderful artist with both a brush on canvas and a computer and mouse, although he had not yet made an effort to make much money with either. Norm's hair was always in a long ponytail, he sported a scraggly beard, and the clothes he wore generally came from secondhand stores. The gang of hoodlums saw him as different enough to deserve a beating. But the tragedy of this case was not that Norm was assaulted, although that was certainly a terrible event. It was not even that Norm was told he was mentally ill after the assault—he was professionally diagnosed as having PTSD. Norm told me that the worst outcome by far was that psychotherapists tried to "fix" the fact that he was "abnormal" in his lifestyle by offering to help him conform to the rest of society. He came to philosophical counseling hoping to regain his former self-respect and to rediscover the passion he once felt for his art and his so-called abnormal lifestyle. The point of this example is this: if a woman who had been displaying her wealth by being dressed in furs and the latest Paris fashions had been assaulted in a similar manner she may also have subsequently been diagnosed by her psychotherapist as suffering from PTSD, but it is very unlikely that her psychotherapist would have tried to "fix" her lavish lifestyle by offering to help her conform to the more modest (normal) lifestyle of the majority of society. Deviation from the norm is not *consistently* defined as abnormal. The economic standing of the individual in relation to the societal norm makes a big difference in how that individual is labeled and treated. Professor of psychology Sohan Lal Sharma points out that "lower-class clients are diagnosed as psychotic (a diseased mind) more frequently than middle-class clients, who are generally diagnosed as neurotic (diseased nerves) with better prognosis."[16]

The definition of normal and abnormal are also often based on preconceived notions of potential harm. In most societies a person's behavior is accepted as normal only when it is relatively harmless, and deemed abnormal when there is believed to be imminent danger of self-inflicted harm or harm to others. An unusually high IQ, musical or artistic talent, and inventive genius are all in fact deviations from the norm and technically abnormalities. A child's peers may even consider her to be abnormal because she is only in the first grade and already able to read at a grade five level. But these positive deviations from the norm are not generally considered clinical abnormalities because they are not believed to be particularly harmful. A man who hears music in his head and uses those auditory hallucinations to write symphonies while neglecting his wife and children is more likely to be accepted as normal than a man who hears music in his head, *doesn't* use it to write symphonies, and still neglects his wife and children. A determination of abnormality in this case is based on the fact that the second man's neglect of his family is not counterbalanced by any benefit to society, such as the writing of music. Sociologist Robert A. Stebbings says that what is defined as abnormal or deviant, and therefore intolerable, in a community at any particular time in history depends

on the current values of those who are collectively powerful enough to shape its legislative, enforcement, and judicial practices and to influence public opinion. In other words, their definition of threat [to the community] is the one by which some forms of deviance are officially treated as intolerable, while other forms are unofficially treated as tolerable.[17]

The problem is, research has shown that human beings are often quick to make the mistaken assumption that what is simply different is dangerous and therefore intolerable. This is why, at various times in history, abnormal individuals were feared and scorned. The execution of women accused of being witches, and the murdering of homosexual individuals, are two of the most graphic examples.[18] Yet the demand for conformity, rather than being a safeguard for society, can be a significant hindrance to its progress. In *On Liberty* John Stuart Mill argued that it is the abnormal individuals or eccentrics in our society who often help bring about the most auspicious changes. In discussing "Individuality, as One of the Elements of Well-being," Mill wrote,

Precisely because the tyranny of opinion is such as to make eccentricity a reproach, it is desirable, in order to break through that tyranny, that people should be eccentric. Eccentricity has always abounded when and where strength of character has abounded; and the amount of eccentricity in a society has generally been proportional to the amount of genius, mental vigor, and moral courage which it contained. That so few now dare to be eccentric marks the chief danger of our time.[19]

Mill's point is that those individuals who are professionally classified as being abnormal may in fact be valuable to society when their different ways of being in the world challenge the members of their society to examine and justify their commonly held beliefs, values, and assumptions. In our present culture the reductionist thinking of many mental health professionals, along with clinical psychology's continual redefinition of various aspects of normal behavior as mental illnesses[20] (which the pharmaceutical corporations are quick to claim require *their* particular designer brand of medication), constitute a significant share of the tyranny of opinion to which Mill is referring. This tyranny in effect creates victims. As contemporary publisher Ariel Gore so aptly put it,

Marketing is the big bummer. For a long time they were just trying to sell women beauty products, so they had to convince us we were ugly. Now that pharmaceuticals marketing is getting really intense, they have to convince us that we are sick and crazy.[21]

Perhaps the most obvious problem with the *DSM* classification system is that there is an implied false dichotomy, an either/or fallacy, being committed in its pages. The *DSM*'s categorization of symptoms divides the world into only two kinds of people: the normal and the abnormal. But in reality the world isn't like that at all. It would be like saying the world is made up of only two kinds of people: the good and the bad, or the beautiful and the ugly. In fact, most individuals fall somewhere in between.

The adherence to an institutionally constructed system meant to classify what is abnormal narrows the permissible range of unique and unusual experiences that have in the past proven to be the progenitors of beneficial human innovation and progress. Therefore, when dealing with a client whose psychological distress may have been labeled by other mental health professionals as abnormal, or assigned a diagnosis that requires treatment within the "behavioral medicine" paradigm, the philosophical counselor should resist the temptation to simply accept that label or diagnosis. Instead she ought to join that individual in an investigation of the underlying philosophical issues to determine whether that client's so-called abnormality isn't in fact something of unappreciated importance, and perhaps even of great value.[22]

Unfortunately, at times a counselor will have as a client an individual whose emotional suffering may be precipitated by a chronic or even fatal physical condition. There may be no hope of improvement, and philosophical counseling will necessarily be only palliative care. Yet even in what may prima facie seem like a hopeless situation there might be cause for celebration.

NOTES

1. Jung, Carl G. "Marriage as a Psychological Relationship" (1925). *The Basic Writings of C. G. Jung*. Violet Staub De Laszlo, ed. New York: Modern Library, 1959. 543.

2. The 2001 edition is in fact titled the *DSM IV TR* (Text Revision).

3. The so-called clinical definition of the abnormality of major depression found in the *DSM* is virtually indistinguishable from the common experience of normal depression.

4. Miller, Nancy. "Diagnosis of Personality Disorder: Psychodynamic and Empirical Issues." *Psychodynamic Treatment Research*. Nancy E. Miller et al., eds. New York: Basic Books, 1993. 131.

5. Foucault, Michel. *Madness and Civilization*. New York: Random House, 1965. 66–67.

6. Rosenau, Pauline Marie. *Post-Modernism and the Social Sciences*. Princeton, N.J.: Princeton University Press, 1992. 151n.

7. American Psychiatric Association. *Diagnostic and Statistical Manual of Mental Disorders (DSM-3-R)*. Washington, D.C.: American Psychiatric Association, 1987. 193.

8. Barham, Peter. *Schizophrenia and Human Value*. London: Free Association Books, 1993.

9. Kendall, Kathleen. "Mental Illness—Tales of Madness: From Asylum to 'Oprah.' " *Social Control in Canada*. Bernard Schissel and Linda Mahood, eds. Toronto: Oxford University Press, 1996. 143.

10. Symptoms such as loss of temper, arguments with adults, and refusal to comply with adults' requests are part of the diagnostic criteria of "oppositional defiant disorder;" while bullying and fighting with others, staying out late at night despite parental prohibitions, and running away from home are said to be symptoms of "conduct disorder." Hales, Dianne and Robert E. Hales. *Caring for the Mind*. New York: Bantam, 1995. 647–667.

11. On September 5, 2001 CTV news discussed recent medical research which has found that the behavior of up to 40% of children diagnosed with ADHD is the result of lack of sleep. Treatment consists of medication to alleviate recurring nightmares which are causing dream-sleep disruptions. There was no mention of the cause of the recurring nightmares.

12. Kächele, Horst and Rainer Richter. "Germany and Austria." In *The Challenge to Psychoanalysis and Psychotherapy*. London: Jessica Kingsley Publishers, 1999. 50.

13. From an essay by Christina Hoff Sommers in *The Atlantic Monthly*, May 2000. Cited in *Utne Reader*, November–December 2000. 28.

14. Foucault, 215–216.

15. For a more detailed discussion of the history of insanity up to 1800 see Foucault's *Madness and Civilization*.

16. Sharma, Sohan Lal. *The Therapeutic Dialogue*. Albuquerque: University of New Mexico Press, 1986. 25.

17. Stebbins, Robert A. *Tolerable Differences*. Toronto: McGraw-Hill Ryerson, 1996. 5.

18. Thomas S. Szasz argues that a strong parallel can be drawn between the victimization of women accused of being witches and the treatment of individuals who simply did not conform to societal definitions of normal—today termed "mentally ill"—in his book *The Manufacture of Madness* (London: Routledge & Kegan Paul, 1971).

19. Mill, John Stuart. *On Liberty*. 1859. New York: Hackett, 1978. 62–64.

20. For a discussion of the "Psychology Industry" and its alleged creation of markets, see Tana Dineen's book *Manufacturing Victims*. Montreal: Robert Davies Publishing, 1996.

21. From an interview in *Utne Reader*. November–December 2000. 117.

22. Roy Porter offers a fascinating insight into the consciousness of a number of individuals who were labeled mentally ill by means of a detailed examination of their written works in his book *The Social History of Madness* (New York: Weidenfeld & Nicolson, 1987). He demonstrates that, although these individuals were deemed abnormal by the society in which they lived, they exhibited a very insightful, and often ingenious, understanding of the world around them which helped them to survive it.

Chapter 14

Celebrating Affliction

When an individual is chronically ill he is considered an invalid. In a sense the afflicted person is judged to be "in-valid" because she is believed to be null and void according to the conventional standard of usefulness. The view that a person who suffers from a debilitating injury, an incurable disease, or who is "constitutionally sick," as Plato put it, is relegated to an unproductive idleness and is therefore simply useless both to herself and to society has a long-standing tradition. Plato made this argument over 2,000 years ago in Book 3 of his *Republic*, and it is accepted as valid by many ailing individuals in our consumer-oriented society where one is defined as either a contributor to the production of consumable goods or a burden to those so occupied. This pervasive belief in the diminished worth of the "dis-abled" and the "in-firm" within modern society has driven some individuals with afflictions such as AIDS, multiple sclerosis, ALS (amyotrophic lateral sclerosis, or Lou Gehrig's disease), Parkinson's, and cancer to intentionally put an end to their presumed worthless lives. Others have sought relief from their self-condemnation by consulting with psychotherapists and philosophical counselors.

The distress that often accompanies chronic illness or physical impairment can be one of the most difficult issues for a philosophical counselor to deal with. Physical illness can cause anxiety, depression, confusion, anger, frustration, and a profound sense of failure. In his book *Existential Thought and Therapeutic Practice* Hans W. Cohn writes that "all physical illness is also emotionally charged." Because of this reciprocity between the physical and the emotional Cohn warns that a psychotherapist should never "rule out the effectiveness of a physical remedy in the case of a psychological disturbance."[1] But what if there is no remedy available for the physical ailment; what if there is little or no likelihood of recovery? The onset of a chronic illness can mark the beginning of a period of mourning for the lost life of health and vitality, and for the missed rewards of a future that will never be realized. An ailing person may experience the very same five emotional stages postulated by Elisabeth Kübler-Ross in her book *On Death and Dying*—denial, anger, bargaining, depression, and acceptance—even when actual death is unlikely.

In counseling this can seem like a hopeless situation because the afflicted individual approaches the philosophical counselor in the hopes of gaining some sort of affirmation of place within a society which the counselor and client both know typically does not value nonproductive individuals. And since we all always see ourselves as social agents, that is, we see ourselves as participants in the meaningful activities which all humans share, the philosophical counselor will no doubt be faced with a client whose involuntary nonparticipation is accompanied by severe self-deprecation. What is left for the philosophical counselor to do when a comforting platitude, such as "Don't worry; things will get better," is simply untrue?

One possible approach is for the counselor to focus attention on the positive aspects of the situation. This does not mean convincing the client to search for the cliché "silver lining," to put on a happy face for the sake of others, or to make the best of a bad situation by attempting to be productive at a reduced level. It means helping the client to conduct a phenomenological or objective investigation into the positive aspects inherent in his affliction.

Terry March has a private philosophical counseling practice on the east coast of Canada. She writes that her practice includes many clients who have gained new successes that are a direct result of their illness. She offers the following example.

"Joan was a psychiatric nurse at the Camp Hill Hospital in Halifax. Joan was one of a number of people at the hospital who developed environmental illness. Her recovery was long and painful. She had little support from others around her. And she felt strongly that she could not return to the environment which had made her ill in the first place. In counseling Joan realized that she could be someone who could lead others to lobby for change. Her efforts resulted in public awareness of the potential hazards of institutional environments. She organized and lobbied for major changes within Canadian Maritime hospitals. The most significant change has been the adoption of a scent-free policy at all the hospitals. Joan also did a practicum at the Environmental Illness Centre in Houston. She now uses her knowledge and her personal experience of illness to counsel patients with severe environmental illness."

But Vaughana Feary, a philosophical counselor in New Jersey and herself a cancer survivor, cautions that celebrating an affliction may lead to the neglect of a very important therapeutic element: the acknowledgment of rational beliefs about the possibility of pain, disability, indignity, and death. Feary argues that

The primary responsibility of anyone counseling cancer patients should be to help them fight cancer through exploring grounds for hope, assisting them in rational decision making about treatment, and helping them to cope with factors often associated with serious disease (fear, stress, guilt, diminished self worth, etc.). . . . With the exception of hospice counseling situations, the focus of the sessions should be on wellness, not affliction.

Feary maintains that clients should be encouraged to explore ways in which anything positive associated with the cancer experience can also be experienced when they are well. "Nothing positive comes from cancer," she says. "It comes from meeting the challenge of cancer successfully."

She also points out that "Christianity's celebration of suffering and death, together with the influence of the natural law tradition on American political and legal philosophy explains why the paternalistic prohibition on physician assisted suicide continues in most states. People afflicted with terminal illness have a right to the counsel of philosophers (and to the help of physicians) in celebrating life as long as they can, and in terminating it when they find nothing left to celebrate."

But Feary's position raises the question, Is life only to be celebrated when it is free of affliction? Can't affliction and illnesses themselves be recognized and acknowledged as an important part of life, as powerful catalysts to changes in life which deserve to be celebrated?

Terry March offers a second example.

Although I have clients, such as Joan, who have managed to turn their lives around as a result of recovery from their illness, the most striking example that comes to mind is that of a personal friend—Spencer. Spencer is a paraplegic. The circumstances of his disability are as tragic as his disability is. Spencer used to lift weights and one day while lifting particularly heavy barbells he felt a strange sensation in his spine and a weakness in his legs. He went to his doctor who told him that he had pulled a muscle and to go home and rest. By the next morning Spencer was paralyzed from the hips down. He was taken to the hospital by ambulance. Unfortunately, little was done for him, and tragically he had a subsequent hemorrhage into several of his vertebrates, which resulted in increasing paralysis.

Initially Spencer was severely depressed and suicidal. Having been a rather difficult individual, he had few friends. He was also a single parent who now lost his job. He felt terribly isolated and impotent. However, he had always had a good mind and so he started ruminating on the meaning of his life. But answers were not forthcoming.

He heard of a philosopher—Peter March—who went out into shopping malls and discussed philosophy with ordinary people. Spencer started attending the discussion groups and came to realize that other people had greater challenges in their lives than he had. In philosophy and through subsequent counseling, Spencer discovered that his life still had considerable value, and that he could continue to contribute in tangible ways to society. He became a teacher to children who were hospitalized with serious behavior disorders. He also single-handedly founded a magazine for people with disabilities—*The Abilities Network*. What made this magazine unique is that almost all of the contributors were disabled themselves, as were all the staff who worked for the magazine. For his efforts, Spencer has won international recognition.

As a result of his accident Spencer, by his own account, has a lot more patience and tolerance of people in general. He was so inspired by how philosophy impacted positively in his life, that he is undertaking the study of philosophy with the hope of becoming a philosophical counselor some day.

March notes that, through their afflictions, both Joan and Spencer found creative ways to improve their lives in general. "Their illnesses have forced them to examine their lives closely and to develop personal philosophies that have meaning and purpose."

It seems then that an illness need not be cured and an affliction need not be reversed in order for it to have a positive influence on a person's life. Being an invalid can lead a person to experience what psychologists have called "secondary gains." That is, being an invalid can lead the person to become more patient; to examine her values and priorities more carefully; to question his own life and goals, making him more contemplative and insightful; to change her being in the world so that life is lived more consciously rather than automatically; to acquire a practicality and maturity in decision-making procedures; to give up identifying himself exclusively with his body or his employment activities; to relinquish the belief that all of life is under personal control, and thereby to gain an adaptive flexibility which easily accommodates physical limitations; and to develop previously unconsidered activities. Furthermore, an illness can bring friends and family members closer together; it can motivate the one afflicted to learn more about health and illness; it can stimulate positive personality changes—for example, from domineering aggressiveness to humility and empathy; it can develop courage; it can motivate the afflicted to take time for physical self-care; it can enhance spirituality or bring spiritual enlightenment; and finally, it can bring the gratification that comes with experiencing the depth of one's own well of willpower, toleration, and stoicism.

But this is not merely a theoretical wish list of hoped-for benefits. Internationally renowned theoretical physicist Stephen Hawking said in a television interview that if he had not been afflicted with ALS he might never have taken the time or trouble to develop the theories which have brought him so much fame. Psychiatrists Mindy Greenstein and William Breitbart have been leading a group psychotherapy program for people in the advanced stages of terminal cancer. They have found that, among other things, participants have reported many positive changes in themselves which they attributed to their illness. These cancer patients said they have become much more responsible, they are more social, they have developed closer relationships with family and friends, they have become more compassionate and open, they feel motivated to being well-adjusted, and they have learned that they were stronger than they had believed themselves to be.[2] And all these positive events in the difficult lives of these individuals will in turn have a positive effect on society at large if that society, rather than devalue, celebrates the afflicted one.

Admittedly all of these benefits could theoretically be experienced by a person in good health, but many nonafflicted individuals procrastinate indefinitely, believing the comforting fiction that there is always another day in which to do with life what has been put off for today. The nonafflicted often fail to recognize that their good health can in fact be a kind of affliction which prevents them from gaining what the truly afflicted gain from life. But this begs the question, What is it that should be gained from life? What exactly is the purpose or meaning of life?

NOTES

1. Cohn, Hans W. *Existential Thought and Therapeutic Practice*. London: Sage, 1997.

2. Greenstein, Mindy and William Breitbart. "Cancer and the Experience of Meaning: A Group Psychotherapy Program for People with Cancer." *American Journal of Psychotherapy*. Vol. 54, no. 4, Fall 2000. 486–500. "The House That's on Fire: Meaning-Centered Psychotherapy Pilot Group for Cancer Patients." Ibid., 501–511.

Chapter 15

The Meaning of Life*

Ask the question, What is the meaning of life? of anyone and the first thing you typically hear in reply is nervous laughter. This question, What is the meaning of life? has the power to make us profoundly uncomfortable because of both its scope and the frightening implications inherent in a number of possible replies. It's not the sort of question we're used to hearing asked seriously, and it's not the kind of question for whose response our parents taught us some ingenious little maxim. In fact, one of the worst ways to reply to someone who has asked this question in all earnestness is with a snappy automatic answer. In philosophical counseling this question arises fairly often.

But before the question, What is the meaning of life? can be answered properly, whether within a philosophical counseling situation or elsewhere, it's essential to discover *why* it's being asked in the first place; within what frame of reference or existential context is the questioner expecting the answer to be located? What is the questioner after?

The question, What is the meaning of life? and its response may be situated within three very different contexts: the academic, the religious, and the personal. The context within which the question has been asked dictates the appropriateness of any given response. In the introduction to his recent book *The Meaning of Life* (one of surprisingly few philosophical books exclusively devoted to this topic), editor and professor of philosophy E. D. Klemke writes,

---

*This chapter was presented as part of the Existential Philosophy Symposium at the International Conference on Searching for Meaning in the New Millennium, Trinity Western University, Vancouver, British Columbia, Canada, July 13–16, 2000 under the title "Philosophical Counseling and the Meaning of Life."

In turning to possible answers to the question of the meaning of life, we find different approaches or stances:
I. The theistic answer
II. The non-theistic alternative
III. The approach that questions the meaningfulness of the question.[1]

Klemke's point is that an answer can be given in one of these three different modes. But I believe that in order for the answer to make sense, and to be meaningful to the one asking the question, the answer must be given within the context in which the question was asked in the first place. It must take into account the ground from which this question has emerged. Problems arise whenever the offered answer simply disregards the context of the question, or assumes the context incorrectly. For example, a theistic answer presented within the context of an anthropological or sociological discussion will most likely prove unsatisfying to the questioner; likewise, questioning the meaningfulness of the question itself while in the company of the religiously devout may be perceived by them as a callous display of disrespect for their spiritual concerns.

Therefore the important question about the answer to the question, What is the meaning of life? is not, How should the answer be framed? but rather, Within what context was it asked: was it within the academic, within the religious, or within the personal?

Having achieved an academic doctorate and having taught at the university level, having been born and raised a fundamentalist Christian, and presently being an agnostic philosophical counselor have given me the wonderful opportunity to gain an insight into the meaning of the question and the sort of replies that may be gratifying within each of these three contexts.

THE ACADEMIC

In the classroom the question, What is the meaning of life? is usually based on a simple scholarly curiosity and generally leads to just one more intellectual exercise among many. Students soon notice that this question is not easily answered by means of a phenomenological investigation of the constituents of life because such a dispassionate description of a life tells you nothing about its meaning. An empirical or scientific inquiry won't produce an answer that makes any sense either because empirical science is concerned with intrinsic properties and measurable effects—such as size, weight, and velocity—not with meaning. For example, a scientific investigation into a game of tennis may result in a lot of information about the ball, the court, and even the biology of the players but none of it will reveal why those two individuals are engaged in smacking a ball back and forth over a net under a blazing sun in the first place. The meaning of the game to its players is of no concern to empiricists. This may lead the academic instructor to point out to his students that the British philosopher and mathematician Bertrand Russell said the study of science and scientific study can make the world seem even more purposeless and more void of meaning than we might have feared on our own.[2]

The instructor will no doubt point out that meaning is not an intrinsic property of anything in nature; it's always a human investment. He will remind his students that sociologists call it "symbolic interactionism" when we humans assign meanings to stimuli, such as events and objects, and act not on the stimuli directly but on those meanings. For example, an octagonal piece of tin painted red with the white letters S, T, O, and P on it has no intrinsic meaning. But we stop when we see it because we understand what it means. The study of the meaning of signs is called semiology, and semiology doesn't concern itself with the meaning of life, because life is not a sign, it's perhaps more like a process or an event.

And the instructor might also caution those students who harbor any sort of belief in a spiritual life after death that the British empiricist philosopher David Hume warned that if we judge by natural reason alone there is no evidence to suggest that life has any meaning past one's time spent living here on earth.[3] Furthermore the instructor may mention that various philosophers have said different, and often contradictory, things about what constitutes a meaningful life. Three centuries before Christ the Epicureans held that in order to live a meaningful life a person needs to fulfill her desires, while the Stoics held that a meaningful life is only possible when a person completely constrains her desires, a position that was later adopted by the Christians.

The instructor will no doubt mention that the modern American philosopher Thomas Nagel writes that we humans are able to look at life from within as well as from without, and that it's precisely because we humans can take an objective perspective on life that it has the potential to seem absurd. Nagel explains that subjectively life makes perfect sense because the conditions that help life make sense, such as happiness and unhappiness, achievement and failure, love and isolation, are simply experienced. But Nagel warns that the philosophical study of the meaning of life threatens to disintegrate that very meaning into absurdity because the study takes the search for a disinterested meaning of life as though it were a serious undertaking.[4] The instructor may offer for example the great literary writers Albert Camus[5] and Leo Tolstoy,[6] who both fell victim to trying to find objective meaning in what is a subjective experience. They testified to the existential absurdity of life—Camus because life observed from the outside seemed to his fictional character like repetitive drudgery, and Tolstoy because he could see no higher purpose to the activities in his privileged personal life. These two writers seem to prove Nagel's point that an attempt to philosophically analyze the meaning of life from an objective perspective has the potential to make life seem existentially absurd despite the fact that it's not subjectively experienced as absurd at all. The instructor may then tell his students that philosophically analyzing the meaning of life is something like analyzing the experience of love: the more objectively and dispassionately love is scrutinized the more absurd it seems. But just because we're unable to objectively and philosophically define the meaning of love doesn't mean we may dismiss love as an absurdity. The same holds for life.

It's possible that students will eventually arrive at the conclusion that asking the question, What is the meaning of life? in an academic context is a kind of category mistake;[7] it's like asking, What color is Beethoven's Fifth Symphony? And finally they will probably decide that no matter what the great philosophers have said, without a belief in some Higher Power nothing about human existence can have any meaning anyway because in a few million years from now our sun will explode, the orderly orbits within our galaxy will degenerate into chaos, and all life will be brought to an end either by fire or by ice. But for most students none of this really matters anyway because it's just another academic exercise, unless, of course, there's going to be a question about it on the final exam.

THE RELIGIOUS

An academic response is clearly not appropriate when the question has been asked in a religious context. When the question, What is the meaning of life? is asked in a religious context it may involve issues as varied as the desire for doctrinal clarification, a search for spiritual revitalization, or a plea for pastoral comforting.

That is, it may be a request for more information about the travel plan or road map that some superhuman Force or Intelligence has charted; a yearning for confirmation that we're on the right course. If meaning is never intrinsic but only attributed, then in a religious context it's understood as self-evident that meaning always only flows from some higher Force or supernatural Being. Many religiously devout individuals believe that even while each person may be the author of his or her own life there is nonetheless at least a rough outline that must be followed, one that has been drawn up by some far more talented Author, and into which each individual narrative of a life must flow if it's to have meaning in the larger scheme of things. So the question, What is the meaning of life? in this context typically asks for clarifying information: How should I write my life in order for it to constitute a meaningful chapter in this Grand Cosmic Book?

At other times it's a question of teleology; it's an end-point or goal-oriented question asking where all of life is headed: What is the ultimate purpose of life? This is in contrast to Heidegger's existentialist assertion that each of us has been "thrown into life"[8] through no will of our own and left completely at the mercy of happenstance. It's based on the assumption that one's life has a purpose though we may not be aware of it, that one's personal goals ought to be consistent with the goal of Life in general, and that one's life is only a means to an end with the ultimate question being, Exactly what am I to strive for? It's the wish to be secure in the knowledge that every personal decision that is made within a particular life will bring that individual a step closer to God's ultimate purpose for all of humankind. It's the desire to understand God's will regarding the orderly unfolding of the universe. In effect it's a desire to read the mind of God.

It's asking the same question Aristotle asked 2,000 years ago when he wrote, "If, then, there is some end of the things we do . . . will not the knowledge of it have a great influence on life? Shall we not, like archers who have a mark to aim at, be more likely to hit upon what is right?"[9]

Human beings are the only creatures on earth who are able to take a perspective that is separate from, while at the same time participating in, the experience of life.[10] We're the only creatures able to ask ourselves, What is, and what should be, the purpose of the life I'm living? But David Hume pointed out that it's impossible for human beings to discern the meaning of life by themselves. He writes,

It's not only impossible for a man to decide, in any given period, of the progress of his existence, of what utility or consequence he may be to society; but without the faculty of prescience, it's still more impracticable for him to divine what purpose he may be intended to serve in the many mysterious revelations of futurity.[11]

Hume would be the first to admit that only a superhuman Intelligence would be capable of such foresight. Within the religious context it's accepted that the most accurate answer to the question, What is the meaning of life? can come only through the contemplation of sacred texts and teachings, through meditation, or through direct revelation in response to prayer. The affirmation that these activities will indeed be rewarded with insights into the meaning of life can have a refreshingly vitalizing effect on a person's spirit.

And yet the question, What is the meaning of life? may not be a request for doctrinal clarification or spiritual revitalization at all but rather a symptom of existential angst. It may be an expression of doubt about the significance of one's own humble spark of life within the brilliant fireball of cosmic vitality. That is, it may be an expression of acute anxiety over one's trivial worth. Furthermore it may be an expression of fear over what to expect in the afterlife, in other words an expression of post-existence angst: Will I be rewarded or punished for how I have lived my life? Then again it may not be an expression of anything at all but rather, as in the case of the biblical Job, it may simply be a rhetorical question over the suffering that has to be endured. It may be asking, Why do I deserve these hardships that have befallen me? In this case it's not a request for an explanation of the cold, hard facts about the purpose of life as such but rather an appeal for the warmth of human empathy and the comfort of Divine compassion.

When the question, What is the meaning of life? erupts from a condition of such personal anguish and despair within the context of pastoral counseling it may benefit from an approach not unlike the one found in philosophical counseling.

THE PERSONAL

Dear Peter,
Would you be so kind as to share with me your personal views as to what it is that gives your life meaning? For example, when you set the scales of life before you, and where no external influences/reinforcements are there (including the influence of some Deity) to distract you from assessing and assigning what you perceive is the value in life, what does your internal voice say that induces you to remain a life participant when it's quite apparent that the other side of the scale is so much more heavily weighted with reasons not to remain?

This is how the message began that I saw on the computer screen in front of me. It was dated June 30, 1997, and was a personal e-mail message addressed to me in my capacity as a philosophical counselor. In subsequent messages I learned that the highly educated professional woman who sent it was suffering from suicidal despair because her physical ailments had become so debilitating that she was unable to practice the profession that had previously given her life its meaning. Over the next three years our discussion focused not so much on answering the question from either an academic or a religious perspective as on coming to terms with the surgery she required, the recovery that was necessary, the low self-esteem she felt in connection with not having been able to prevent several suicides in her immediate family, and her inability to meet her own perfectionist standards at her place of work. When this was done we turned our attention to discovering new and meaningful projects that she would be physically able to handle.

In philosophical counseling the question, What is the meaning of life? is asked most often within this personal context. It's in the context of the personal that this question is most immediate and subtle, and it's in the context of the personal that the answer to this question fulfills the most vital role. Here, in the context of the personal, the person asking the question always has a vested interest in the answer. Here the problem of the meaning of life is often a sort of skepticism about motivation, that is, it involves the underlying question, Why should I bother to live my life when it hurts so much to continue?[12] The implicit request is not for an increase in meaning but for a decrease in pain.

A careful observation of human affairs, especially within the life narratives presented in a counseling setting, suggests that contentment is a natural state of being, and that for most people life is full enough of meaning when it's not filled with distress. For most of us, the meaning of life manifests itself precisely by virtue of escaping our attention. A child that is well loved and well cared for will be so engrossed in planning the kinds of projects and experiencing the various adventures that present themselves unexpectedly throughout a young life that the question of the meaning of life simply never comes to mind. For adults meaning is found not only within the immediate act of participation but also in the long-range relationship between our actions and among our projects and commitments.[13] As sociologist Anthony Giddens puts it,

The threat of meaninglessness is ordinarily held at bay because routine activities, in combination with basic trust, sustain ontological security. Potentially disturbing existential questions are defused by the controlled nature of day-to-day activities within internally referential systems.[14]

It's when the day-to-day activities of life seem to lose their previous internal connection to our hopes and dreams, when life becomes an arduous struggle, and when it begins to feel the way Camus[15] described it—like a heavy boulder that must be repeatedly pushed up a steep mountain—that the question, Why is this happening to me? or What is this all about? worms its way into awareness. From someone for whom life has become a burden the question, What is the meaning of life? is the desire to know where the shrieking-and-running-around joy of youth has disappeared to. It's not necessarily a search for meaning as much as it is a search for a childhood paradise lost. Certainly the question may arise in moments of complete contentment, while basking in the sun beside a tropical ocean or while gazing up at the stars from a comfortable lawn chair on a summer's night. But at these times the question is meant not as a catalyst to serious metaphysical inquiry but simply as an expression of personal—and often passing—curiosity about the transcendent mysteries of life. It is merely academic.

When the question, What is the meaning of life? arises early on in a philosophical counseling context it is generally safe to assume that something has seriously compromised what that client once held life's meaning to be. The e-mail message above is one example. Another comes from an essay found on an Internet web site: "Occasionally I get bummed out and begin asking, "What's the purpose of life?" I ask this because I see that most people live without purpose, without caring about others or about any cause. For me, that life is not worth living."[16]

Notice that the essay begins with the words, "Occasionally I get bummed out." Rather than the question about the meaning of life being the cause of this individual's getting bummed out, it's in fact the feeling of being bummed out that precipitates the question. To the philosophical counselor this suggests that this individual is asking the question because life has somehow become so difficult that it seems—at this juncture in time at least—not worth living. The question may simply be a cry of despair, not about life in general, but about a number of unpleasant or distressing particulars which have converged to make a previously satisfying life overwhelmingly discouraging. Sigmund Freud warned that "the moment a man questions the meaning of life and value of life he is sick. . . . By asking this question one is merely admitting to a store of unsatisfied libido to which something else must have happened, a kind of fermentation leading to sadness and depression."[17]

But is asking for meaning in life out of suffering, despair, or anxiety always a sign of some sort of psychical sickness or mental illness? Contrary to Freud, clinical philosopher Peter Koestenbaum insists that it's precisely the *denial* of existential anxiety that produces the symptoms of mental illness such as neurosis, maladjustment, melancholia, and so forth.[18] But as a practicing philosophical counselor I have learned that both existential anxiety and the denial of that anxiety are simply nonexistent when life is experienced as pleasure rather than pain. The question of the meaning of life in a philosophical counseling situation is usually associated with incomprehensible misfortunes that have made a formerly good life unbearable, like the loss of a loved one through sudden death or divorce, serious damage to personal identity due to complex life changes or conflicting values, or the disruption of meaningful connections with significant others.

For example, one of my clients began by telling me he would like to discuss the meaning of life. But through a series of sessions he revealed that he was feeling alienated from his wife and children, he was unable to keep up with the oppressive work load of his profession, and he had a very low opinion of himself because he seemed to be failing at everything: being a good husband, being a good father, and being a good employee. As it turned out what he really wanted was not to discuss the meaning of life at all but help with reducing the stress and distress in his life so that he could enjoy it once again. Another client who said she wanted to discuss the meaning of life eventually revealed that her life had been turned upside down when she finally admitted to herself and her religiously devout parents that she was a lesbian. Again, the issue she really wanted to deal with was not the meaning of life at all but how to maintain her self-esteem in light of the antihomosexual position of the church her parents regularly attended. These two clients, like many others, had begun with the prosaic question about the meaning of life in general, but behind it there lurked a profound feeling of defeat brought on by the difficult particulars life had forced on them.

What both psychoanalysts and existentialist philosophers sometimes fail to notice is that when life is expressed as meaningless, that expression neither is a symptom of psychopathology nor does it always indicate the client's total awareness of the philosophical conundrum that generated it. For the suffering client it is first and foremost reference to a *feeling*, but one that has been precipitated by difficult and complex life circumstances. What philosophers and others have described as existential angst, nausea, anguish, absurdity, and meaninglessness are in fact not mental illnesses or intellectual states at all; they are felt by the client as powerful *emotional* states which often succeed in completely camouflaging the moral, political, spiritual, and practical reasons behind their emergence. Consequently it seems very unlikely that the elimination, on a personal level, of either existential anxiety or the meaninglessness of life could be achieved through medication or some abstract theoretical discourse on meaning. It can be accomplished only through a mitigation of the feelings of distress and hopelessness by means of the practical resolution of their antecedents, namely the detailed events and beliefs the client experiences as her overwhelming everyday problems in life.[19]

This is not to say that a discussion of the meaning of life cannot be undertaken on a more abstract level once a client's immediate personal problems have been resolved. A number of simple strategies are available to the client whose expressed desire to inquire into the meaning of life isn't compelled by suffering. For example, it could be suggested to the client that he should consider his desires, hopes, and wishes that have been or have *not* been met as pointing to meaning; he could revisit past personal accomplishments at work or in the family and see these as giving meaning; he could consider his relationships and connections with others as giving meaning; he could consider meaning as not something life intrinsically *has* but as something which he can produce or create and give to life; he could survey his life backward to find a possible thread of choices he has made that give meaning; he could search for meaning within the simple, momentary episodes of his life rather than trying to find it within its whole complex structure; he could imagine that the search for the meaning of his life is itself its purpose and meaning; or he could consider the meaning of life as simply *being*—living in the moment, as a Taoist would put it.[20]

In conclusion, and simply put, when life is kind the question of meaning does not arise on a personal level. In fact I would venture to say that for most people it's not at all necessary to have an answer to that question. So long as life continues to feel good simply living it is its meaning. I also believe it's safe to assume that in the majority of instances in which the question, What is the meaning of life? does arise in philosophical counseling it's rarely the case that it has been asked from an academic or religious perspective. Behind it there is most likely some profound personal dissatisfaction or disappointment with life's present circumstances. The counselor's job is therefore to help the questioner deal with those life problems, regain an earlier contentment with life, and rediscover that place where when the question, What is the meaning of life? was asked it was accompanied by a little comfortable laughter.

NOTES

1. Klemke, E. D. *The Meaning of Life*. New York: Oxford University Press, 2000. 3.

2. Russell, Bertrand. "The Free Man's Worship." *The Philosophy Source* CD. Daniel Kolak, ed. Belmont, Calif.: Wadsworth, 2000.

3. Hume, David. "Essays on Suicide and the Immortality of the Soul." Essay II, sec. 2. *The Philosophy Source* CD. Daniel Kolak, ed. Belmont, Calif.: Wadsworth, 2000.

4. Nagel, Thomas. *The View from Nowhere*. New York: Oxford University Press, 1986. 214–216, 223.

5. Camus, Albert. *The Myth of Sisyphus*. J. O'Brien, trans. New York: Knopf, 1955.

6. Tolstoy, Leo. *A Confession and Other Religious Writings* (1879). Jane Kentish, trans. New York: Viking Penguin, 1987.

7. Gilbert Ryle first coined the term "category mistake" in his book *The Concept of Mind* (London: Butchison, 1949).

8. Heidegger, Martin. *Being and Time* (1927). Joan Stambaugh, trans. New York: State University of New York Press, 1996. 135–137.

9. Aristotle. "Nicomachean Ethics." Book 1, Section 2. *The Philosophy Source* CD. Daniel Kolak, ed. Belmont, Calif.: Wadsworth, 2000.

10. This observation comes from Paul Tillich's *The Courage to Be*. London: Collins, 1952. 54–55.

11. Hume, Essay II, sec. 2.

12. This perspective comes from Nagel's book *The View from Nowhere*. 218.

13. For a discussion of meaning as located in the relationships between projects see Galen K. Pletcher, "Meaning and Awareness of Death." *Awareness of Mortality*. Jeffrey Kauffman, ed. Amityville, N.Y.: Baywood Publishing, 1995. 67.

14. Giddens, Anthony. *Modernity and Self-Identity*. Stanford, Calif.: Stanford University Press, 1991. 202.

15. Camus.

16. Sarles, Sharon. "What's the Purpose of Life" www.ethicalculture.org/aeuves/purpose.

17. In *Letters of Sigmund Freud*. James Stern and Tania Stern, trans. E. L. Freud, ed. New York: Harcourt, 1960. 436.

18. Koestenbaum, Peter. *The New Image of the Person: The Theory and Practice of Clinical Philosophy*. Westport, Conn.: Greenwood, 1978. 231.

19. An interesting discussion on the relationship between happiness and meaning can be found in chapter 5 of John Stuart Mill's *Autobiography* titled "A Crisis in My Mental Life." Also contained in *Vice and Virtue in Everyday Life*. Christina Sommers and Fred Sommers, eds. Fort Worth, Tex.: Harcourt Brace College Publishers, 1997. 554–561.

20. Adapted from a collection of seventeen steps in an inquiry into the meaning of life in Appendix C of my book *Philosophical Counseling: Theory and Practice*. Westport, Conn.: Praeger, 2001.

Chapter 16

Learning to Be Old

Philosophical discussion of the issues around aging are not easy to locate. Standard references, such as *The Oxford Companion to Philosophy*[1] and the ubiquitous *Encyclopedia of Philosophy*[2] make no mention of the topic. The philosophy of aging is not likely to be found listed as a course in college or university calendars. This is both odd and not surprising. It is odd because old age is an experience everyone will inevitably encounter; and it is not surprising because in our Western institutions of higher learning academic philosophy is very theoretically oriented and simply doesn't often concern itself with real-life issues that are likely to have a personal impact on students.

There is no question that aging has an impact, and that it changes everyone. But what there is considerable doubt about is whether those changes are good or bad. For example, from a positive perspective it may be said that the physical strength of youth changes to strength of character in old age; the functional cleverness of the young changes to wisdom about life; and the beauty of outward appearance changes to the beauty of inner tranquility. On the other hand, from a negative perspective, it may be said that the strength of youth is lost to quivering muscles and brittle bones of old age; cleverness is forgotten by a poor memory and slow thinking; and as outward beauty falls away fear of death increases. Life in old age can be either rewarding or depressing depending on which one of these two perspectives a person has learned to adopt.

The trouble is, being old doesn't come naturally, and how to grow old is not something we are taught by our parents or teachers. From the time we're very young our parents, our teachers, our peers, our clergy, and the media all make an effort to teach us what it takes to be an upstanding member of the community or at least a good person. But what most of us are never taught is what it takes to be a valuable *old* person, how to age gracefully, and how to live with dignity when physical strength and good looks are on the decline. Perhaps the reason for this is that the positive aspects of old age simply don't mesh with our high-speed, technologically oriented, computer-driven society. Old people are variously called senior citizens, the elderly, or old timers. These terms will generally bring to mind individuals of negligible or even negative value in our society not because the words themselves are somehow inherently disparaging but because we have come to believe that the higher a person's age the lower their usefulness to our society. Perhaps the words elder, matriarch, or patriarch are positive valuations, but how often are these words used in our everyday affairs? The disrespectful "old fart" is a term that is much more commonly heard. But this negative attitude toward old people, so prevalent in our Western culture, is not found everywhere in the world. As Lin Yutang explains,

In China, the first question a person asks the other on an official call, after asking about his name and surname is, "What is your glorious age?" If the person is anywhere over fifty, the inquirer immediately drops his voice in humility and respect. That is why all old people, if they can, should go and live in China, where even a beggar with a white beard is treated with extra kindness.[3]

In a culture where the wisdom of old age is valued, the progression from youth to middle age to old age is accepted as natural, and each stage of life is eagerly anticipated as offering unique rewards not available at the previous stage. In highly industrialized cultures, where wisdom is not required for mass production and massive consumption, old age is resented and feared. In a mass media culture dominated by images of the young, the strong, and the beautiful, becoming old is an embarrassment. In a nation in which independence is held to be the cornerstone of society, becoming old and dependent on others is downright unpatriotic. And in a predominantly Christian society that follows the Protestant work ethic, in which the merit of a person is measured by their productivity, becoming old is almost a sin.

The problem with aging in many societies is not only that the young fail to value the withering members of the preceding generations, but also that those seniors consent to that low valuation from the young because they themselves equate their own advanced years with worthlessness. It is no wonder then that in Christian, capitalist, computerized, consumer-oriented societies most people try their best to avoid becoming old. But the assumed worthlessness of the elders in a society is a question of ontology: are elders in fact worthless, or are they merely perceived as worthless because of the socioeconomic norms and epistemic assumptions of their society?

Becoming old is not something that can be avoided. It is estimated that by the year 2010, one in four Americans—or some 74.1 million people—will, unavoidably, be over 55; one in seven will be 69 or older. A few people will accept growing old as a part of the accustomed flow of life, and with serenity and grace as though it were a gentle gift. For most others the realization that they're growing old comes to them unexpectedly as an "aha!" experience. At worst, it's like a slap in the face, because aging has been denied or forgotten; the time passing within has gone unnoticed because of the external distractions of our youth-oriented culture. For these people aging can be the unsettling experience of having to reconcile their chronological age with the predominantly negative myths surrounding the elderly. But for still others old age is like a cancer which, if it cannot be simply denied, must be raged against with medications, darkened with dyes, covered with makeup, and even cut away with surgery.

The transition from adulthood into old age can be every bit as turbulent as the transition from childhood to adulthood. But while the teenager rebels against his former powerlessness as a child, the person in late maturity rebels against the forced relinquishment of power that is concomitant with growing old. For the philosophical counselor the issues around growing old will rarely, if ever, be presented in plain view by the client. They will instead be surrounded by other issues such as questions about the meaning of life, concerns about changing relationships, confusion over social or familial roles, and disappointments over the failure to realize youthful dreams. Some clients will be most concerned about their physical changes and decline; others will be worried about the perceived degeneration of their mental or intellectual capacities; many will feel vulnerable to social and cultural biases; and the underlying issues for still others will be a sense of existential and even spiritual disconnection. How should a philosophical counselor deal with a client whose concerns about aging are making his or her midlife a misery?

One important, although perhaps obvious, fact that the philosophical counselor must keep in mind is that our society accepts men's aging better than women's aging. This means the transition into old age can be very different for women than it is for men. And yet there are also many similarities. For "Gail" life had always been full of challenges. She had set many goals for herself and reached most of them successfully. But one goal she hadn't reached was to find a man with whom she could spend the rest of her life. She told me she didn't mind the fact that she didn't have any children to call her own; this was not something she had ever wanted. Not having a good man to wake up with in the morning, however, left her feeling empty. And the worst part of it all, she told me, was that she was growing old and the chance of anyone wanting her was rapidly diminishing with every passing day. Gail felt that, since she was in her late 40s, she would have to accept the fact that she might be alone for the rest of her life despite having many good friends. Added to this she regretted the fact that she never "made anything" of herself—neither as a professional person nor as a mother—and she resented the fact that she had wasted so much time searching for a man instead of putting more energy into a career or a profession. Gail wanted philosophical counseling to help her decide what to do about what she considered to be "the downward slope" of her life to make it less painful.

"Scott" came to see me for philosophical counseling because his marriage was falling apart and his relationship with his teenaged son was deteriorating despite his best efforts. He said he wanted to discuss the meaning of life. We started out by

talking about relationships, specifically what elements must be present for a relationship with a spouse to add meaning to life. We inquired into what it takes to be a
good father, and we examined his relationships with both his own son and his own
father. But the more deeply we looked into these relationships the more we began
to realize that perhaps the worst relationship Scott was having to endure was his relationship with himself. And the primary reason this relationship was so bad was
because Scott insisted on seeing himself, and trying to live his life, as though he
were still a 25-year-old. In reality he was nearing 50. Scott was a corporate executive, and a workaholic both in his professional life and at play. Every weekend was
a working weekend, and work continued during the holidays by cell-phone; he was
unable to play a sport for relaxation, approaching every family outing on skis or bi-
cycles as a competitive event; and he demanded of his wife that their sex life be as
frequent and as vigorous as it had been early in their marriage. By the time Scott
came to see me he had already had a brief affair with a much younger woman, one
which he had admitted to his wife and which he regretted deeply. Scott had initially said he wanted to discuss the meaning of life, but what eventually helped him
the most was learning how to be old.

PHYSICAL CHANGES

Learning to be old means, first of all, becoming consciously aware of bodily
changes, and accepting these as natural. Physical aging means going from dependent youth to competitive adult and active wage-earner, and eventually to dependent elder. The road of life leads metaphorically from being a spectator to
competitor to coach and back to spectator again. The sharp and exciting pains of
youth are gradually overgrown by the dull and tiresome pains of old age. There is a
decline in vision, smell, taste, and hearing, at the same time that there is an increase
in joint, heart, and digestive system problems. The aging process also brings a decline in the nervous system, muscle tone, reflexes, and balance. There may be
more of a reliance on medication, natural remedies, and dietary supplements simply to achieve what was once a state of normal functioning. For men getting old is
seen as a deterioration of physical vitality, and a creeping loss of potency in a number of different senses of that term. For women aging is associated with loss of
beauty and sexual attractiveness. Serious problems may arise for men and women
who see their identity as dependent on their appearance, their physical prowess or
allure, or their sexual performance.

Yet a loss of memory, teeth, sex drive, and general physical health are not necessarily part of aging. They are often due to poor personal care, depression, and an
improper diet. But fears of these losses can become a self-fulfilling prophecy. David Hilditch is an adjunct professor of philosophy at Webster University in St.
Louis, where he is a practicing philosophical counselor and a facilitator of philosophy cafés. Hilditch agrees that retirees are very concerned about their declining
health. They are acutely aware of the gradual loss of their earlier physical vi-
brancy. Hilditch writes, "But here's the clincher—they are also aware, now more
than ever, that decisions made earlier in life will affect the degree to which they

suffer health problems. Late age physical decrepitude is made more or less certain by bad habits (unless you have great genes). Many older people express regrets at not having lived more health-mindedly, e.g., by exercising, eating a healthy diet, and so on." In other words, the physical suffering brought on in old age can be largely avoided if in middle age the body isn't subjected to the damage caused by aggressive contact sports, the drive to win or be popular at any cost, and the poor dietary habits of youth—including the excessive use of alcohol and so-called recreational drugs. Hilditch says a philosophical counselor may reduce the middle aged client's anxieties about declining health by suggesting he or she take a closer look at present-day self-punishing habits in his or her lifestyle. Beyond this, Hilditch believes it's also useful to point out that many elderly people continue to participate in sports such as tennis and swimming, although at a recreational level, and live healthy lives because of it.

There are many dietary programs, hair dyes, and approaches to cosmetic surgery that claim to keep a person young forever. But these are only tempting if one is convinced that there is something wrong with being old. No reasonable person demands that an adult should have the same physical energy and the same naïvely optimistic perspective on life as a child. Why then is there the demand that in old age a person should have the same physical energy, and live life at the same naïvely optimistic pace, as in midlife? Some people, rather than being humiliated by the expectations of their youth-oriented culture to stay perpetually young, blame themselves, as though getting old is something they are personally responsible for. They feel a profound sense of guilt for not being able to keep up with the young, to act, and feel, and even look as they did 30 years earlier.

In dealing with the physicality of aging, the philosophical counselor's primary job is to help the client accept the process of growing old, and to feel comfortable with gray hair and wrinkles and all the other so-called failings of the body. I remember my father telling me, "I may look 50 to you but I still think of myself as being 20." This seems to be a fairly common way of thinking in aging individuals, and it may be beneficial in the sense that a positive attitude is conducive to good health. I found it poignant but not particularly problematic because my father was not living a life of self-deception; he understood that his interior self-image was only an image. He was living his life like a man of 50, not within the fantasy of lost youth. But I have found that some clients project and live this self-deception, and it makes their lives, and often the lives of loved ones, both physically and emotionally unbearable. By trying to live the physical self-image of the past they miss the rewards of the intellect, the spirit, and the emotions that come with accepting old age in the present.

Hilditch says he was amazed at how many of the participants at one of his philosophy cafés still saw themselves as being young in their "mind's eye."

"Indeed, in most cases, their self-image was stuck back in their late teens and early 20's. (I also remember my Mother, who is elderly, telling me that she still thought of herself as 18.) From what I could gather, a lot here hinges on one's physical self-image—to the point that one is nearly always surprised when one sees just how old one really is in the mirror. But there's also a sense in which the life narrative—so important for constructing a sense of self—can't be stretched to include old age. And yet a few of my participants seem to stand in sharp contrast to this—they embrace their old age and seem to be on a different footing from everyone else."

Hilditch says that the happiest retirees seem to be the ones who are the most active and thereby less focused on themselves. They do things with one another, and many are involved in volunteering (such as adult literacy programs), in taking classes, and in being members of hobby clubs, social clubs, or dance clubs. The key point, he says, is that growing older doesn't necessarily imply inactivity. When a philosophical counselor has a middle aged client who is worried about how meaningless life will become in old age, Hilditch says, "It is important to ask that client how diverse his or her interests are *right now*. I've known some 42 year old workaholics who may have reason to fear retirement since they are living one-dimensional lives already. On the other hand, the 70ish husband of a client of mine (he happens also to suffer from non-Hodgkin's lymphoma) uses his spare time to keep up with his life-long hobby of playing the drums—he still goes out to play with other musicians at various senior functions. Another retired woman who participates in one of my cafes, has some severe physical debilitation with Parkinson's disease, but she is a passionate reader of classical literature and is involved in reading discussion groups in her community." This suggests that perhaps the philosophical counselor ought to suggest to the middle aged client that he or she develop active interests right now, other than working or watching TV, that can later be carried into old age.

Of course, it could be argued that playing the drums or reading literature in old age are meaningless and trivial pastimes. The response to this is to ask, Isn't happiness or at least contentment an adequate goal for any activity? What greater goal than happiness or contentment is achieved by so-called less trivial activities, such as working to make money? While middle age may be perceived as the loss of one's usefulness to employers, it can also be seen as a phase in life in which one gains the time to care for oneself and to do things for which there was never time available during the hectic days of child rearing and career building.

The client in philosophical counseling who is troubled about growing old will typically speak in terms of personal loss: loss of the innocence of youth, loss of vitality, loss of looks, loss of work, loss of sexual appetite, and so forth. Some individuals will actually go through a kind of mourning for these losses. The philosophical counselor may then be faced with a client who is going through the five stages of grieving associated with death and dying: denial and isolation, anger, bargaining, depression, and acceptance.[4] The philosophical counselor's job is to remind the client that although she is no longer the person she once was, she is nonetheless still a person of value and significance. And while life may no longer consist of the fast-paced work and intense passions of youth, life is not overall a losing proposition; life is cumulative; it consists of continual maturation, evolution, and gain. Clinical philosopher and septuagenarian Peter Koestenbaum writes that

Only a body-model of the person identifies evolution with the suppleness and strength of the body. A field-of-consciousness theory of the person identifies experience, wisdom, knowledge, and understanding with authentic evolution, an evolution in which bodily growth is merely one phase or element.[5]

The philosophical counselor may want to remind the client that what constitutes her as a person is not only her aging flesh and bones and her diminishing physical abilities but also her assumptions, beliefs, biases, and feelings. These are the personal cognitive, conative, and affective elements of life, developed within the milieu of family, community, and culture. Because of their impermanent nature and the fact that they are constantly evolving, these assumptions, beliefs, biases, and feelings can be intentionally altered and developed within a counseling setting. A philosophical inquiry into the underlying reasons that have led a client to see old age in negative, physical terms may help her to alter her perspective to a more positive one.

It may also be helpful to explain to a client that it's a mistake to conceive of life as being like a tree which goes through only four seasons, the bloom of spring, the productivity of summer, the decline and loss of autumn, and the barrenness of winter. In fact a tree goes through these seasons many times. And the leaves which are lost to the winds of change in the autumn of one year sprout anew the next. A tree losing but then regaining its foliage through a number of life cycles is like a person losing the "foliage" of the various stages in life, youth, adolescence, early adulthood, and midlife, and "sprouting" the exciting new foliage of the next stage. The life of an individual is not a simple decline from birth to death; it consists of multiple regenerations.

MENTAL/INTELLECTUAL CHANGES

Middle and old age can take a heavy emotional toll. It can be depressing to know that the unencumbered young have the ability to change their lives at a moment's notice, while the older person is fettered by responsibilities to the young, financial limitations, and a gradually decelerating body. Old age means realizing that some plans, goals, and dreams will never be fulfilled. Middle age is often considered to be the state of attainment,[6] but old age can be distressing if there is a sense of failure to attain earlier in life. Research in psychology has shown that people under the age of 45 tend to see their own lives as having an infinite horizon. It isn't until a person is over the age of 45 that he or she develops a sense that life is indeed limited, and the realization that there simply isn't enough time or energy available any more to reach those goals not yet attained.[7] Not having reached one's goals can be disheartening and hard on self-esteem if it is perceived as one's having failed to live up to not only one's own expectations but those of parents (perhaps already deceased), peers and associates, friends, spouse, and children.

One of my clients was in distress because he had been thinking about how old he would be by the time he finished his degree. He had started at age 40 and would be 46 if he wanted to achieve a Master's degree. He had two arguments for not starting: first, there is no point in starting since, at this age, he could drop dead tomorrow; and second, he would be 46 before he finished. My response was, "What if you don't drop dead tomorrow? You will have squandered today thinking about a future possibility that never happened. If you do this every day, you'll end up never having lived your life at all." In response to his second argument I told him about a similar conversation I had had with my wife some years previously. When I said to Anne, "There's no point in my even starting college at 40 because I'll be 50 by the time I get my doctorate," she simply replied, "You're going to be 50 anyway." The point is, life is best when it is lived, regardless of at what age one is living it. If it were reasonable to sit back and not live life simply because of the possibility that it may end the next day, no one would make it out of the cradle. I suggested to my client that life can be a protracted preparation for death or a wonderful celebration of living, but the choice is completely up to him.

Advancing years and declining physical vitality can be especially difficult for the person with a leadership type of personality, one who is used to being in control, and who has been known as someone who has always been able to make things right. It can be distressing to see that death is imminent and that it is not something that can be fixed. There is helplessness, frustration, and anger in being unable to either prevent death in loved ones or avoid it oneself. This may be accompanied by regrets about how life might have been better if other choices had been made in the past, and other forks in the road had been taken—for example, in selecting a marriage partner, having/not having children, career choices, and so on. The elderly person may have the feeling that his or her self-identity has been miscreated by the lifelong tasks that he or she was expected to perform at work or at home. This may all lead the elderly to suffer from dreams of a lost youth. Nostalgia can bring on a painful homesickness for "the good old days."

The philosophical counselor may want to remind the client, however, that many young people suffer from being young: they are often disregarded or not taken seriously in adult interactions; in their youthful curiosity and exuberance they are often unfairly suspected of bad intentions; they will unavoidably inherit the mistakes of the previous generation; and they rarely have the resources to make their dreams come true. Even early middle age brings its own disadvantages such as having to work to maintain a home, raising a family, and keeping a steady job. What is often forgotten by the elderly is that the so-called good old days of earlier years were often filled with their own struggles, upheavals, and confusion. Youth and middle age are simply concerned with different problems, not less of them. Old age can bring with it a certain freedom from the expectations of others, and thereby a peace of mind rarely experienced by those of younger years.

When my son Tim was about 10 years old he commented one day that he could hardly wait to get old because old people are so wise. Of course, wisdom does not come automatically with old age, but in old age one can leave behind that frenzied pursuit of the practical knowledge necessary for the activities of life, or what some authors call the "praxis of life." In senior years one can spend time in gaining philosophical and spiritual wisdom and in sharing knowledge about the more subtle aspects of life with grown children.[8] But it may be difficult for some individuals to cope with the fact that they are now at an age at which they're *supposed* to be wise but find they're not any smarter than they were when they were young. The elderly person may believe this is a time for shame and embarrassment, but the philosophical counselor can point out that it is in fact the perfect opportunity to take the time afforded by the slowed pace of life to once again give oneself the time for self-education that is lost during the mercantile years of midlife.

While mental and intellectual maturity may stagnate or grow rigid in old age, this happens only by choice or neglect, not by necessity. Two of the fundamentals on which philosophical counseling is based are first, that our lives are not absolutely determined by our early childhood experiences, and second, that old age does not end moral, intellectual, or spiritual growth. Maturation is in fact a continuing process that isn't reached at any particular age. In our fast-paced world, in which each generation of technology is estimated to be only about seven years, seniors are often expected to be merely the repositories of antiquated knowledge. But this raises the question, Why can't they also continue to be accumulators and even generators of new knowledge? One woman in Hilditch's philosophy café group put it this way: "I have become a history addict. I feel like I have a lot of catching up to do. I knew about the Cuban Missile crisis when it took place, but I didn't really know many of the details—I didn't know how close we were to war. Now I'm learning all about it." Interestingly, in some areas such as international diplomacy and governmental policy making, the knowledge and experience of men and women well past traditional retirement age are valued as essential to avoiding past mistakes.

SOCIOCULTURAL CHANGES

Although the knowledge that comes with age and experience is a valuable resource to any society, there are times when one generation must make room for the next. As mentioned earlier, in youth and in midlife a person is metaphorically on the competitive "field of play." In many fields, when a person reaches old age she is forced to either coach or retire completely. Unfortunately, some people continue to want to be on the "field of play," and refuse to make room for the next generation of "players." Not only will this cause problems in terms of employment, but also women can create problems for themselves by wanting the attention of younger men; men can get into difficulties by imagining they are still sexually attractive to younger women; high school teachers and college professors can find themselves in serious professional and personal difficulties if they allow themselves to imagine that they are being seduced by their young students; and parents can cause problems for their offspring by attempting to control their lives well into adulthood. Refusing to leave the competitive field of play to the next generation can mean, among other things, the unwillingness to give up a position of power in the workplace, the determination to retain popularity within the social circles of the young, and the attempt to live the lives of younger family members vicariously.

When a philosophical counselor is faced with a middle aged client in distress over his or her changing social status, Hilditch suggests explaining to the client that concern over social status is simply a waste of energy. While "the good life" for the young often means having the highest social status and the most material possessions possible, for those of advanced years these need not be important. In fact, according to Hilditch, older people live happier lives by ridding themselves of furniture, cars, and the like.

For the older person the decision to either agonize over a lack of status and material possessions or enjoy old age free from these concerns is a decision that the philosophical counselor can help his client make in a very intentional or conscious way. As one woman in Hilditch's philosophy café put it, "You decide to be content with what you have—it's a decision you make, it doesn't just come upon you." Another participant pointed out that with the loss of status there is also a reduction in responsibility to others, and therefore an increase in freedom. "When you're old you have the ability to spend time the way you want. You no longer have to do what someone else tells you to do. You have time to help others, to do things for others."

Unfortunately for some, growing old may mean becoming absolutely dependent on the children who were once dependent on them. But what may be perceived as a one-way dependency of the old on the young is only an absolute dependency in cultures where value lies primarily in the physical and economic abilities of the young. In cultures where the wisdom and spirituality of the old are valued there is an interdependence between aging parents and their offspring, with the young providing economic support and the old supplying intellectual, emotional, and spiritual support.

For both men and women growing old can be a painful time when it is accompanied by the scattering of the family, with married sons and daughters and their children moving away to begin life far from the retirement home. But for many growing old brings relief from the burden of attending to the incessant needs of children.[9] It allows an increase in connectedness within the marriage, a strengthening of relationships with remaining siblings, a time for recovering past friendships which were abandoned during hectic younger days. Of course, old age also means becoming a grandparent. This can be experienced as the heartbreak of realizing one's mortality or the joy of participating in the continuing cycle of life. As one elderly café participant put it, "Retirement is really a mixed feeling. For so many years I had obligations and was needed. Now there are no real obligations and I feel so useless sometimes. We work so hard to make sure our children are independent. And then they become independent." The philosophical counselor can help the client come to appreciate that the independence of children is also a cause for celebration, and that peace can be found in the knowledge that she has done a good job in raising her son—or he has done a good job in raising his daughter—who is now autonomous and quite capable of raising a son or daughter in turn.

The issue of being needed by the younger generation was explained by one senior this way: "You're needed at one time. And then you're not needed at all. Why am I here? I said this to my children, and they said 'Mom, we need you to pray for us.' So I know that, no matter what, I'm needed to pray."

EXISTENTIAL/SPIRITUAL CHANGES

It is possible that the middle aged person who decides to attend church, synagogue, or temple after a long absence may feel like the biblical prodigal son returning to spirituality from the fear of what death outside religion may bring. Some people may suffer from grave religious doubts due to the fact that in the past their religion encouraged them to believe they would never grow old. They had come to believe that God would literally destroy the wicked and bring in a new world order of peace, joy, and harmony in their lifetime, allowing them to remain perpetually young. Now they find themselves having to cope with being old in the real world which, unexpectedly, continues on uninterrupted. This may prompt a client to raise the question of whether it is even necessary to attend a place of worship in order to be spiritual. The philosophical counselor may be called upon to help the client to either restore a previously abandoned religious belief or develop a new spiritual worldview, one that is not eschatological in nature but much more mundane in its forward looking perspective. The question of how much religious discussion a philosophical counselor should engage in with a client is considered in greater detail in chapter 18.

Not only may middle age bring a newly discovered interest in religion, but also it can bring the shock of noticing that the past is now longer than the future which was previously believed to be infinite, and that the future now has a very definite personal horizon which is drawing ever closer. The feeling of youthful indestructibility and immortality is lost to the realization that everyone's future can be seen to have an end if one is willing to look courageously in that direction. Kenneth Doka, professor of gerontology at the College of New Rochelle, explains that the first glimpse of a limited future may not necessarily be a time filled with the serenity of calm acceptance.

The awareness of mortality strikes at a time when that recognition can be quite problematic. Family responsibilities and financial constraints may be at their peak. Career commitments may be at their apex. Life goals, even as reassessed, are likely to be incomplete. Under such conditions, the knowledge that one will die is likely to provoke great anxiety. It could be expected then that death anxiety would be at its highest in mid-life as the adult becomes increasingly cognizant of the paradox of both heightened responsibility and limited time. . . . Aware of limited time, even if it is measured in decades, a mid-life adult becomes deeply concerned that one's life has meaning.[10]

Midlife anxiety, or the so-called midlife crisis, is brought on (in part) not by the intellectual acknowledgment that life is finite, but by the internalization—that is, by the application to oneself—of the knowledge that one's own experience of life will some day come to an end while the rest of the world continues on unaffected. The philosophical counselor may be called upon to help a client deal with a very real fear of how death will strike, what it will feel like, and what sort of existence, if any, may be expected to follow. This is when discussion of Stoicism, Epicureanism, and other philosophies, as well as an examination of the beliefs about life after death in both Western and Eastern traditions, may bring some comfort.[11] The client may also ask the counselor for help in determining the meaning of life. This was already discussed in chapter 15, but it may be useful to note in addition that some clients, although claiming that they wish to discuss the meaning of life, may in fact simply want to find some comfort in connecting with a fellow traveler on the unmarked road ahead.

One of the most grievous consequences of aging is the gradual loss of parents and their cohorts. The death of family members, friends, and peers can leave a person feeling isolated and out of touch with the community. There is some truth to the poignant joke in which the 60-year-old person at the funeral of the last one of his parents says, "I guess I'm an orphan now." Psychologists point out that parents are perceived by their offspring as their protectors long after childhood, and when a parent dies it represents the removal of a buffer against death. "As long as the parent was alive the child could feel protected, since the parent by rational order of things was expected to die first. Without this buffer there is a strong reminder that the child is now the older generation and cannot easily deny his or her own mortality."[12] Recognizing that death will come can create in the client a desire to see that the remaining years are spent in the best, most meaningful, way possible. This is when the philosophical counselor can help the client in gathering and assessing the life options still available. The philosophical counselor can also remind the client that the recognition of one's own mortality need not be depressing. Accepting the finiteness of personal time can add a new vitality and zest to life, and a renewed appreciation for the tedious routines of compulsory daily tasks.

Also of benefit to the middle aged client are discussions with the philosophical counselor concerning meaningful personal goals for the years still remaining. The client can be asked, How do you want to be remembered? This goes well beyond the questions of earlier times in life which centered on material possessions, wealth, and status, that is, How do you want to live? As Kenneth Doka puts it, the middle aged person "must consider what one has been, what one wished to be, and what one still can become. In essence, one begins to consider what one could leave behind."[13] Perhaps the most salient description of a person's 'soul' is how that person is kept 'alive' as a memory in the minds and hearts of others. The person in midlife or old age, such as Scott above, who anguishes over the fact that his obsession with wealth and power has led him to neglect his family and friends, must be helped to redefine himself and re-present himself to those individuals in whose memories he wishes to be welcomed. When the pace of life in the middle years is intentionally slowed down, and when living is recognized as a natural progression rather than a suicidal act, then life after 40 will be a time of exploration and learning rather than simply a gradual approach to dying.

NOTES

1. *The Oxford Companion to Philosophy.* Ted Honderich, ed. Oxford, U.K.: Oxford University Press, 1995.

2. *The Encyclopedia of Philosophy.* Paul Edwards, ed. New York: Macmillan, 1967.

3. Yutang, Lin. "On Growing Old Gracefully." *The Importance of Living.* New York: William Heinemann, 1931. It's possible that this sentiment does not exist as strongly today

as it did when Yutang wrote this passage, but there is certainly still more respect for the elderly in China than in most Western societies.

4. See Elisabeth Kübler-Ross's book *On Death and Dying.* New York: Macmillan, 1969.

5. Koestenbaum, Peter. *The New Image of the Person. The Theory and Practice of Clinical Philosophy.* Westport, Conn.: Greenwood, 1978. 354.

6. Grollman, Earl A. *Suicide: Prevention, Intervention, Postvention.* Boston: Beacon Press, 1988.

7. Gould, R. "The Phases of Adult Life: A Study in Developmental Psychology." *American Journal of Psychiatry.* 129. 1972. 521–531.

8. For a discussion of knowledge development later in life see for example "Toward a Neofunctionalist Conception of Adult Intellectual Development: Wisdom as a Prototypical Case of Intellectual Growth" by F. Dittmann-Kohli, and P. B. Baltes in *Higher Stages of Human Development.* C. N. Alexander and E. J. Langer, eds. New York: Oxford University Press, 1990. 54–78.

9. According to sociological research the "empty nest" syndrome is a fiction. See Marlene Mackie's *Constructing Women and Men: Gender Socialization.* Toronto: Holt, Rinehart and Winston, 1987. 180.

10. Doka, Kenneth J. "The Awareness of Mortality in Midlife: Implications for Later Life." In *Awareness of Mortality.* Jeffrey Kauffman, ed. Amityville, N.Y.: Baywood Publishing, 1995. 111–120.

11. For a good discussion of various perspectives on death see *The Metaphysics of Death.* John Martin Fischer, ed. Stanford, Calif.: Stanford University Press, 1993. See also *Death and Philosophy.* Jeff Malpas and Robert Solomon, eds. London: Routledge, 1998.

12. Moss, M. and S. Moss, "The Impact of Parental Death on Middle Aged Children," *Omega,* 14. 1983. 65–76.

13. Doka, 116–117.

Chapter 17

Suicide as Self-Defense

We have recently entered a new millennium, one that is, for the most part, free of the threat of global nuclear war and out from under the oppression of all but a relatively few misguided political despots and terrorists. But there are many people who turn their backs on all that the future seems to promise, and choose instead to walk the lonely road that winds down into the valley of the shadow of death. Worldwide, more men and women between the ages of 15 and 44 die from intentionally self-inflicted damage than from warfare or AIDS or heart diseases. In the United States alone, between 1980 and 1992, the rate of suicides by children aged 10 to 14 increased by 120%. Every 17 minutes someone in the United States commits suicide. The frequency may be even higher because many cases of suicide are officially reported as accidental death in order to spare the family additional grief. For every person who succeeds approximately 100 others will have tried and failed.[1] Sadly, in most instances those who are left behind have no idea why their loved one has chosen to take such an irreversible journey. They are left with the self-recrimination, anger, guilt, and shame that come from having been unable to intervene in what they believe to be the mysterious alchemy behind such a solitary denial of life. Relief may come eventually by means of the assumption that the one who took his own life surely must have been crazy.

Some psychotherapists have in fact argued that the most common element in suicide is psychopathology or mental illness. They claim that from 90 to 95% of people who commit suicide were suffering from a diagnosable psychiatric illness.[2] But it seems clearly mistaken to conclude either that every attempted suicide is a symptom of some sort of mental disorder or that every successful death is, by definition, the result of a chemical imbalance or neurobiological disease in the brain which could have been cured with the appropriate analeptic medication. While statistical data show that the incidence of suicide is higher among certain populations, such as those who have been diagnosed with schizophrenia or antisocial personality disorders, there is no evidence that this correlation is actually a *causal* relationship. In other words, there is no evidence that schizophrenia or antisocial personality disorders cause a person to attempt suicide. In fact it may be that there is some other causal factor, or several, behind *both* the diagnosed mental illnesses and the suicides.

A case in point is what has been happening in some of the northern indigenous (or First Nations) communities of North America. Government social workers discovered that in one remote village more than 50% of the teenagers have attempted suicide.[3] These teens are part of a community whose traditional way of life—self-sufficiency primarily by means of hunting and fishing—has been effectively extinguished. The government relocated these people far from access to game and fish and from their ancestral burial grounds, and obliged them to accept absolute dependency on social assistance from the government as their only means of survival. The radically unfamiliar lifestyle they have been forced to adopt in this desolate region has led to a catastrophic rise in alcohol abuse among adults and a contagion of drug and solvent abuse and suicides among the young. But it would surely be at least a category mistake, or at worst a misdiagnosis, to claim that every teenager who has attempted suicide in this unfortunate village is suffering from some sort of mental illness, and that each attempted suicide was merely caused by a chemical imbalance in that teen's brain which could have been cured with medication. It does not require an advanced degree in psychology to imagine correctly why the inhabitants of this "artificial" village suffer from such a disproportionately high rate of suicide. But if a counselor chooses to retain the notion that suicidal ideation is always symptomatic of mental illness, which in turn is explainable as a chemical imbalance in the brain, then she will miss the actual causal factors which are often fairly obvious and frequently philosophical.

"Philip" is a very energetic man. He has been twice married and divorced. He was extremely bright in school, receiving several prestigious mathematics awards and scholarships to college. His father was very domineering and demanded that Philip and his three brothers become either doctors or lawyers. Although Philip's mother often told him she loved him, she was very critical of almost everything he did. He remembers she once called him a "fucking bastard" when, as a young boy, he got his shoes muddy while playing in the yard. One pleasant summer's evening the second youngest of Philip's brothers committed suicide by dousing himself with gasoline and setting himself on fire in front of the dining room window in plain sight of the family gathered around the dinner table. Philip became a real-estate agent like his father, because he thought this would make his father proud of him, but his business failed and his marriage failed. He lost his wife, his children, his home, his car, and his self-esteem. When final divorce proceedings were about 60% completed Philip felt he needed help figuring out what his life was all about, so he decided to consult a psychiatrist. The psychiatrist diagnosed him as schizophrenic and put him on a strict regimen of potent medications. After a number of months on medication, and after the drugs' side effects had caused him considerably more problems than they had relieved, Philip decided to slit both his wrists. This is the story Philip told me when he first came to see me in my philosophical counseling office about a year after his suicide attempt. He added that he was feeling somewhat depressed about life lately, and had begun thinking once again about ending his life.

A client who reveals to a philosophical counselor that he has tried to kill himself in the past, or who confesses that he has been thinking about suicide recently, is one of the most terrifying clients a counselor can encounter. Such a client can lead a counselor to seriously doubt her own abilities as a helper, to question her right to have a role in the life or death decision making of another human being, and to jump to hasty conclusions about both what causes suicide and how best to prevent it. Philosophical counselors pride themselves in helping individuals make their own decisions, in enhancing client autonomy, and in fostering an independence of will based on good reasoning. What is a philosophical counselor to do when a client admits the desire to carry out what appears to be one of the most irrational acts executable by a supposedly rational human being?

The problem is compounded for the philosophical counselor by the fact that historically philosophers have not all agreed that suicide is an irrational act. Furthermore, even where secular laws permit it, the common belief in many Christian communities is that not only does common decency preclude self-murder but, more importantly, God explicitly forbids it.

THE BIBLE

The fact is that suicide is rarely mentioned in the Bible, and when it is it's generally considered part of God's plan and therefore not condemned. For example, Ahithophel, a member of King David's council, gave advice to David's enemies on how to overthrow David's kingship. But this advice was ultimately disregarded and Ahithophel killed himself in disgrace. The account is found in the Bible at 2 Samuel chapter 17, verse 23: "When Ahithophel saw that his counsel was not followed, he saddled his donkey and went off home to his own city. He set his house in order, and hanged himself; he died and was buried in the tomb of his father." The Old Testament does not condemn this act; it treats it in a very matter-of-fact manner, as though it were in accord with God's overall plan for his people. Another Old Testament account of suicide is the case of Zimri. He assassinated Elah, king of Israel, and reigned as king himself for only a week. When his city was besieged he burned the palace down around himself. He killed himself in disgrace, but his death is explained as justified for the sins he committed. The Bible record at 1 Kings chapter 16, verse 18 states:

When Zimri saw that the city was taken, he went into the citadel of the king's house; he burned down the king's house over himself with fire, and died—because of the sins that he committed, doing evil in the sight of the Lord, walking in the way of Jeroboam, and for the sin that he committed, causing Israel to sin.

The suicide of Judas is the third, and probably best known, of only four cases of suicide mentioned in the Bible. Judas was the apostle of Jesus who betrayed him, but later returned the silver he'd been paid, and killed himself out of repentance and remorse. His self-inflicted death is not condemned. Instead it is described as the fulfillment of the prophecy of Jeremiah. Differing accounts of this suicide can be found at both Matthew chapter 27, verse 5, and Acts chapter 1, verse 18.

The fourth case, found at 1 Samuel chapter 31, verse 4, is that of Saul, military leader of Israel. After the enemy had killed all of Saul's three sons in a fierce battle, and Israel was hopelessly besieged, Saul asked his armor-bearer to run him through with his sword. When the servant refused, Saul fell on his own sword. His servant subsequently did the same and died with him. One other mention of suicide is in the story of the long-suffering Job. The Bible tells of how Job was both pious and prosperous. Satan argued with God that if he took Job's material possessions away his piety would soon end. So God agreed to let Satan test Job to see if his love of God was indeed based on his wealth. The Devil makes life so miserable for him that Job actually entertains thoughts of suicide. But since God finally intervenes, Job's life is spared.[4]

These biblical accounts of actual suicide and thoughts of suicide lead to two important conclusions: first, there is no prohibition in the Bible against a person taking his or her own life; the Bible makes no explicit reference to the sinfulness of suicide. In fact sometimes a suicide is treated as an acceptable act which was necessary to advance God's plans for the future of humankind. And second, the prevalent and powerful Christian condemnation of suicide must have originated elsewhere.

Socrates lived many centuries before the Bible was written and compiled. He claimed that taking one's own life is wrong because life does not belong to the one living it. He told his students "the gods are our keepers, and we men are one of their possessions. . . . We must not put an end to ourselves."[5] But Socrates *did* put an end to himself! His is one of the most famous suicides in all of recorded history. And it was not as though he had no choice in the matter. He was given several opportunities and a number of options which would have allowed him to continue his life, but he chose not to take them, and drank the poisonous hemlock instead. How did he reconcile his claim that suicide is wrong, and yet take his own life? He simply argued that a person must not intentionally end life "until the gods send some compulsion like the one which we are facing now."[6] The compulsion Socrates felt he was facing was the fact that the State had forbidden him to continue his public philosophical inquiries. For him this was reason enough to kill himself because he believed "the unexamined life is not worth living."[7] But what made suicide so appealing to Socrates was that he believed religiously that his soul was immortal and that he would continue on in an afterlife.

While the Athenians had Socrates, Christianity offers the story of Jesus Christ as the paradigm example of the virtuous nature of a willing death in response to evil. The problems created by people killing themselves to escape the sins and suffering of the mortal world in order to attain the glorious rewards of life in heaven became so overwhelming during the Middle Ages that the Christian church, led by its primary medieval spokesman St. Augustine, devised the argument that to commit suicide was a greater sin than any that could be avoided by it. Augustine invoked the sixth commandment, "Thou shalt not kill," and applied it to self-killing.[8] The paradox of any religion is that if the promised afterlife is made to seem more rewarding, or even just more tolerable, than the believer's present miserable life on earth, then suicide is a reasonable response to earthly suffering. This means that, in order to dissuade believers from acting reasonably and intentionally ending their earthly suffering, the tenets of all religions that claim supernal rewards must contain a threat of a punishment for suicide that both exceeds the misery experienced in life and denies the rewards of an afterlife.

This is why, in the thirteenth century, St. Thomas Aquinas spoke of the infernal and eternal punishments of Hell. He again took up the Socratic position that life is a gift from the gods (in Aquinas's case, a gift from God) which may not be discarded. But Aquinas added two other arguments which, in combination, proved to be an incontestable ban against suicide for the next four centuries. He wrote in his voluminous *Summa Theologiae*,

It is altogether unlawful to kill oneself, for three reasons: [1] everything naturally keeps itself in being. Wherefore suicide is contrary to the natural law and to charity; [2] because every man is part of the community, and by killing himself he injures the community; [3] because life is God's gift to man, and is subject to His power. . . . Hence whoever takes his own life, sins against God.[9]

But during the Enlightenment era of the seventeenth and eighteenth centuries this absolute prohibition against suicide became subjected to the same sort of scrutiny and criticisms leveled against other tenets of the major religions which had, up to this time, been obediently accepted as absolute Truths. The eighteenth-century secular philosopher David Hume, borrowing from the writings of several predecessors, was able to formulate devastating arguments against Christianity's foremost theologian. He responded to Aquinas's first point by arguing that taking one's own life is not against natural laws any more than any other of man or beast's activities can be said to contravene the laws of nature. For Hume, it is simply an impossibility, and the height of presumption, to suppose that one could go against the God-created laws of nature. Hume wrote,

Since therefore the lives of men are for ever dependent on the general laws of matter and motion, is a man's disposing of his life criminal, because, in every case, it is criminal to encroach upon these laws or disturb their operation? But this seems absurd. . . . Every action, every motion of a man innovates in the order of some parts of matter, and diverts, from their ordinary course, the general laws of motion. . . . It is a kind of blasphemy to imagine that any created being can disturb the order of the world, or invade the business of providence.[10]

Hume's response to Aquinas's second point is one that is often made by those who are thinking about ending their own lives. Hume argued that, rather than a person causing harm to his community by ending his life, perhaps his suicide will bring more good than harm. Of course this argument rests on the probability that the suicidal person who assumes his death will bring more good than harm is in fact making a *correct* assumption. Concerning the third point, Hume argues that if God has allowed men the freedom of will to choose how to live their lives, why would He have reserved the right to choose the time of a man's death for Himself? Hume reminds his readers that there is not a single text of scripture in the Bible that prohibits suicide. While the Bible condemns the murder of another human being "over whose life we have no authority," suicide, he says, is clearly not the murder of another, and therefore cannot be a sin against God.[11] Unfortunately, with Hume's solid arguments in hand, humankind was once again faced with the dilemma which caused so many problems for the earlier mediaeval Christian church: suicide too easily justified, and therefore far too appealing to the struggling masses. But can a cogent argument, such as this one made by Hume, motivate a person to take his own life? Or put another way, What is it exactly that makes a person decide to carry out this final and fatal act?

PHILOSOPHY OF SUICIDE

If suicide cannot always be instantly and categorically defined as a symptom of organic brain disease or mental illness then some other cause or reason must exist in its place. And while suicide cannot be judged from a moral perspective if it is in fact caused by organic brain disease or mental illness, other reasons a client may offer a philosophical counselor for wanting to do it may be seen by the counselor as morally reprehensible. This can cause serious problems for the counselor since one of the guiding principles of philosophical counseling is that the counselor is willing to help the client reach any goal that is reasonable *and moral*. So before discussion can begin concerning what a philosophical counselor ought to do when faced with a client who is talking about wanting to commit suicide, it is important to first of all determine whether the client's goal of bringing about his or her own death is indeed reasonable and morally permissible.[12] In other words, it is vital to examine why it is that a person might want to end life in the first place, and then to determine the moral status of those reasons.

Philosophers and psychologists have, over the years, presented many perspectives on why someone might want to take his or her own life.[13] But the one overriding feature of their speculations has been to maintain that the person who wants to end life always feels there is sufficient reason to do so. Hume put it this way: "I believe that no man ever threw away life while it was worth keeping."[14] What makes a person want to commit suicide is typically unendurable physical or psychological pain brought on by needs which have not been met in life. Since in our modern world most physical pain can now be alleviated by various medical means, the philosophical counselor will generally be faced with a client suffering from predominantly emotional or existential pain. The suicidal person feels helpless to change a hopeless situation; he desires that the suicide itself will either be heard as a cry for help or that it will act as a solution.[15] And suicide seems to be primarily immediate-goal oriented. The person who commits suicide does so *not* because he does not want to experience the next year or even the next day but because he does not want to experience the next moment. The suicidal person believes that the future will not be an improvement over the present, and that it will hold at least as much misery if not more. Psychiatrist Ludwig Binswanger called suicide an "existential retreat"[16] By this he meant that the woman who wants to end her own life is looking for relief in death from, for example, the agony of a breakdown in a significant relationship, or the man who killed himself did so in order to overcome some deeply embarrassing financial situation, or perhaps both have found the struggle with sexual identity unendurable. In other words, according to Binswanger, suicide is a retreat from an unbearably painful existence.

Of course, many individuals would say that this is not a justifiable moral reason for suicide. In fact, after Socrates killed himself in ancient Athens, Aristotle, one of his brightest students, said that such an escape from the troubles of this world is a cowardly act. Aristotle wrote,

> To kill oneself to escape from poverty or love or anything else that is distressing is not courageous but rather the act of a coward, because it shows weakness of character to run away from hardships, and the suicide endures death not because it is a fine thing to do but in order to escape from suffering.[17]

But contrary to Aristotle's position, there is no doubt that suicide takes courage. Even to merely talk about ending one's own life is not an easy task whenever and wherever there is a strong taboo against it. The suicidal person knows that self-destruction will inevitably bring accusations against his family and community. And at a time, in a family, or in a culture where there is no strong collective belief in life after death killing oneself simply cannot be the act of a coward. Conversely, even if there is a strong religious belief in an afterlife, taking one's own life can be even more difficult. For example, practicing Catholics believe that the person who kills herself will burn in Hell for all eternity. Yet many practicing Catholics, and others who truly believe God punishes those who kill themselves, still do so. This takes courage. The level of courage involved in suicide depends on metaphysical conviction. An analysis of suicide in relation to this conviction looks like this: if there is certainty that an afterlife (of some sort) will be pleasant then it takes no courage; if there is certainty that the afterlife will be painful then it takes great courage; if there is uncertainty whether the afterlife will be pleasant or painful, or that there even is an afterlife, then it also takes courage. A similar analysis holds for a suicide in relation to a belief in reincarnation: it always takes great courage when there is an expectation of a future filled with suffering and punishment, or if there is metaphysical uncertainty. And for most individuals there is no certainty.

Immanuel Kant argued in the seventeenth century that an act is only an act of will if it goes contrary to one's natural inclinations.[18] Suicide must be an act of will rather than merely a cowardly surrender because it goes utterly contrary to every individual's most powerful natural inclination: the primordial survival instinct which makes the body kick and struggle up from the depths to break the surface and to breathe in life no matter how painful it may be. In the eighteenth century,

German philosopher Arthur Schopenhauer argued that suicide is not at all a weakness of character. In fact, he said, it is quite the contrary.

Far from being denial of the will, suicide is a phenomenon of the will's strong affirmation. For denial has its essential nature in the fact that the pleasures of life, not its sorrows, are shunned. The suicide wills life, and is dissatisfied merely with the conditions on which it has come to him. Therefore he gives up by no means the will-to-live, but merely life, since he destroys the individual phenomenon.[19]

For Schopenhauer, then, suicide is a strong-willed act. And it is a courageous act because it resists willfully the overwhelming urge to survive. It is not at all a rebellion against all of life, but against some particularly monstrous life which is brutalizing its owner. If life is a gift from the gods then the suicidal owner of this life chooses to return to the gods what is considered to be a worthless (or harmful) gift. It is therefore not an immoral act against all of life, which could never be anyone's personal possession, but an individual act of moral outrage against the intolerable conditions of one torturous life. But the blame for a suicide does not always belong solely to that one troubled individual. While there may be only one actor, there are often many others who have, either knowingly or unwittingly, set the stage. Twentieth-century German philosopher Jürgen Habermas argues that a solitary suicide can incriminate an entire community.

Notwithstanding the Stoic view which held that this final, desperate act reflects the imperious self-determination of the lone individual, the responsibility for suicide can never be attributed to the individual alone. This seemingly loneliest of deeds actually enacts a fate for which others collectively must take some of the blame, the fate of ostracism from an intersubjectively shared lifeworld.[20]

In a sense Habermas is saying that suicide is at times a form of *sociocultural homicide*. Societal standards can be such that a person becomes marginalized or ostracized. Cultural traditions and norms (such as an arranged marriage, or the inferior status of women) or cultural prohibitions (such as against a particular sexual orientation) or cultural demands (such as that a person be rich, beautiful, or famous) can lead a person to feel so inadequate, and so alienated from, or shunned by, his community that death seems kinder. Even bullying is a form of homicide if it leads the victim to see death as preferable to the treatment received at the hands of others. It is what French sociologist Émile Durkheim called *anomic* suicide.[21] In this case suicide is a form of social criticism or political protest against being victimized by society—even if it is only a protest against the politics of one's own family or peers—and not at all an immoral act since the intention is not merely self-serving. The self-killing by the person who is being victimized sends a message; it makes a statement; it is the cry of the powerless, a symbolic reclamation of control over one's own destiny; it is an attempt to purchase societal reform at a shocking price.

Of course, suicide is not always so altruistic. It can be a reaction against the expectations of family and peers that are so high that failure is recurrent and inevitable. In such a case suicide is not an immoral act either since it is the plea of a victim; it is an accusation; it is a cry for help that is heard too late. Durkheim uses the term *egoistic* suicide as self-death brought about by "man's no longer finding a basis for existence in life."[22] This may be the merely self-centered justification for death which involves comparing one's own inadequate accomplishments in life with those of the superstars of sports and screen or the fantasy characters of fiction. Suicide thereby becomes the romantic *good death* of the mythological hero which conquers the boredom of mundane life, and sabotages the natural but ignoble passing away in ordinary time.

Not only is taking one's own life praised as heroic by some, it can also be admired as downright "macho." Young people especially can interpret self-killing as a show of strength in the face of despised authority figures. "Suicide by police," in which an individual taunts and tricks a police officer into firing the fatal shot, has become a common method for combining reckless defiance with fearless self-destruction. Suicide can thereby be anger turned outward—a silent but violent "I don't care"; an act of revenge against police, parents, and teachers. It can also be anger at others turned inward—a defiant act of rebellious refusal to live life as others would have it. The immorality of these manifestations of suicide is obvious since they are merely a veiled attempt to inflict pain on others through the agency of one's own body.

Psychiatrist Sigmund Freud wrote that at its most mysterious suicide comes about indirectly as the result of a perplexingly subtle death wish. Freud maintained that an "unconscious suicide" could occur as a result of an unintentional overdose of medication or illicit drugs, or an accidental injury which brings death through "semi-intentional" carelessness.

Whoever believes in the occurrence of semi-intentional self-inflicted injury—if this awkward expression be permitted—will become prepared to accept through it the fact that aside from conscious intentional suicide, there also exists semi-intentional annihilation—with unconscious intention—which is capable of aptly utilizing a threat against life and masking it as a casual mishap. . . . More than one case of apparently accidental misfortune has become known to me whose surrounding circumstances justified the suspicion of suicide.[23]

But Freud's so-called death wish has been severely criticized by psychologists as being an after-the-fact explanation of either a suicide or an accident that is completely unsupported by empirical evidence, and therefore without scientific validity.[24] Furthermore his postulation of "unconscious suicide" leaves philosophers with the enigmatic question, How can a suicide which is unconsciously self-inflicted be judged to be either moral or immoral? In other words, since an unconscious suicide is not merely a morally neutral act of nature but is still the intentional murder of a human being by a human being, what moral status would such an unconscious human action have? Perhaps it would count as a case of what Socrates called *akrasia*. But *akrasia* is defined as intentionally choosing that which you know is bad for you. If this choosing of suicide is done with "unconscious intention" can it even be said that the victim—he or she—is doing the choosing? Put another way, claiming that a suicide was committed with *uncon-*

scious intention raises the curious question, What is the moral standing of the unconscious *agent* whose intention is to kill the conscious person?

For most, suicide is an intentional act that is considered the lesser of two evils: the known and already experienced evils of life, and the unknown and not yet experienced evils of death. And while it is not an act of murder, as Hume argued, I believe it is in fact often an act of killing in self-defense. It may seem to be a blatant contradiction to say that suicide is self-defense since its "successful" outcome is the annihilation of the self, but suicide committed as self-defense is, again, having chosen what is believed to be the lesser of two evils: the evil of an *authentic* death (in which the act of ending one's life is in one's own hands) over the evil of an *inauthentic* life (in which others have the power to dictate and control one's life). At the height of the Cold War the battle cry of many fervently nationalistic Americans was, "Better dead than red!" What these patriots were proclaiming with this slogan was that they preferred death over having to live life according to an ideology not of their own making. But they did not prefer death over life per se. Death represented the desire not to end their democratic or capitalistic lifestyle but to preserve in temporal stasis what is left of a preferred lifestyle in the face of overpoweringly destructive external forces.

The person who commits suicide in self-defense is doing something very similar: he is attempting to preserve in temporal stasis what is left of a self-constructed life in the face of overpoweringly destructive external forces. These external forces need not be a hostile foreign power; they may be as close to home as an abusive parent or bullying peers. In other words, as self-defense, suicide is an act believed to counteract these self-destroying external forces (either real or imagined, and either institutional or individual). It is meant to counteract the annihilation of the self, to prevent the total loss of self-image (even if it is idealized), and to preserve what little remains of personal dignity and self-respect. It is the last desperate act of a struggle to retain, albeit in self-annihilation, some semblance of power and control over oneself. Suicide as self-defense is manifest overtly in any number of means for violent self-destruction, and indirectly in addictions to various harmful substances, in participation in clearly life-threatening leisure activities, and in bulimia, anorexia, and so on.

Psychologist Roy F. Baumeister comes close to describing suicide as self-defense in his discussion of suicide as a form of escape from a definition of the self which has been created by the external problems in life. Baumeister writes,

The suicide attempt thus can be seen as an escalation of the person's efforts to escape from the definition of self that has evolved from recent problems or setbacks. The old self is no longer tenable, and no new definition of self has emerged to replace it. The person can neither let go of the past meanings [in life] nor accept them. In such circumstances, the appeal of suicide is mainly oblivion. It is not an aggressive catharsis, or whatever, but rather simply an ultimately effective form of escape. It makes the world stop.[25]

But suicide in self-defense is not simply a form of escape from recent problems or setbacks; it is not merely a desire for oblivion or to make the world stop. It is a final, desperate act of trying to maintain self-possession and self-control; it is thereby a genuine attempt at self-preservation, and, of course, at the same time a hopelessly paradoxical achievement.

Elena, one of my clients, put it this way:

I had so many pressures on me, so many people were expecting me to be there for them in so many different ways, that I was worried I was losing myself. I didn't want to disappear completely. I mean, I wasn't able to look after my own needs because I was looking after so many other people's needs. At my lowest point, I was totally convinced suicide was the only way to keep the last little bit that was left of me from sliding away.

Suicide cannot be immoral when it is an act of self-defense since self-defense is always considered morally permissible except by the extraordinarily saintly. Suicide as self-defense embodies the philosophy of passive resistance so well exemplified by a number of outstandingly virtuous figures in both past history and recent times. And as an act of self-defense suicide is therefore also comparable to a biblical good Samaritan's act of kindness, albeit toward oneself. Still, the desire to commit suicide as an act of self-defense is nonetheless a serious problem for the philosophical counselor, and very difficult to deal with because of the paradoxical nature of its justificative rationale. But while it may be morally permissible under some circumstances for an individual to take his or her own life, perhaps it is also ultimately avoidable.

PHILOSOPHICAL COUNSELING

I don't know of any cases in which a suicidal person has gone to a philosophical counselor looking for permission to go through with it. In fact such a request could not be fulfilled by a philosophical counselor since philosophical counselors do not pretend to have the authority to grant or withhold permission to do so. Any talk of giving permission for suicide is a paternalistic stance that is absolutely antithetical to the philosophical counselor's respect for the client's autonomy. The question of whether a philosophical counselor can ever give permission to a suicidal person is therefore simply a nonissue. It is imperative that the philosophical counselor find out what the client wants, even so far as to ask directly, "What do you want from counseling?" Individuals who turn to philosophical counseling are typically hoping that the philosopher will be able to help them find an agreeable alternative to suicide, one which they themselves have not been able to imagine.

No one picks suicide as his first choice when there are other options available. Suicide is always a last resort, like any desperate and violent act of self-defense, when all other options appear hopeless or have already failed. Hume wrote almost three centuries ago that "age, sickness, or misfortune may render life a burden, and make it worse even than annihilation."[26] Today's philosophical counselor is faced with a far longer list of reasons why a person may want to end life:

- when a young person has negative interpersonal relationships, or is considered by others to be a "loser," a "geek," or a "fag"

- being gay or lesbians, or being labeled as such
- when a boyfriend or girlfriend ends a relationship
- when academic efforts are in decline or a job stagnates
- when the support network of family and peers has collapsed
- when family and peers are overly critical and demanding
- being addicted to alcohol or drugs at any age
- being addicted to medication
- being a member of a visible minority in an urban environment, such as blacks, Asians, or aboriginal, especially the young and especially in intolerant areas
- belonging to one of the indigenous peoples in a rural setting, especially as a young person who is not yet able to be self-sufficient, in an isolated community, where it is impossible to follow traditional ways
- when marital difficulties arise such as separation, divorce, child custody disputes, in-law conflicts, religious differences, and so on
- when suffering financial stress, bankruptcy, joblessness, loss of the farm, business, house, or car
- when a physician (or other professional) at the peak of his or her career is overly self-critical, or has suffered recent humiliation or tragic loss, or becomes a substance abuser
- being the veteran of a war which lacks public endorsement, such as Vietnam
- having suffered the victimization of war, or being a refugee
- when a middle aged person is overwhelmed by the disparity between expected achievement that is unfavorably compared with perceived actual accomplishments
- bereavement, especially widowhood during the first year of the death of spouse
- when an elderly person is abandoned[27]

The items on this list are not endogenous diseases, intrapsychic conflicts, or diagnosable neurobiological causes. They are existential, interpersonal, ethical, and political reasons which stand to benefit more from philosophical discussions than from medication.

In training for a suicide crisis line I was taught to remember that individuals who take the time to make the call and talk about killing themselves probably don't want to die. Those who really want to die do so almost unhesitatingly, and they choose the most effective means—those which will not allow others to come to their rescue. But I wondered, If the caller does not want to die, then what is the call all about? Similarly, if the client who is talking about suicide in the philosophical counselor's office doesn't want to die, then what does she want?

In all likelihood she is hoping to find a way to regain control of her life. This may include the following:

- the hope that the daily activities of her life will become meaningful once again
- the desire to have the counselor's acceptance of who she is—regardless of who she is—including the shocking fact that she has been thinking about killing herself
- the need for relief from undesirable external controlling influences

- the need for relief from the self-damnation and guilt which, in our culture, are socially conditioned side-effects of suicidal ideation
- the craving to once again feel comfortable with her own definition of herself, which may have been denied for some time
- a longing to find different and better options

The philosophical counselor is faced with a client who is often convinced that she is in a dilemma for which there is no resolution: the dilemma of either being a quitter and coward if she backs out of her suicidal plans, or being a quitter and coward if she goes ahead with them. But there is a way the philosophical counselor can help the client avoid interpreting this situation as a dilemma. The counselor can point out to the client that her decision to commit suicide is in fact a reasonable choice *if* the quality of her life has diminished to the point at which death is equal to or better than all other options available to her. But this is a monumental "if." Suicide may seem like a reasonable option at this particular time, given the information at hand, the present options, and current emotional support available. But given enough time and some exploratory work the situation may change, other information may surface, more options may become available, and individuals may be found who are willing to offer their strength and care in support. Over time the option of suicide may no longer be a reasonable option. The problem is, a philosophical counselor deals with a client in time, in the present moment, with all the attendant shortcomings and failings of that client's life. The challenge is to have the client see that over time life can be improved, and that the decision to commit suicide at this moment in time cannot be reversed once it is carried out. It is vital for the client to remember that suicide is not of the same nature as other life decisions. While many life decisions can be reconsidered, ~~correteedd~~ corrected, and rewritten like a word on a page, suicide is always final. The decision to commit suicide, and its ultimate completion, are not at all like a natural death which has been described as the satisfying period at the end of a good sentence. Instead, suicide is like a sentence left unfin

Imagination plays a pivotal role at this point, both in the suffering individual's attempt to articulate a reasonable justification for committing suicide and in its avoidance through philosophical counseling. The person who believes suicide is the best alternative has imagined the future as inevitable and unbearable, while the philosophical counselor can help the client to use the imagination to discover alternate perspectives, and to create alternative solutions to replace those which have already been discarded. The philosophical counselor can help the client to discover and invent options which make the option of death seem less reasonable and less desirable. Imagination can also help in the examination of significant life changes. The philosophical counselor can point out to the client that changes in life can seem like the end, but they are often just *transitions* to other stages or phases. In fact the only change which may actually be an end is death itself. And while it may be obvious to some clients that change is indeed part of life, what is often much less obvious is that suffering is also part of life. Suffering is a significant and important contributing factor to human development. In our remarkably well-educated, marvelously automated, and overly medicated society we tend to forget that comfort is also a tranquilizer. A time of suffering, when it is neither extreme nor endless, can focus the mind, sharpen the senses, and create meaning in life.

Clients who visit a philosophical counselor out of their own free will are always eager to help the counselor help them to overcome their suicidal thoughts. They make every effort to answer the counselor's questions honestly, and to reveal as much of their lives as they think necessary to resolve their problems. A client who visits a counselor is always hoping that there are undiscovered options available other than death that have the potential to solve their problems.

But there is one problem which a client may present that has taken on mythic proportions because it has seemed to be unresolvable to many philosophers: the belief or feeling that life is absurd. This is connected with the problem or question of meaning of life which has been dealt with in chapter 15. The so-called absurdity of life seems prima facie to be sufficient reason for ending it in oneself. But the Algerian French philosopher Albert Camus argued that the absurdists cannot condone suicide because in order for life to be hopelessly absurd it must continue.

The final conclusion of the absurdist process is, in fact, the rejection of suicide and persistence in that hopeless encounter between human questioning and the silence of the universe. Suicide would mean the end of this encounter, and the absurdist position realizes that it could not endorse suicide without abolishing its own foundations. . . . Absurdist reasoning thereby recognizes human life as the single necessary good, because it makes possible that confrontation. . . . To say that life is absurd, one must be alive.[28]

But the client who agonizes over the absurdity of all life is rare, or perhaps totally extinct already. Suicide is always personal even when the reasons for it are put in terms of generalized or universal justifications. While novelists, playwrights, sociologists, and philosophers may propose concepts such as absurdity, anomie, and nihilism as the lofty motivations behind suicide, the person contemplating suicide is thinking and acting in terms of existentially perceived positive and negative actualities in just his own life. By this I mean he is either reacting against what life *is* (painful, confusing, unfair, etc.) or against what life *is not* (enjoyable, rewarding, fulfilling, etc.); he is reacting against what others think *of* him and what they *fail* to think of him; he is reacting against what others are *doing to* him and what they *fail to do for* him; and he is reacting in response to what he thinks *of* himself, and what he *cannot* think of himself. But while suicide is always personal, the personal is also always philosophical. The philosophical insights woven together from formal academic training can be a sturdy lifeline when the philosophical counselor offers it gently with empathy and compassion.

Organic brain disorders and so-called mental illness are negligible as causal factors in the majority of suicidal clients who request the services of a philosophical counselor. Although a person's emotions or concerns may have been clinically diagnosed as some type of psychopathology, the reasons for depression, melancholy, or despair will soon become apparent in a careful and care-full philosophic inquiry.

"Elena" had been raised by her family to believe that a woman's role is to help others. She had been told many times by family, friends, and coworkers how strong and capable she was. She prided herself on being able to handle any situation with confidence and composure. But she reached a time in her late 30s when the demands of others for her time and energy were too much to bear. She found that she couldn't confide in anyone since everyone believed her to be so strong and capable. She felt completely overwhelmed and helpless to change her predicament. So she attempted suicide by taking an overdose of sleeping pills, but a friend of hers found her and took her to the hospital. She was diagnosed with clinical depression and put on medication. She confessed that her stay in the psychiatric ward of the hospital not only gave her some time to take care of herself, but also sent the strong message to friends and relatives that she was not willing to be their champion any more—a message she had never been able to bring herself to communicate to them.

But when Elena came to see me she was once again thinking about suicide. The support and acceptance she had experienced in the hospital were no longer there to sustain her in the real world, and the old expectations of family, friends, and coworkers were once more bearing down on her. Her attempted suicide was, in effect, the desired "death" of the old Elena, but her family and friends had not understood this well enough. They saw only her smile, her eagerness to be helpful, the familiar in her. They didn't understand that suicide is, in many cases, a last desperate attempt to bring an end to the familiar. This is why it is often an act of self-defense. In Elena's case, as in so many others, the desire to defend against the familiar was very strong, but what was lacking was her ability to recognize both that desire and the familiar for what they were. This is where philosophical counseling comes in because it is only when the reasons for wanting to end the old life are finally understood that a new life can begin.

For some this new life may include adopting some form of religion or spirituality as a means to comfort; for others it may mean exactly the opposite: giving up previously held intellectually and emotionally stifling religious beliefs. But talk about religion or spirituality within a counseling setting that is said to be philosophical is sure to raise the question, What does God have to do with it?

NOTES

1. The facts and statistics about suicide in this chapter come from Kay Redfield Jamison's book *Night Falls Fast: Understanding Suicide.* New York: Vintage, 1999. 309.

2. Jamison, 100. Bernard Gallagher states what is the common opinion among many professionals this way: "Although some consider it risky to assume that a person who commits suicide is mentally ill, it is safe to assume that a suicidal person is at least temporarily disturbed" (*The Sociology of Mental Illness.* Englewood Cliffs, N.J.: Prentice-Hall, 1987. 255).

3. This village, located near James Bay, was the focus of a Canadian Broadcasting Corporation documentary aired in January 2001 on CBC TV.

4. Job chapter 3, verse 21, and chapter 7, verse 15.

5. Plato. "Phaedo." 62 a–c. *Collected Dialogues* (c. 375 B.C.). Edith Hamilton and Huntington Cairns, eds. Princeton, N.J.: Princeton University Press, 1961.

6. Ibid.

7. Plato. "Apology" 38a. *Collected Dialogues* (c. 375 B.C.) Edith Hamilton and Huntington Cairns, eds. Princeton, N.J.: Princeton University Press, 1961. Clitophon says Socrates also believes, "someone who doesn't know how to use his soul is better off putting his soul to rest and not living at all." *Clitophon* 408b in *Plato: Complete Works.* John M. Cooper and D. S. Hutchison, eds. Indianapolis: Hackett, 1997.

8. See *The Encyclopedia of Philosophy.* Vol. 8. Paul Edwards, ed. New York: Macmillan, 1967. 43.

9. Aquinas, Thomas. *Summa Theologiae: A Concise Translation* (1274). Timothy McDermott, ed. London: Methuen, 1991. II. ii, Q. 64, A 5.

10. Hume, David. "Of Suicide" (1779). *Writings on Religion.* Anthony Flew, ed. La Salle, Ill.: Open Court, 1992. 43–47.

11. Ibid., 49.

12. An interesting discussion on the moral permissibility of suicide is Elliot D. Cohen's "Permitting Suicide of Competent Clients in Counseling: Legal and Moral Considerations" in the *International Journal of Applied Philosophy.* Volume 14: 2, Fall 2000. 259–274. Besides the moral question of whether suicide is ever morally permissible in general terms, Cohen also discusses the question of whether a philosophical counselor may ever *give* permission to a competent client wishing to commit suicide. I personally believe this is a nonissue since granting permission, or forbidding, is paternalistic and is thereby antithetical to one of the foundational principles of philosophical counseling: client autonomy. I believe the proper response to a client who is seeking permission to commit suicide is to say that no authority exists in a philosophical counselor to either grant or deny such permission. That authority always only rests in the competent client.

13. In fact many notable writers and scholars have themselves attempted to do so. See the list of artists, writers, and scientists who have tried to commit suicide in Jamison, 365, note 181.

14. Hume, 49.

15. Adapted from *Crisis Intervention Strategies.* Burl E. Gilliland and Richard K. James. New York: Brooks/Cole, 1997. 193.

16. Binswanger, Ludwig. "Being-in-the-World." *Selected Papers.* J. Needleman, trans. New York: Basic Books, 1963. 258.

17. Aristotle. *Ethics* Book 3, vii.

18. Kant, Immanuel. *Groundwork of a Metaphysic of Morals* (1797). H. J. Paton, trans. New York: Harper & Row, 1964. 66.

19. Schopenhauer, Arthur. *The World as Will and Representation.* Quoted in *The Dictionary of Philosophical Quotations.* A. J. Ayer and Jane O'Grady, eds. Oxford, U.K.: Blackwell, 1994. 414.

20. Habermas, Jürgen. *Moral Consciousness and Communicative Action.* Translated by Christian Lenhardt and Shierry Weber Nicholsen. Cambridge, Mass.: MIT Press, 1996. 200.

21. Durkheim, Émile. *Suicide: A Study in Sociology.* Quoted in *The Dictionary of Philosophical Quotations.* A. J. Ayer and Jane O'Grady, eds. Oxford, U.K.: Blackwell, 1994. 120–121.

22. Ibid.

23. Freud, Sigmund. "Psychopathology of Everyday Life." *The Basic Writings of Sigmund Freud*. A. A. Brill, trans. and ed. New York: Modern Library, 1995. 91–93. It is interesting to note that Freud extrapolates this theory of an unconscious death wish to "a sexual attack on a woman, in whom the attack of the man cannot be warded off through the full muscular strength of the woman because a portion of the unconscious feelings of the one attacked meets it with ready acceptance" (93n.). Freud equates the "unconscious" wish to die with a woman's supposed "unconscious" wish to be raped.

24. Hall, Calvin S. and Gardner Lidnzey. *Theories of Personality*. New York: Wiley, 1970. 71.

25. Baumeister, Roy F. "The Self Against Itself: Escape or Defeat?" *The Relational Self*. Rebecca C. Curtis, ed. New York: Guilford Press, 1991. 250.

26. Hume, 49.

27. Adapted and expanded from *Suicide: Prevention, Intervention, Postvention*. Earl A. Grollman. Boston: Beacon, 1988. 74.

28. Camus, Albert. *The Rebel*. Quoted in *The Dictionary of Philosophical Quotations*. A. J. Ayer and Jane O'Grady, eds. Oxford, U.K.: Blackwell, 1994. 81.

Chapter 18

What Does God Have to
Do with It?

In North America philosophy is often misunderstood. Not only is it frequently believed to be only a rather useless academic pastime, but also it is regularly confused with so-called New Age spirituality. A local neighborhood bookstore is likely to shelve philosophy books in the most unlikely places: Immanuel Kant's books on the metaphysics of morals will often be with books on magic for mortals; Thomas Hobbes' *Leviathan* with books on the Loch Ness monster; and René Descartes' meditations with books on the Maharishi's meditation techniques for senior citizens.

People also often confuse philosophy with more traditional religious activities. One man calling to find out more about the philosophical counseling I offer asked me, with a suspicious tone of voice, "You're not promoting some sort of religion, are you?" An e-mail message sent to me by a young man who had found my web site asked me to please send him some prayers he could use that God would be sure to listen to. These are clearly cases of mistaken identity: a philosopher has been mistaken for a theologian or priest or, worse still, some sort of New Age guru. These examples are not meant to illustrate that all personal problems that involve God or spirituality are automatically unsuitable for philosophical counseling. But philosophical counselors are often approached by clients who have a mistaken conception of what philosophy is and how philosophical counseling works. Philosophical counselors are therefore sometimes reluctant to deal with clients whose problems seem at first glance to be religious.

The connection between philosophy and religion, as well as their hostility toward each other, goes back to antiquity. The eighteenth-century German philosopher G.W.F. Hegel points out that up to and including his own day there has always been a love/hate relationship between the two. Theologians have condemned philosophers as heretics while at the same time they have used philosophical arguments to help believers enhance the strength of their convictions, and philosophers have condemned religion as nonsensical while at the same time they have been fascinated by the philosophy that has turned up when inquiries were made into the various aspects of religious beliefs.[1]

The fact that contemporary religion demands of its followers that they accept its most incredible claims on faith alone—such as that everyone is born sinful, that prayer will bring solutions to all personal problems, or that all the world's woes will be eliminated by a Savior—can make some philosophical counselors very uncomfortable and reluctant to accept for counseling those who hold strong religious beliefs. Tim LeBon is the editor of *Practical Philosophy*, the journal of the British Society of Consultant Philosophers, and a philosophical and existentialist counselor in London. LeBon believes he would find it very hard to work with someone whose personal problems involved religion or spirituality.

I'm an atheist myself, and find it hard to reconcile the philosopher's search for truth with religious dogma. Obviously as a counselor I try to "bracket" my own worldview and help the clients explore and develop theirs. But with religion I think I would find this very difficult. I had an e-mail client from the States once who, in her first e-mail, made it clear that she was quite religious. In my first e-mail back (before I had taken her on as a client) I made it clear that I did not share her religious perspective, and said that although I would be willing to work with her, she'd probably be better off finding someone more sympathetic to religion. She said she'd think about it, and we did not proceed further. In retrospect I think this was right. Religious belief can be very comforting, and even if as a philosopher I want to question it, as a counselor I realize this could be quite harmful to my client.[2]

LeBon's position raises the question, What is it specifically that makes so many philosophers uncomfortable with the comfort others find in their religious faith? The answer to this may at least in part rest with the difference between the philosopher's state of mind and the state of mind of the religiously devout. The philosopher prides himself or herself in having an inquiring mind which takes nothing for granted, on having the diligence to question everyday assumptions, traditions, and beliefs, and on having the courage to challenge any position, including his or her own, whose supporting reasons seem weak, inconsistent, or nonexistent. A philosopher will rarely claim to hold a belief strictly on faith. It might be said that most philosophers place their faith in not putting their faith in anything which is not at the same time supported by adequate evidence or reasons. In contrast to this, the state of mind of the religiously devout person is, as William James put it, one in which

the will to assert ourselves and hold our own has been displaced by a willingness to close our mouths and be as nothing in the floods and waterspout of God. In this state of mind . . . the time for tension in our souls is over, and that of happy relaxation, of calm deep breathing, of an eternal present, with no discordant future to be anxious about, has arrived.[3]

In the soul of the philosopher tension is created by the unanswered—and often unanswerable—questions behind every conviction. There is a thirst for knowledge, but no irresistible urge to satisfy this thirst absolutely. And it is this unquenchable but agreeable thirst which is absent in those who simply depend on the "waterspout of God" to bring them relief from difficult questions. This creates a fear among philosophical counselors that having a philosophical discussion with a religiously devout person will callously create an uninvited 'dehydration of the soul' destructive of the "happy relaxation" that religious certainty seems to bring to such a person.

But philosophy doesn't need to disturb religious conviction. While LeBon admits he has difficulty in working philosophically with religious clients who wish to explore *religious* areas he believes he would have no problem working with a religiously devout client who wanted to discuss, for example, career issues.

Why should I have any more trouble with, say, a Catholic if I am atheist than with, say, a Kantian if I were a utilitarian? It's perhaps something to do with religion providing a crutch I would not want to remove, without replacing it with something else. But also I wonder if religious beliefs have to some extent become a "sacred cow" which says it's a person's right to have a belief which should not be challenged. In which case perhaps, as philosophical counselors, we should only be exploring religious ideas in an agreed-upon joint inquiry with clients, as with any other issues, and help them replace religious values with their own only if they actually lose their religious faith as a result of the inquiry.

It is not at all a given that when a philosophical inquiry is conducted into a religious concern or problem it will cause the client to lose his faith. But exactly how can a counselor give counsel on religious matters when she is not a believer herself, or when she is of a different faith than that of the person asking for her help?

In my previous book I discussed the case of "Clarence," a dedicated Christian who asked me to help him restore his connection with God.[4] Clarence's request did not require that I present theological reasoning or biblical arguments. What helped Clarence was, first of all, my coming to an understanding of his personal conception of God and what he meant by his "connection with God," and then working with Clarence, not to criticize his faith from my subjective perspective, or to change it, but rather to question it from *within his own* belief system in order to help him find the contradictions in his beliefs that were preventing him from finding a resolution to his problem consistent with his faith. Philosophy was easily up to the task, and the issue of my own belief or nonbelief in his God was never a factor.

In a more recent case, I was confronted with a question that was clearly religious in nature, and which the client obviously thought was within the scope of philosophy. The client said, "I'd like to ask you some questions about our almighty God: In the beginning, it's written, God's spirit was on earth and we were made in the image of God, and in the New Testament it says that Jesus Christ has a soul. Does this mean God has a soul like we do? Can you also please enlighten me on the difference between soul and spirit and between our spirit and Holy Spirit."

I responded by saying, "My understanding of Christian beliefs is that when Jesus was on earth and had a human body he also had a soul like all humans have. But Christians believe he *is* spirit when in heaven. God also *is* spirit and does not have a soul. Of course things get very complicated if you believe that Jesus and God are one. I learned that when we are told we're made in God's image it means we have God's attributes of love, kindness, compassion, etc. The problem is that I also learned we're all born with original sin, which came from Adam not God. Having been made in God's image seems to me to conflict with being sinful because of one person's actions. When you ask me these questions I'm not sure if you want to know what Christianity says about such matters or what philosophy says. They would give you two different answers. As a philosopher I find many Christian beliefs to be very troublesome and contradictory. That's why believers are asked to simply accept them on faith, which I can't do. I'm not a traditional Christian; I am an agnostic (I'm undecided about what I believe). If you would like to discuss Christian beliefs some more I suggest you talk to a priest or minister. They are better trained to answer theological questions such as yours than I am."

While the questions in the case above have undeniably arisen from the client's religious conviction, in some cases the metaphorical vines of a religious belief can so entangle the client's life story that they will have overgrown and obscured the *philosophical* path that needs to be taken in order to mitigate the problem. To put it another way, a person can become so enraptured by her spiritual community's supernatural ideology that it blinds her to the fact that she still needs to function within the human environment here on earth. This is especially true of the recently converted or "born again" whose spiritual point of view is all-encompassing. Stephen R. Palmquist is associate professor of religion and philosophy at Hong Kong Baptist University and a philosophical counselor. At their first meeting one of his clients said he was deeply religious and this was causing conflict in his personal life. But, as it turned out, his religious beliefs really weren't at the heart of his troubles. His problem was a typical relationship issue. Palmquist therefore suggests that it's important for the philosophical counselor to keep in mind that life problems are not always contingent upon religious beliefs. In a situation where the person's religious beliefs really aren't the source of their problems Palmquist thinks that the responsible counselor "can't do much more than try to help the person *see*, as clearly as possible, what their beliefs really do imply about the situation at hand, and then *act* on that implication. If they do, and the problem is solved, then who are we to say that their (to us) overly-narrow beliefs are bad for them? And if they do and the problem remains unsolved then it brings the person one step closer to a genuine spiritual search."

Philosopher Christopher Borst, who says he practices "the radical challenging of received opinion through community organizing" in Toronto, Canada, thinks that religion is, after all, just a subset of philosophy—the matters involved are often the same matters as elsewhere in philosophy, and the method of counseling involved equally so. Borst argues that the counselor must listen attentively to the client's concerns; he must try to carefully articulate, in as concrete a set of terms as possible, what is really at stake; he must then pose questions to try to identify contradictions between opinions or between opinions and actions; and he must try to resolve such contradictions, sticking as much as possible to the set of opinions, beliefs, or worldview within which they are already working.

Borst provides three examples, one that was not particularly successful, and two that were.

I was speaking with a student. He experienced a great deal of torment over the fact that he masturbated, for he was an Evangelical and had aspirations to the ministry. I found that at that time I had a great deal of difficulty being useful to him, for I found his belief in the immorality of masturbation to be so obviously wrong as to be laughable. Nonetheless, I did try to provide direction to him, suggesting routes of inquiry he might follow, books he might read. Now, however, I can think of many ways in which I could have been much more helpful to him when I spoke to him.

Borst sees his failure in this case located in his "inability (or unwillingness) to see the problem as a problem, to accept the terms in which it could appear as a problem." Borst admits his initially harsh judgment of the client's beliefs prevented him from simply dealing with the client's issues as presented.

In the second case he was speaking with a man who worked in a bank, while putting himself through graduate school, and who understood himself to be a Wiccan priest.

He was disturbed because he felt he had been making the appropriate sacrifices to his patron god, yet was not receiving the largesse in return which he felt was his appropriate due. I had to work my way into the situation via my reflections on Nietzsche and the Iliad (specifically on the notion of nobility), but I was able to bring the discussion around to a reflection on his calling, and his progress within that calling. I posed the suggestion that, since he seemed still to be in his apprenticeship, it was only appropriate that he be experiencing a certain hardship. I suggested that he ought to be mining his experience for the insights it would allow him later on, when he moves into the journeyman stage of his progression.

In a third case Borst was speaking with a woman in the seminary to become a Presbyterian minister.

We had been discussing the various ideas to understanding the way of the Cross. She explained how she was having major problems reconciling her school, its pedagogy, and its curriculum, with her relationship to her children. She felt the formal instruction she was receiving about the way of the Cross neglected its relevance or connection to her daily struggles with her children. I found it particularly easy to turn these ideas back to her and the sufferings she was experiencing, and to point out how she perhaps needed to exemplify God's love in her interactions with both her instructors and her children—and that the whole point of the Cross was that such interactions were inextricable from suffering. Not only did this give her a way of approaching her own actions, it also gave us a context in which to discuss why some of her colleagues might be resistant to the very ideas she had been espousing.

Borst claims that the success in these two cases lay not in any particular religious biases he might have had but in his willingness to delve deeply into the terms in which the client was putting the discussion. In other words, Borst was willing to deal with his client's problems within the client's worldview.

I do not identify myself as either a Wiccan or a Christian, but I was able to work with the conceptual sets which these offer to me. And, this is in many ways the important part: the conceptual sets which were needed were not, ultimately, all that far removed from each other, or all that far removed from anything I had read by any philosopher. We talked about suffering or hardship or how things were going otherwise than they might wish. We talked about what they were trying to achieve, who they really were and what was truly important to them. And we talked about how their particular hardships could be understood as part of what they were trying to achieve, and what they had to do if they were going to approach them in such a manner.

As for a really difficult issue, such as how to counsel a fundamentalist about abortion, Borst recommends the same procedure. Many important questions need to be asked and answered, such as, "What is the issue? Is the person unsure of their own stance, and afraid that this might mean their exclusion from their spiritual community? Are they faced with an unwanted pregnancy? Are they trying to decide whether to participate in protests outside an abortion clinic? And so on. What are their fears, insecurities, and worries about this issue such that they feel it necessary to see a philosophical counselor? What do those fears reveal about their deeper commitments? Are those deeper commitments consistent with their professed beliefs? If not, why not? What *do* they really *believe*? What *do* they really *want*? How can they get that, in general and in the current situation? The answers to these questions and more will ultimately point out a course of action they are likely to feel comfortable with."

But the issues inherent in religious beliefs, and even the personal religious beliefs of the philosophical counselor himself, need not always be hidden or "bracketed" when the counselor is seeing a deeply religious person. In fact, the faith of the counselor may itself be a therapeutic role model to the client. Stephen R. Palmquist claims that his own religious beliefs, rather than being a hindrance to good philosophical counseling, at times actually enhance it. Palmquist enjoys counseling all the more, and finds discussion all the more fruitful, when his client is already open to genuine spiritual searching: "In such cases I find that there is usually little or no issue of interference (with their beliefs) arising. The person has come to me precisely because he or she is already questioning his or her religious beliefs, sees me as someone with a religious background who has gone through (is going through!) such questioning and yet still somehow manages to remain religious, and therefore views me as a potential source of guidance on the road ahead."

But Palmquist warns that the philosophical counselor must be on guard against the danger of inappropriate interference with a client who is in the process of abandoning his current religious convictions, and in search of new ones to replace them.

Sometimes such a person comes with *such* an open mind that he or she might well want to make "a new religion" (in the worst sense of that phrase) out of anything I say. When the client is a very religious (or maybe I should say, a fundamentalist) person, the expectation that the counselor will help him to be more religious or to become more spiritual can be quite dangerous, and the philosophical counselor needs to be careful not to become for the client just a substitute "guru." That is, I can envision a situation where a naturally religious person who, for one reason or another, has become dissatisfied with his traditional beliefs, might come to a philosophical counselor expecting and hoping to have "wisdom imparted." In this case, the counselor could turn herself into the "power-source" that effectively robs the client of the experience of reasoning through the tough issues. For this reason I generally try to avoid anything that could be construed as advice-giving or even truth-preaching.

Dennis Polis agrees. Polis describes himself as "a Catholic and a non-academic philosopher committed to the notion that philosophy can help us lead lives of integrity." He argues that while fundamentalists generally have an anti-intellectual bent that would probably preclude their seeking philosophical counseling, there are many orthodox Christians, Jews and Muslims who may find pastoral counseling inadequate to their needs and who would benefit from philosophical counseling from a philosopher who is open-minded. "I myself was in a position where the religious dimension of my dilemma left a psychiatrically trained counselor without the tools to deal with my case—as she frankly admitted. It was this, coupled with the failure of pastoral counseling, that first caused me to see the need for an alternative type of counseling."

Polis suggests that if the counselor feels she can prove with metaphysical certitude that the client's faith position is incoherent, then she ought to tell the client this, and allow the client to determine whether he wants to proceed along those lines. But he adds that it must be remembered that "the client is typically under considerable intellectual stress from the problem that has initiated the search for help, and so is not entirely in a position to rationally judge what is an attack on his belief system, nor is he in such a state as would allow him to articulate and defend his beliefs as well as he might at some other time. Thus, the potential is there for an intellectually dishonest and ego gratifying victory on the part of a counselor. This would be unethical and must be guarded against."

Assuming that the client decides to proceed, Polis offers some things for the counselor to bear in mind as she formulates an approach to the problem at hand:

(1) Beliefs are not philosophical *per se*. The content of beliefs very often entails matters that cannot be decided philosophically. If the client has chosen to believe that the universe was miraculously created in seven days, we may say that we do not find that view coherent with what we see—but, however unlikely, it is logically possible.

Another way of saying this is that beliefs are not the result of any intellectual vision of the truth of their content, but are instead, like doubts, acts of will. Beliefs are the result of commitments made either by reflective choice or by default. If they are by default, then a philosophic counselor may suggest that their grounds be examined, but ultimately the choice of commitments belongs to the client alone.

(2) The commitments made by a client are part of that client's reality, and need to be

treated as such. If the client is committed to the position that killing a fetus is actual or probable murder, then that is part of the client's moral landscape, and any counselor who chooses to ignore this is simply closing her eyes to this reality.

If the counselor does not share this position, then unless she can prove with metaphysical certitude that it is not murder, it is part of her faith position. As philosophers, we may share our beliefs as to the realities of a case, and our reasons for belief, but we may not actively seek to replace the client's faith position with our own.

(3) While there is one reality, there are many ways in which it can be experienced, and even more ways in which the experience may be articulated. If we recognize this, we can often bridge gaps between the client's belief system and our own by looking for what the client sees that we have not yet seen, or have articulated in a different way. It is much more fruitful to look for the common reality underlying our diverse positions than to look first for errors. Once we are on the same side of the table, sharing diverse experiences of the same reality, then there is the possibility of mutual growth as we each incorporate the other's vision with our own.

Again, taking the abortion issue as an example, Polis points out that if the philosophical counselor is pro-life,

she needs to see that being pro-choice entails a vision of freedom of conscience and moral agency that is well-grounded. If she is pro-choice, she needs to see that being pro-life entails a vision of the value of the individual and of the sacredness of human life that is equally well grounded. In fact, each position is a different articulation of the intrinsic values entailed in being a moral agent. Obviously, if the counselor thinks there is no basis in reality for the client's position, then she will be unable to see any common ground or grow in the client's vision. Similarly, she can offer the client no basis for accepting the vision she offers. If such is the case, she had best disqualify herself and suggest that the client seek help elsewhere.

Philosophical counselors sometimes worry that they will be called on to make sense of the religious tenets their client adheres to which they know to be false, inconsistent over time, or blatantly contradictory. For example, a church may forbid its members to accept blood transfusions as part of their medical care on the basis that it constitutes a sort of God-forbidden cannibalism. And yet that same church may allow its believers to accept organ transplants.[5] If a philosophical counselor were faced with this situation it would prove to be very troubling indeed. But a philosophical counselor will rarely, if ever, be called upon to alleviate confusion over a church's internal and fundamental doctrinal issues. The question of what to do with an apparently contradictory doctrine will only arise when the believer is already in the process of questioning doctrine. The philosophical counselor will then not be expected to help the client end his doubt and strengthen his conviction, but to help build a meaningful life removed from adherence to such troublesome doctrines.

Even when the client and counselor know that their separate deeply held convictions clash with each other, there are times when the client asks to know exactly what the counselor personally believes about some issue and why. Rather than being a cause for concern, the counselor's unhesitating truthfulness and unreserved openness in such a moment can offer the suffering client the comfort of an authentic connection with a caring and thoughtful human being whose beliefs are not simply based on faith alone.[6] Stephen Palmquist says he often shares his own religious experiences with his clients, and finds doing so very rewarding. "When the client sees that it is possible for one person to question their fundamental beliefs to the very core and yet still perceive life as meaningful, it tends to fill them with courage to pursue their *own* course more wholeheartedly."

But while working with religiously devout clients may be rewarding for some philosophical counselors it may also present an issue for which most philosophers are not very well prepared. The religious beliefs of some individuals lead them to understand their dreams as being messages from a spiritual source, and they may want to discuss these dreams with a philosopher. Not only have philosophers rarely dealt with the issue of the religious content of dreams, they also have for the most part avoided the topic of dreams altogether. This raises the question, What should a philosophical counselor make of his client's dreams?

NOTES

1. Georg Wilhelm Friedrich Hegel makes a similar point in his *Lectures on the Philosophy of Religion*. R. F. Brown et al., trans. Peter C. Hodgson, ed. Berkeley: University of California Press, 1988. 77–80.

2. Quoted comments from Tim LeBon, Stephen R. Palmquist, Christopher Borst, and Dennis Polis are from personal e-mails to the author and are used with permission.

3. James, William. *The Varieties of Religious Experience* (1902). New York: Penguin, 1958. 53.

4. Raabe, Peter B. *Philosophical Counseling: Theory and Practice.* Westport, Conn.: Praeger, 2001. 137–142.

5. This was the official position of Jehovah's Witnesses at the time this chapter was written.

6. For a detailed discussion of this issue see the chapter titled "On Professional Neutrality" in my book *Philosophical Counseling: Theory and Practice.*

Chapter 19

Dream Interpretation

I know I am not dreaming right now. I can say this without the slightest doubt. People who are not ill or on medication are easily able to determine confidently and correctly whether they are dreaming or awake. It's only academic philosophy instructors who still goad their students into spending hours agonizing over this so-called problem of epistemology. The philosopher who is perhaps the best known for his struggle with the question of how he could be sure whether he was asleep or awake was seventeenth-century French philosopher René Descartes. He put it this way in his *Meditations*:

How often has it happened to me that in the night I dreamt that I found myself in this particular place, that I was dressed and seated near the fire, whilst in reality I was lying undressed in bed! At this moment it does indeed seem to me that it is with eyes awake that I am looking at this paper; that this head which I move is not asleep, that it is deliberately and of set purpose that I extend my hand and perceive it; what happens in sleep does not appear so clear nor so distinct as does all this. But in thinking over this I remind myself that on many occasions I have in sleep been deceived by similar illusions, and in dwelling carefully on this reflection I see so manifestly that there are no certain indications by which we may clearly distinguish wakefulness from sleep that I am lost in astonishment. And my astonishment is such that it is almost capable of persuading me that I now dream.[1]

Gottfried Wilhelm Leibniz, a German philosopher of the same century, reflected Descartes' skeptical position when he asked rhetorically, "What prevents the course of our life from being a long and well-ordered dream, a dream from which we could be awakened at any moment?"[2]

At first glance the apparent credibility of the idea that life is just a long dream (or "an unusually persistent and recurrent nightmare," as British philosopher Bertrand Russell put it[3]) can send a frigid finger of existential terror up the spine of any philosophy freshman. But once neophyte students have been given the freedom and accepted the responsibility of thinking for themselves, rather than simply having to memorize what reputed experts have said, many of them quickly consider Descartes' epic epistemic struggle a rather silly academic exercise that is not worthy of further consideration. Other students, after more careful reflection and discussion, judge his declaration—that there are no certain indications by which we may clearly distinguish the state of being awake from being asleep—to be a remarkably hasty conclusion which is obviously false. They point out that dreams are often brief, chaotic, and fantastic worlds whose erratic events defy logic and causal relationships, and lack the kind of continuity and predictability we can depend on in waking life (Descartes also came to this conclusion, but not until his "Sixth Meditation"). They argue that, while there are times when a dream may seem real enough, in fact most dreams don't seem real at all, and that if you say all of life is a dream just because last night's dream seemed real then you are drawing an unwarranted conclusion and making a hasty generalization. What is often far more interesting to students of philosophy, and to most other people as well, than the question of how they can be sure they are not living a life trapped within a dream is the question of why they have dreams in the first place, and what their dreams might mean.

Despite the fact that there has been a great deal written about the function and interpretation of dreams in academic psychology books and journals, in science and medical journals, in so-called New Age publications, and in the self-help manuals of popular psychology, philosophers generally appear reluctant to venture into this territory.[4] Sigmund Freud said at one time that it is vain to expect philosophy to yield information about dreams.[5] He then succeeded in putting such a powerfully paradigmatic psychological stamp on dreams that many of today's philosophers and philosophical counselors are worried that if they show even the slightest professional curiosity about their clients' dreams, or if they discuss the theories of dream interpretation with any sort of enthusiasm, they will be accused of having abandoned "real" philosophy (this actually happened to me when I gave a public seminar on this topic). But if philosophy is the attempt to come to a better understanding of the complexities of human life, and sleep and its dreams are a significant part of that life, then why can't an inquiry into dreams be part of modern philosophy?

Perhaps the best approach for arriving at how a philosophical counselor might interpret the enigmatic contents of a client's dreams is to begin by systematically investigating the most significant theories that have been formulated to explain them. Therefore, the first section below briefly examines what some of the earlier philosophers had to say about dreams. The second and third sections summarize the familiar theories formulated by Freud and Jung respectively, and highlight some of the critical weaknesses and limitations inherent in each. The fourth section then presents the clinical findings of sleep and dream researcher Ernest Hartman, and explains why Hartman's lesser known theory of dream interpretation is a more empirically sound alternative on which to base philosophical counseling. And finally, the fifth section discusses how to integrate Hartman's conception into actual practice.

1. WHAT IS A DREAM?

In order for the examination of anything to make sense, especially when that examination is meant to produce a theory of meaning, it is first of all necessary to understand what the nature and function are of the items under examination. Philosophers have spent relatively little time discussing dreams. For example, *The Oxford Companion to Philosophy* allows only 2½ column inches for the subject of dreams, consisting of three unanswered questions (it gives the same amount of space to the subject "snow is white"), while on the other hand devoting a full 15 pages to academic logic.[6] Macmillan's classic eight-volume *Encyclopedia of Philosophy* allots only slightly over two pages to the topic of dreams but logic-related essays span a massive 150 pages over two volumes.[7] And yet a much larger portion of our lives is taken up by our engagement in the mysteriously private, and yet biologically necessary, activity of dreaming than in puzzling over the complexities of formal logic. Are dreams being treated by philosophers the way our tonsils were treated by physicians at one time, when they were dismissed as mostly vestigial and generally unnecessary for human well-being? Or are dreams simply too mysterious, too impenetrable, for philosophers who feel the subject is better left to empirical scientists, clinical psychologists, and shamans?

The discussion of dreams has not been avoided by all philosophers. The ancient Greek philosopher Plato postulated that dreams are "residual motion" from waking life when we have fallen asleep. Such motion engenders "visions within us, . . . which are remembered by us when we are awake and in the external world."[8] Plato's student Aristotle agreed that a dream is a kind of phantasmic vision, "a presentation based on the movement of sense impressions."[9] Yet in order to differentiate the illusory dreams of the average human being from the revelatory dreams of those claiming to be prophets, seers, and messengers from the gods, Aristotle simply called ordinary dreaming a kind of imagination which occurs in sleep. But Plato went further still, noting that dreams are not as innocent as a person's waking imagination. For him dreams indicated that "there exists in every one of us, even in some reputed most respectable, a terrible, fierce, and lawless brood of desires, which it seems are revealed in our sleep."[10] For Plato, then, dreams were a rather nasty exhibition of the unspoken desires of even the most respected members of his society; unspoken because these were not just ordinary desires, they were a "terrible, fierce, and lawless brood."

Thomas Aquinas (said to be the greatest philosopher-theologian in medieval times) believed that dreams are partly caused by memories of what the dreamer felt and thought while awake, partly by internal and external stimuli occurring while the dreamer is asleep, and partly by God or demons influencing the dreamer's imagination. Aquinas held that dreams sometimes influence future events and may therefore be used by the dreamer to choose an appropriate course of action, and that at other times dreams can actually foretell what is fated to happen in the real world regardless of what the dreamer may choose to do while awake. While Aquinas wisely recommended that it would be advisable to rely only on those dreams that are of divine origin, he failed to suggest a serviceable methodology for accurately determining which dreams are divine and which are demonic.[11]

Writing some 400 years later, during the period of history in which the authority of scientific empiricism was beginning to seriously overshadow the authority of religious ideology, British philosopher John Locke proposed that dreams are not at all visions from God or demons. In Locke's opinion dreams are "for the most part, frivolous and irrational" because they are simply "made up of the waking man's ideas, though, for the most part, oddly put together."[12]

These three theories of dreams—Plato's belief that dreams are a kind of exhibition of dark desires, Aquinas' belief that they are imagination influenced by God or demons, and Locke's belief that they are frivolous nonsense—sum up the predominant theories of dreams still held today. The most important question for the practice of philosophical counseling is, Are any of these theories appropriate as an approach to the interpretation of dreams presented by a client in a philosophical counseling situation? And if not one of these then what?

It goes without saying that the most precarious approach is the one that holds dreams to be somehow connected with the supernatural or paranormal. It is, first of all, imprudent from a pragmatic perspective because it may lead a counselor to help a client base an important decision or action on what is believed to be a message from God that turns out in fact to be demonic. Second, it is reckless from a scientific perspective in that the counselor simply assumes the supernatural nature of dreams, which is an assumption that has not yet been rigorously tested and proven to be true. The current body of research evidence concerning the paranormal powers of dreams—such as the ability of dreams to foretell the future, communicate with the dead, or view distant locations—is still intensely controversial and convincingly inconclusive. This is not to say that dreams are never supernatural, only that philosophical counselors do not work in that area.

2. SIGMUND FREUD

The theory that dreams are the release of "a terrible, fierce, and lawless brood of desires" which are normally held in check during waking hours may have been first suggested by Plato before the Christian era, but it was brought into prominence by a nineteenth-century neurologist and psychopathologist named Sigmund Freud. However, Freud went beyond Plato in that he did not stop at merely trying to identify the function of dreams; he developed a theory, or actually two theories, of how this "brood" of dreams are to be interpreted. A number of different approaches have been developed by psychotherapists for the interpretation of dreams, such as Jungian analysis, Gestalt techniques, the body feeling approach, and others, but the methods developed by Freud were the first and are considered foundational to all other methods.

According to Freud dreams are messages from an area of the mind—the unconscious—that is completely concealed from, and inaccessible to, the individual when she is awake. Freud postulated that most dreams have two aspects to them: the *manifest* dream content, which is the images, sounds, and emotions of the dream experienced by the dreamer, and the *latent* dream content, which is the deeper meaning hidden within the dream's maze of symbols. Because he defined the unconscious as inaccessible to the dreamer, Freud was able to maintain that to understand the latent content of a dream it is necessary for the dreamer to consult an expert who can unlock its secrets with a special interpretive "key." It is interesting to note that Freud's interpretation of his patients' dreams was not a new invention. In fact it was a revival of a very old tradition that harks back to at least ancient Biblical times. Both Joseph and Daniel of the Hebrew Scriptures or Old Testament presented themselves as having God-given interpretive skills that would let them explain the meaning of the symbolic features of other people's dreams.[13] But Freud's approach was unique in that he claimed to have developed a means of dream interpretation that did not rely on divine inspiration. Freud claimed that his method was scientific, which is a claim no one before him had ever dreamed of making.

For Freud the *manifest* content of a dream always acts like a screen which blocks or censors its substantive core. The *latent* content of a dream is almost always, according to Freud, a forbidden childhood desire (predominantly sexual in nature) that has been hidden in the unconscious.[14] This means that "the interpretation of dreams is the royal road to a knowledge of the unconscious activities of the mind."[15] To get at these unconscious activities Freud taught his followers to use two very different "keys": free association and translation of what he believed to be the archetypal or universal symbols found in all dreams.

Unfortunately, there are several major problems with Freud's approach. First, regarding dreams themselves, there is what Freud himself cited as the problem of "dream-distortion," or "disagreeable" or "counter-wish" dreams. These are dreams whose manifest content is distressing and which display events clearly contrary to those the dreamer would actually wish to experience. Freud explained these in several ways. At first he wrote that disagreeable dream content "serves only to disguise the thing wished for. . . . Dream-distortion proves in reality to be an act of censorship." According to this explanation a wish hides within a dream within a disguise, and requires the dream analyst to examine first the disguise and then the dream it disguises in order to ferret out the wish that the dreamer wants fulfilled. A few pages later Freud claimed that the seeming contradiction of his wish-fulfillment theory can be explained "with the principle that the non-fulfillment of one wish signified the fulfillment of another." As an example he offered the instance of one of his patients who dreams what she would never wish for: traveling with her mother-in-law to a place they would both spend the summer. When she told this dream to Freud as a counter-example to his wish-fulfillment theory, Freud argued that the dream "was her wish that I should be wrong, and this wish the dream showed her as fulfilled." In this sort of case, according to Freud, a "counter-wish dream" is just symptomatic of the patient's state of neurotic resistance to his psychoanalytic investigations. But then again a distressing dream, such as one in which the dreamer is the victim of brutal violence, may merely *seem* to contain "unwished-for content," wrote Freud, while in fact it may be "nothing more than wish-fulfillments, which satisfy their [the dreamer's] masochistic inclinations. . . . Even dreams with a painful content are to be analyzed as wish-fulfillments."[16] Counter-wish dreams then, according to Freud, are not at all counter-evidence against his wish-fulfillment theory of dreams, and this can be easily proven by going not only behind the manifest dream to its latent wish, but behind its latent wish as well, that is, behind the latent dream's "disguise," during the psychoanalytic process. The question this raises is, can the disguised latent dream content itself be disguised, and so on, in an absurd infinite regress?

Regarding the interpretation of dreams, in the method which Freud called "free association," and which he first documented in 1900, the patient is asked to simply say whatever comes to mind. The patient is encouraged to resist self-censorship, to "eliminate the critical spirit in which he is ordinarily in the habit of viewing such thoughts," to consider himself as having "but one task—that of suppressing criticism," and to relate even what may seem absurd, unrelated, or embarrassing.[17] The patient is asked to report on each separate element in the dream so that the analyst may work backward through a chain of associations to the original material that is believed to have formed the dream. Elements of the dream that come up repeatedly in the form of recurring thoughts or wishes are what Freud refers to as the latent dream that is buried in the dreamer's subconscious. The unearthing of this latent dream is the revelation of the dreamer's desires and wish-fulfillment fantasies.

One of the problems with this method of dream interpretation is that many people find it exceedingly difficult to adopt the particular attitude which is required to articulate their freely rising ideas. The act of free association at the heart of psychoanalytic dream interpretation is not an easy feat—although Freud argued that it is not difficult to learn.[18] Second, the process of free association can be absolutely endless. Saying everything that comes to mind about every element of a dream can lead to an overwhelmingly disparate, and ultimately discouraging, amount of material. The third, and perhaps most troublesome, problem is that free association may bring to the patient's mind thoughts that don't necessarily constitute the thoughts and material that originally formed the dream. Many factors other than the dream's content may be intruding on the patient's thoughts at the time he is reporting on his dream such as his mood on that day, his feelings about the therapist, some recent annoyance, and so on.

Freud's other approach to dreams, which he developed from 1909 to 1914, is based on the idea of universal or archetypal dream symbolism. Freud maintained that the relationship between dream elements and symbols is constant. This facilitates the translation process so efficiently that the dreamer may simply be left out of the interpretation process altogether.[19] Among the most common imagery Freud found universally in all dreams was sexual symbolism. He wrote that

All elongated objects, sticks, tree-trunks, umbrellas (on account of the opening, which might be likened to an erection), all sharp and elongated weapons, knives, daggers, and pikes, represent the male member. A frequent, but not very intelligible symbol for the same is a nail-file (a reference to rubbing and scraping?).—Small boxes, chests, cupboards, and ovens correspond to the female organ; also cavities, ships, and all kinds of vessels.—A room in a dream generally represents a woman; the description of its various entrances and exits is scarcely calculated to make us doubt this interpretation.[20]

This method of symbol interpretation raises the question of whether in the interpretation of, say, sexual imagery the analyst is correct in making the concretistic or simple symbol-to-organ translation Freud advocates. In other words, how does the analyst differentiate those times when a dream about an umbrella symbolizes a male sexual organ and when it is simply a dream about an umbrella? Furthermore, problems can arise when the analyst takes into account not only the dream's symbolism but also its supposed inherent wish-fulfilling function. When a female client dreams of an umbrella is this to be interpreted as her having unconscious wishes about some other individual's male sexual organ, or her unconscious wish to have such an organ of her own? Or when various male clients dream of an umbrella does it necessarily signify homosexual wish-fulfillment fantasies in *all* of those clients?

Despite its inherent problems, the interpretation of dream symbolism has become very popular among the general public. Hundreds of so-called dream dictionaries have been published which catalogue thousands of stereotyped interpretations of dream motifs claiming to reveal their hidden meanings. They are sold as the keys that allow for effortless dream interpretation with the highly incredible implicit claim that, just like a single horoscope is accurate for millions of individuals worldwide, likewise, an umbrella has the same sexual meaning in every culture and for every person in whose dream it may appear. Of course the irony of these dream dictionaries, like the irony inherent in published horoscopes, is that the meanings which various dream dictionaries attribute to a particular symbol often blatantly contradict one another.

An additional element of Freudian dream interpretation, related more to free association than to dream symbolism, involves what has been called the anagrammatic approach. This is a process whereby the individual concepts and words connected with dream imagery are meticulously scrutinized by the analyst. For example, in their book about Freud, professor Nicholas Rand and psychoanalyst Maria Torok attempt to prove that the rather obvious inconsistencies and contradictions in Freud's model of psychoanalysis were caused by his deeply unconscious struggle with an unresolved trauma that he experienced as a nine-year-old boy: the arrest of an uncle for counterfeiting and the scandal this brought to the Freud family name. Rand and Torok proceed to reanalyze one of Freud's own dreams, which he originally analyzed himself. They claim to demonstrate where he is wrong in the interpretation of his own dream's imagery in order to prove their point.

It is important to bear in mind that the 52-year-old Freud had a severe nicotine addiction (he would eventually undergo numerous surgical procedures to remove malignant tumors from his palate), and he often suffered physically from the discomfort and pain of hemorrhoids. In the preface to the second edition of his book

The Interpretation of Dreams Freud also explains that he had undertaken his self-analysis in October of 1896 in reaction to his father's death earlier that same year. In his nightmare he observed

a dissection of the lower part of my own body, my pelvis and legs. . . . The pelvis had been eviscerated, and it was visible now in its superior now in its inferior aspect, the two being mixed together. Thick flesh-coloured protuberances (which, in the dream itself made me think of hemorrhoids) could be seen. Something which lay over it and was like crumpled silver-paper had also to be carefully fished out.[21]

By using a classical Freudian anagrammatic approach to this dream Rand and Torok argue that Freud's dream suggests the following interpretation:

The crumpled *silver-paper*—to be "fished out," in the original German, to be carefully pieced together one by one (= *ausklauben*)—leads us to the like-sounding *syllable* (in German, silver = *Silber*: *Silbe* = syllable). Did the dream's syllables get crumpled or mixed up? Did the words describing Freud's self-dissection condense other words concerning his family's counterfeiting affair? The German names of the two bones that make up the pelvis, on which Freud chose to operate, are no doubt telling about Uncle Josef's impact on the family: a *cross* and a *shame* (sacrum = *Kreuz*bein: cross bone; innominate bone = *Scham*bein: shame bone). Freud's self-analytical operation seems to hover around these hidden thoughts. If, in this immediate context, we piece together the syllables describing Freud's self-dissection, they very closely approximate the words *false* or counterfeit *banknotes*. We interpret the German original as follows: Freud operates on his legs = *Beine*, his pelvic *bone* = *Beine*, and *flesh*-colored = *fleisch*-rote = flesh red protuberances = *Kno*llen. These syllables yield bein-fleisch-kn-ote-n; unscrambled, they are nearly identical in pronunciation, through *fleisch*: *falsch* = false and *Bein*: *Ban*, to *falsche Ban-kn-ote-n*: *false* or *counterfeit bank notes*.[22]

It seems incredibly far-fetched to imagine that Freud's unconscious was hiding this important message from him like some sort of backward masking on the soundtracks of his mind, and then leaking only cryptic hints about it through his dreams.[23] It is more likely that Rand and Torok found the meaning they wanted to find, something like discovering a face in a cloud. Yes, of course the face is there in the cloud, but the impetus for it being there is located in the observer, not in the cloud. Naturally, if we were to believe that the unconscious does in fact leak such ambiguous clues about what the mind keeps hidden from its owner, then that would prove to be a convenient justification for the existence of psychoanalysts who claim exclusive expertise in their discovery and interpretation. Granted, Rand and Torok present their fantastic interpretation as only a possibility; they make no claim to hard evidence that would prove them correct. A more plausible approach to interpreting Freud's dream, however, would be to keep in mind that Freud was not only dealing with the anguish of having lost his father, he was also attempting what no one had ever done before: a self-examination of the very intimate material in his personal dreams by means of a controversial form of analysis which he was still developing. He knew this "self-dissection" would expose to his colleagues and to the public at large not only his nascent psychoanalytic method but, in a sense, his own interior (cognitive and affective) mechanisms. Again, Freud was struggling with a severe nicotine addiction and the physical pain of hemorrhoids. These issues in Freud's life at middle age easily lead to the conclusion that perhaps a more credible interpretation of his dream is that it simply represented his emotional concerns about both his own mortality (due to the death of his father) and his physical problems in combination with the metaphorical "opening up" inherent in the publication of his pioneering attempt at self-analysis.

Then again, perhaps Freud's dream was just so much nonsense, as Locke would have it. But the theory that dreams are just random nonsense is also counterintuitive. There are often times in which the dreamer is easily able to recognize in retrospect the people in his dreams as those individuals he came into contact with during the previous day; or the dreamer may recognize the story line of his dream as having a close resemblance to the plot of a movie he watched before going to sleep; and so on. These dream elements would not be nonsense at all to the dreamer. They would be something more like recent, although somewhat jumbled, memories. Freud himself acknowledges that while a dream may bring to light memories of early childhood, "the dream clearly prefers the impressions of the last few days."[24] Even those dreams whose imagery is extremely bizarre often seem to have an obvious connection to the people or events of the dreamer's waking life. For example, I had a very vivid dream recently in which I was approaching a female bird resembling an eagle sitting on a branch in a nondescript environment. The bird was covered in small but very heavy brass plates which it was struggling, and failing, to remove with its beak. When I tried to help it pick the armor plates off its back it turned and pecked my hand. I tried several times but the bird persisted in trying to peck me. I finally gave up, at which point I woke up from the dream. At first this odd bird perched in a nonidentifiable context seemed like a typically nonsensical and very bizarre dream image indeed. But it was not at all nonsense, and neither was it necessary to interpret the bird in terms of universal symbolism. It was simply a matter of recognizing the feelings I was dealing with in that dream in relation to events of the previous day. My struggle with the bird had felt very similar to the real-life struggle I was experiencing with a troubled client. She was coming to see me for help in sorting out her problems but after several visits she continued to keep me at a distance from her by remaining closed and defensive. This seemed like a perfectly reasonable interpretation to me, and because I understood the imagery in this way the dream certainly did not appear to be either symbolic or random nonsense. The dream helped me to decide to be less insistent in offering my help. Naturally, for a follower of Freud, the question remains, Could there not also be a deeper meaning to this dream that I have overlooked?

Today the views that Freud held regarding dreams and their interpretation are, for the most part, no longer taken seriously by professionals. Many psychotherapists and most experts in sleep and dream research no longer believe, as Freud did, that dreams are irrational or psychotic mental products, that they are the royal road to the unconscious, that every dream is the fulfillment of a childhood wish (typically sexual), that they are disguised products of psychical censorship,[25] that there is a latent dream underlying each manifest dream that needs to be interpreted by an expert (by means of free association, the decoding of universal symbols, or anagrammatic deciphering), that dreams are rife with sexual symbolism, and that the function of dreams is to preserve sleep.[26] But if not according to Freud's model, then how are dreams to be understood?

3. CARL JUNG

One of Freud's best-known disciples, and one of his earliest critics, Carl G. Jung, held a far less sinister view of both the unconscious and the content of dreams. Jung believed that not all dreams are the fulfillment of repressed forbidden childhood sexual wishes as Freud had claimed. Similar to Plato's claim that dreams are "residual motion" from waking life, Jung held that dreams are due to "an incomplete extinction of consciousness."[27] They are not one-sided in either form or content but lend themselves to many different readings of their "text" which can only be successfully accomplished through the combined efforts of the interpreter and the dreamer. Yet Jung agreed with Freud that "average" dreams have a personal character reflecting the dreamer's conscious impressions of day-time activities, and "deep" dreams derive directly from unconscious sources. But according to Jung, deep dreams have a collective character; they are composed of a rich tapestry of symbolic images derived from a "universal unconscious" which contains archaic elements of primitive myths and religions, which he designated "archetypes." For Jung these archetypal images "prove that the human psyche is unique and subjective or personal only in part, and for the rest is collective and objective."[28] As well as common archetypal elements, dreams also contain typical dream motifs such as flying, climbing stairs or mountains, being naked in public, losing teeth, being chased by frightening animals or ghosts, and so on.

Jung observed that a succession of similar dreams can often run into the hundreds and that they "resemble the successive steps in a planned and orderly process of development." He reasoned therefore that these dream-series were "a kind of development process in the personality," the spontaneous expression within the unconscious of the dreamer's individuation. By "individuation" he meant the process of "becoming a single, homogeneous being," a "coming to self-hood or self-realization," "of psychological development . . . in which a man becomes the definite unique being that he in fact is."[29] The function of the dreams themselves in this process of individuation is to counterbalance the individual's conscious attitude held during waking life, so that if the conscious attitude to a life situation is positive while awake then the dream takes the negative side and vice versa. A dream is thereby a compensatory mechanism which aims "at establishing a normal psychological balance and thus appears as a kind of self-regulation of the psychic system." The essential aspect of the "dream action," according to Jung, is "a sort of finely attuned compensation of the one-sidedness, errors, deviations, or other shortcomings of the conscious attitude." The dream may therefore either "repudiate the dreamer in a most painful way, or bolster him up morally."[30]

Interestingly Jung was one of the first psychologists to emphasize the importance of the extreme emotional content of many dreams. But he suggested that emotions in dreams can be understood only by keeping in mind that a deeply meaningful dream generally deals with *collective* emotions, that it is "a typical situation full of affect" which is not primarily a personal experience but rather a *universal* human problem that has forced itself upon the dream's consciousness.[31]

The problem for Jung's etiological claims of dream origins is twofold: first, it is not at all self-evident that because the dreams of people of different cultures, or people of the same culture but of different generations, contain within them what appear to be similar images of gods or demons this means their dreams necessarily spring from a collective unconscious in which the memories of past generations and all cultures are stored. Other, far simpler, explanations are available. For example, evolutionary psychology and evolutionary epistemology maintain that shared biological experiences have produced in human beings a common understanding of the world despite their superficial cultural differences. This has led diverse civilizations to postulate analogous gods and demons to explain the universal occurrences of natural phenomena and human suffering. This existentially generated explanation seems far more plausible than the extravagant ontological proposition that there exists a universal or collective unconscious. Second, there is an inherent, and possibly unresolvable, epistemological difficulty when attempts are made to differentiate between which images ought to be understood as the experiential and intimately personal contents of a dream and which as the universal or collective archetypal symbols. Once this is accomplished—if indeed it can be—there exists the further psychological difficulty of explaining how the dreamer benefits from the so-called counterbalancing effects of the various elements of his dreams. Finally, Jung states categorically that without the unconscious, "the dream is a mere freak of nature, a meaningless conglomeration of fragments left over from the day. . . . We cannot treat our theme (the practical use of dream analysis) at all unless we recognize the unconscious."[32] But this clearly begs the question whether this either/or dichotomy is in fact necessary, whether, without the unconscious, dreams are in fact just "a meaningless conglomeration of fragments left over from the day."

At the end of his work on dreams, Jung acknowledged that although the study of dream psychology had contributed substantially to his understanding of far-reaching philosophical and religious problems, he did not yet possess a generally satisfying explanatory theory of this complicated phenomenon.

4. THE PHILOSOPHY OF DREAMS

There is a significant gap between popular conceptions of what dreams are all about—based on a lay reading of Freud's and Jung's theories—and what modern research is revealing. The director of the Sleep Disorders Center at Newton-Wellesley Hospital in Massachusetts and professor of psychiatry Ernest Hartmann offers a perspective based on many years of his own empirical and clinical research. The conclusions he reaches not only seem more intuitively correct when applied to one's own dreams but also are much more compatible with philo-sophical counseling than the other approaches to dream interpretation discussed above.[33] Hartmann maintains that his own research and the work of other special-ists in the field clearly indicate that dreams are not crazy or random meaningless brain noises, or some form of psychical and symbolic hints concerning previously censored obscene desires stored in the cryptic unconscious which only a highly trained expert in psychology can decipher.[34] Dreams can in fact be explained in a very simple and practical way.

Hartmann suggests that the mind is best imagined as a widespread net, or a net-work, within which there are specific regions that are more tightly organized be-cause they contain well-learned material. This material is stored as memory by means of various interconnections throughout the net. This net, like the ocean, is never absolutely still; it is always busy making connections to some degree, and never completely calm except perhaps in some deeply meditative states. Though continuously active, it is also always trying to settle itself into a condition of least agitation, that is, a relatively calm or stable condition with a minimum amount of disturbance. But because of the constant unsettling inputs from various kinds of external events, especially trauma, stress, and emotional concerns, the calming process is never quite complete and the net requires ongoing ministration. Particu-larly strong emotional concerns, such as the breakup of a significant relationship, a career-threatening workplace confrontation, having to make a major life-directing decision, financial difficulties, or a serious health problem are like localized storms on this net that affect not only a person's wakeful thinking and imaginings but her dreams as well.[35] In the natural world the severity of a storm is diminished, and its potential to cause damage is reduced, if it becomes somehow less concen-trated, that is, if it becomes diffused over a greater area. This is somewhat analo-gous to what dreams do in the mental world.

Dreams, according to Hartmann, make connections guided by the dreamer's emotions and emotional concerns in the "nets of the mind." This is not radically different from the theories of Freud and Jung which state that it is the most power-fully emotional daytime events that most often occur again in dreams.[36] But Hartmann argues that dreaming makes use of our visual/spatial picturing abilities and, rather than being symbolic guides to what is hidden in the unconscious, dreams provide *explanatory metaphors* for the dreamer's emotional state of mind. The difference is that a metaphorical image is meant only as a comparison or an analogy, while a symbolic image is meant to definitely represent something else. Hartmann maintains that people's dreams are simply the mind's metaphorical pic-tures about what is important to them, what they *feel* strongly about. Dreams typi-cally consist of very odd combinations of backgrounds, foregrounds, characters, time periods, childhood memories, recent memories, and real and fictional plots. As Jung puts it, dreams bring together "the most heterogeneous things."[37] But the pictures in dreams are not meant as simple entertainment.[38] Hartmann says the seemingly random dream process serves an important purpose.

The making of connections simultaneously smoothes out disturbances in the mind by integrating new material—"calming out the storm"—and also produces more and broader connections by weaving in new material. It does not simply consolidate memory, but interweaves and increases memory connections.[39]

In other words, the etiology of a dream becomes evident when its two practical functions are understood: first, a dream reduces the localized storms caused by the emotions which were experienced while awake by *diffusing* them across a wide area of connections, and second, these connections to other memories are the mind's attempt to better *understand* those events in waking life which caused the heightened emotions in the first place in order to reduce their negative impact when the dreamer is awake.[40] This teleological theory of dreams is corroborated by a number of other clinicians and researchers. For example, dream researchers Ramon Greenberg and Chester Pearlman in Boston have added their study of Rapid Eye Movement (REM) sleep to earlier research findings. Concerning function, they suggest that the dream is the dreamer's effort to cope with a currently meaningful issue, and they emphasize especially that it is clearly an attempt to solve a current problem. Their studies also suggest that there is an important role for dreams in the mind's attempt to deal with emotionally important situations.[41]

The following example illustrates how a dream will draw from waking events with strong emotional content, located under various "headings" in the memory, and then recombine them in order to diffuse their impact on the dreamer: my wife and I watched a program on TV which I found very troubling about male inmates who were pleading with prison officials for their early parole; I struggled all day to get the wording of one chapter of this book just right; on the late evening news we were told the disturbing story of a woman in hospital who had to give birth to her premature baby by herself because the nurses and doctors, for some reason, had ignored her cries for help; and just before going to bed I looked at my inadequate notes for the class I'd be teaching the next day and worried about how to improve them. One of my dreams that night—the one I recalled most clearly after waking up—was about my being a teacher to only two male students, one of whom was pregnant and was pleading with me because he seemed to be going into agonizing labor.

At first the dream seemed rather silly, but the elements in it from the previous day are actually fairly obvious (when you know what to look for): I am a teacher, and the dream that I had only two students was probably due to my actual concern over my poor class notes; the real-life inmates who were pleading in front of the parole board supplied the image of the pleading student; and the birthing elements could have been furnished by the "birthing pains" I was feeling over the chapter of my book I had been working on, but are probably better interpreted much more simply as the actual story of the woman in hospital. So what may at first have seemed like a totally nonsensical dream actually reflected and dealt with a number of somewhat stressful events from the day before. Medard Boss, professor of psychotherapy at the medical school of the University of Zurich, studied a series of 823 dreams of one of his patients over three years of therapy and found that they closely resembled the patient's mode of existence in waking life. Boss wrote that dreams are *revelations* of existence and not concealments; they "are an *un*covering, and *un*veiling and never a covering up or a veiling of psychic content."[42]

According to Hartmann's theory dreams may be considered a coping strategy, or even a form of self-therapy. Fear and anxiety appear to be overall the most common emotions reported in dreams, and when there are several competing concerns in waking life the individual's dreams will tend to deal primarily with the most serious one.[43] Dreams are palliative care. They ameliorate both physical and emotional suffering by reducing the violence or intensity of the mental impressions of waking experiences. They are the therapy of strong emotions, especially ongoing negative emotions which can contribute to serious physical problems, such as ulcers, heart disease, a weakening of the immune system, digestive disturbances, and even what psychotherapists call mental illness, if they are left unresolved. Dreams are the antibodies of the mind; they are the mind's way of reducing the toxic effects of strong emotions that were felt but left unexpressed, or that were simply too complex and confusing to resolve during waking hours. They are an integral and essential part of the self-restoration and self-preservation mechanisms the human body has developed. They may be related to the automatic self-preservation system which causes a person to descend into unconsciousness when any sort of suffering becomes overwhelming and unbearable. In fact individuals who are suffering from severe emotional stress often have the urge to go to sleep, and then remain asleep far longer than the norm. From this perspective dreaming can be understood to be a much more positive and restorative life experience than presented in the model of the rather secretive and sinister unconscious formulated by Freud. Hartmann also points out that a dream does not need to be analyzed by the dreamer in order for it to have a restorative effect. Even when a dream is forgotten—which they frequently are—that dream has already performed its therapeutic function of diffusing strong negative emotions and reducing the sort of stress that would ultimately prove physically or mentally harmful to the dreamer.[44]

While they work to preserve both the physical and mental health of the dreamer, dreams can only express the dreamer's emotional state and the state of his mind "in terms of the language available in the neural nets as they function in the dreaming, auto-associative mode—visual-spatial imagery and picture metaphor."[45] Again, there is an important distinction to be noted between Hartmann's views and the views of psychotherapists who speak of Freudian "dream symbolism." Hartmann does not claim that the dream translates one object or stimulus into another, or that the unconscious mind produces a concretistic, and Freudian, object-to-object symbolism as an intentional or active concealment of true meaning. Hartmann maintains that his research, and the recent work of other sleep researchers, indicates that the dreaming mind, in dealing with the current emotionally important state, typically uses metaphoric pictures because that just is the language in which it operates.[46]

Another good example of dreams working with the dreamer's daytime emotions—or in response to the suppression of those emotions—is the experience of one of my clients who told me, "In many of my dreams I'm angry. When I'm awake I work hard at controlling my emotions. I was taught to never let my anger show. But when I've held my anger in during the day with some person I'll often meet that same person in my dreams, or just that person's head, and in some very bizarre places, and I find myself arguing very loudly with them. And I'll sometimes even wake myself up because while I'm in the dream argument, and fast asleep, I'll yell something right out loud and it wakes me up. I think I wake myself up because I feel very uncomfortable arguing even in my dreams. In my dreams I often become very emotional, which is something I never allow myself to do while I'm awake."

The recognition that she often does in dreams what she considers wrong to do in waking life helped this client to begin to identify some of the problematic restrictions she and others had placed on her need for the expression of strong emotions. In this case, with the help of a philosophical counselor, the dream brought to light for the client an issue that would prove to be of central importance in the philosophical inquiry into her unhappy life without the need to search for symbols. In a sense this dream had already presented to the client an answer to the question which I was only able to ask her several sessions later: What is troubling you? It seems reasonable to generalize from this that dreams often reveal answers to questions the dreamer has not yet asked, or is simply unwilling to dwell on while awake.

But this is not to say that dreams present answers in an *intentional* manner. A dream does not act like a homunculus, or little man, in the mind which sends cryptic messages to tease the dreamer with something censored and hidden.[47] And the forgetting of a dream is not at all an unconscious and deliberate act full of "hostile intentions" as Freud suggested.[48] A dream is simply a process of the mind which, like digestion, serves an important function in keeping the individual healthy without having to be observed. The restorative process inherent in dreams takes place regardless of whether or not the dream is analyzed, understood, or even remembered. But when dreaming is understood to be a restorative mechanism it can render insights into the most pressing issues and concerns being experienced by the individual having that dream. This will explain why a dream or nightmare will sometimes reoccur night after night: not because it has not yet been clinically analyzed by an expert but because the individual having that dream continues to struggle daily with the same issues or concerns that generated the dream in the first place.

5. DREAM INTERPRETATION IN PHILOSOPHICAL COUNSELING

The advantage of philosophical counseling over other forms of therapy is that the philosophical counselor may use any means of inquiry available. The philosophical counselor is not constrained by any particular school of therapy or systematized methodology. Therefore, although commonly considered a psychotherapeutic approach, an inquiry into the meaning of dreams can be very useful in philosophical counseling as a means of helping a client better understand what is troubling him.

As discussed in my book *Philosophical Counseling: Theory and Practice*, it is not always obvious to a client in the early stages of counseling what the problem is and why he is unhappy.[49] This is when an examination of his dreams can offer some helpful insights. But just as the reasons for his unhappiness are not always immediately apparent to the client, the meaning of a dream can also be very elusive to the client's individual interpretive efforts. A competent philosophical counselor can help a client understand both his emotional distress and his dreams by helping the client examine how the dream images reflect the troubling events in his life. For example, a client may present a dream he has had of rolling down a steep hill in a car with defective brakes. The philosophical counselor knows that in his private life this client is in fact in a turbulent and failing personal relationship which he refuses to give up despite the fact that the future of this relationship is out of his control. He may not necessarily make the connection that the dream of the malfunctioning car is a metaphor for the emotional risk he is taking by refusing to accept that his obsessive drive to maintain the relationship is doomed to end in emotional disaster. Aristotle said, "A good dream interpreter is one who notices similarities."[50] By helping this client to notice the similarities between his life and his dream, the philosophical counselor can help him to recognize that his dream is dealing with the concern he is feeling regarding his own well-being which he has not allowed himself to dwell on while awake. In this way the dream, rather than being a symbolic concealment of unconscious material, becomes heuristic: it has explanatory value in philosophical counseling.

Hartmann maintains that ordinary dreams are simply concerned with solving interpersonal problems, ethical concerns, or personal problems dealing with one's health or one's work, in order to diminish the emotional and somatic disturbances those concerns are producing.[51] Given Hartmann's clinical research into dream function, it is reasonable for the philosophical counselor to assume that the client's dream material will show the way to serious emotional concerns which have been carelessly neglected, intentionally ignored, unintentionally forgotten, or sometimes simply missed while awake. The astute philosopher will recognize that strong negative emotions in dreams are a guide to the subtle areas of the client's distress or perplexity, and that they are a clear indication that there is some sort of interpersonal issue, ethical conflict, or emotional problem—all related to his waking life—with which the client is struggling.

When it comes to the most serious disturbances in a person's life it is important for the philosophical counselor to keep in mind that in the earliest dreams after a traumatic event, terror and fear usually predominate. Sometimes these are followed by dreams of extreme vulnerability, after which survival guilt may surface. Research on dreams and nightmares after trauma shows that, although a trauma itself may sometimes occur in a dream, dreams very seldom replay a trauma realistically and exactly as it occurred.[52] A person who has been extremely terrified by an auto accident, absolutely overwhelmed by a family disaster, or anxious about a difficult upcoming event may find her distress and concern metaphorically pictured in her dreams as a burning house from which she can't escape, a tidal wave break-ing over her, or being chased by a gang of thugs. Similarly, the daytime worries and fears of children often manifest themselves in dreams of mythical monsters, fierce animals, and bogeymen. But while these images may exhibit a common theme among various individuals, and even among various cultures, they are not at all the kind of childhood sexual wish fulfillment fantasies hypothesized by Freud, nor are they the primitive archetypal symbols arising out of a collective uncon-scious postulated by Jung.

Dreams following trauma or severe stress, as well as so-called normal dreams, don't need to have each little detail interpreted in order to be of practical value. A dream is like a jigsaw puzzle in that the overall picture can be understood long be-fore the last tiny piece has been set into place. Useful subjective insights can be gained when the fragmentary material in a dream is correlated with the overall context of the dreamer's waking life.[53] This is not at all contrary to some aspects of the approach to the interpretation of dreams presented by both Freud and Jung.

But there can be a significant difference between how a philosophical counselor will use dream material to help the client examine his life, and how that same mate-rial is acted upon by a Freudian or Jungian therapist. For example, in his essay "The Practical Use of Dream Analysis" Jung offers the case of a man with "humble beginnings," a peasant who, by virtue of ambition, hard work, and talent, had had an extraordinarily successful career but suffered from a sense of anxiety and inse-curity. The man related two dreams to Jung, both exemplifying his insecurity about his own career successes. In the first dream he ignores some former class-mates while walking in his own village. This is interpreted by Jung as meaning "You forgot how far down you began." The second dream—actually more of a nightmare—involves the man missing a train he was trying to catch on the way to work. He explains that the track has a dangerously sharp S-curve in it but "the en-gine driver puts on steam, I try to cry out, the rear coaches give a frightful lurch and are thrown off the rails. There is a terrible catastrophe. I wake up in terror."[54] Jung then analyzes the dream as follows:

Here again no effort is needed to understand the message of the dream. It describes the pa-tient's frantic haste to advance himself still further. But since the engine-driver in front steams relentlessly ahead, the neurosis happens at the back: the coaches rock and the train is derailed.[55]

Jung says that this dream gave him not only the etiology of his patient's neurosis but a prognosis as well. Jung furthermore believes it tells him exactly where the treatment of his patient should begin. He proclaims, "We must prevent the patient from going full steam ahead" because this is what the patient's dream (and his un-conscious) has told the patient himself. But the man does not agree with Jung's ap-proach and he does not remain Jung's patient for very long.[56] Jung writes, "The upshot was that the fate depicted in the dream ran its course. He tried to exploit the professional openings that tempted his ambition, and ran so violently off the rails that the catastrophe was realized in actual life."[57] So, based on this eventual unfortunate outcome, Jung concludes that the dream was a kind of premonition of doom, a warning to the man from deep in his unconscious that he should not forget his peasant beginnings, and that he should stop his upward striving. But is this in fact what the dream was trying to tell Jung's patient?

In light of Hartmann's empirical research into dreams, Jung's reading of the dream should be troubling to any philosophical counselor. His interpretation and suggested treatment not only recommend a paternalistic interference in the course of a patient's career but also advocate bringing into actuality the patient's own neurotic dreams of failure as, paradoxically, the best way to counteract his fear of failure. In other words, first, while Jung would paternalistically prevent his patient from striving for more success in his career, the philosophical counselor would never take such an autocratic position. And, second, while Jung considers the dream to be a sure sign of impending doom, and while he would therefore intentionally "derail" his patient's career by preventing him from going "full steam ahead" (making the man's nightmare of failure come true), the philosophical counselor would consider the dream to be only a metaphorical indicator of the fear of the *possibility* of failure that is worrying her client. She would not presume to know as categorically as Jung did that the best thing she can do for her client is to stop him in his tracks. She would instead empathetically offer to discuss with her client why his success is causing him such anxiety and insecurity, find out if he still wants to continue his efforts to advance his career, and if so help him to examine what options are available to him to keep his extraordinarily successful career on track. Put in another way, rather than force him to stop his career because of a dream based on his fear of the possibility of failure (thereby creating a self-fulfilling prophecy), the philosophical counselor would understand his dream as an insight into his worries, help him resolve those worries, and then help him come to terms with the possibility of even greater success.

Furthermore, when Jung's assumptive diagnosis of the man's supposed endogenous pathology is viewed from a feminist perspective it is clear that Jung's approach to the dream amounts to Jung's (unconscious?) attempt to maintain the status quo by having the man with the peasant background stop advancing in his career into the realm of the upper class of which he is not a member. The philosophical counselor's approach, on the other hand, would be to help the man overcome the exogenous social barriers put up by both his peasant friends and members of the upper class (including Jung), which barriers are exacerbating the man's anxiety and insecurity.

So the fact that the man's career did eventually crash was not at all due to his having reached the highest point of his career and having exhausted his strength, as Jung contends. It was in fact due to Jung's erroneous assumptions about the premonitory meaning of his patient's dreams, his attempts to paternalistically dissuade his patient from pursuing his life goals, and the man's subsequent disillusionment with, and abandoning of, Jung's misguided directive therapy.

But, obviously, a dream can only be made use of by a philosophical counselor if and when the client remembers it. What is to be done if the dreamer can't recall the dream? Hartmann recommends that five general facts about sleep and dreams be kept in mind when attempting to mitigate this problem: (1) developing a conscious interest in dreams will usually increase dream recall; (2) recording a dream immediately after having it, and in only a few words, will help recall it later; (3) reviewing a major problem or emotional concern at bedtime will stimulate dreaming in that area and will prompt those dreams to be more vivid; (4) getting a good night's sleep is essential to dream recall; less than six hours of sleep substantially reduces the likelihood of dream recall. And if all else fails he suggests (5) working with daydreams since they function somewhat similarly to dreams although in a more limited capacity.[58]

In summary, the function of dreams is best understood as analogous to the diffusion of a storm, and to the physical body's self-restorative system. It is in sleep that the body engages most actively in its physical healing, growth, and repairs, and it is in dreams that the mind carries out its own healing, growth, and repairs. In dreams mental connections are made which help to diffuse the dominant emotional concerns of the dreamer. This restorative process takes place regardless of whether or not the dreamer understands or remembers the dream's connective metaphors. Understanding dreams as this sort of restorative mechanism explains why an individual can suffer from sleep/dream deprivation if not enough hours have been spent sleeping, and why it is not possible to store up sleep/dream hours ahead of time. Just as the body is not always able to deal adequately with severe physical trauma in just one night's sleep, serious emotional trauma may require more than a single night's dreams to ease the pain of that sort of injury. And just as physical pains often benefit from being attended to by a caring individual skilled in the practice of medical therapy, mental and emotional pains can likewise benefit from the attention of a caring individual skilled in the practice of philosophical counseling. Philosophical counseling can also help alleviate the distress caused by a recurring dream or nightmare by bringing to light, and then dealing with, the troubling daytime issues and concerns that generated it.

Dreams need not be treated as meaningful symbols to be interpreted as the exhibition of malevolent or forbidden desires which the mind has somehow inexplicably hidden from itself in its own inaccessible unconscious; neither does the dream state need to be feared as some sort of competing illusory reality meant to confound the human condition. Dreams are most often simply an attempt of the mind to resolve one or several troubling issues stored among the complex interconnections of daytime memories. Although psychoanalysts may hold dreams to represent repressed desires and fears, the interpretation of dreams within a philosophical counseling setting will be most profitable if dream events are seen as metaphorical road signs pointing the way among the complexities of the client's daily life. And contrary to Freud's dictum that the analyst should never analyze himself, as a philosophical counselor one ought to consider the examination of one's own dreams as part of one of the most important duties one has to perform: namely, the duty to oneself.

NOTES

1. Descartes, René. *Meditations* (1641). *The Philosophy Source* CD. Daniel Kolak, ed. Belmont, Calif.: Wadsworth, 2000.

2. Leibniz, Gottfried Wilhelm. "Letter to Foucher" (1675). *Philosophical Essays*. Roger Ariew and Daniel Garber, ed. and trans. Indianapolis: Hackett, 1989. 4.

3. Russell, Bertrand. *Our Knowledge of the External World* (1914). London: Routledge, 1993. 101.

4. The only account I'm aware of in which a philosophical counselor discusses a client's dream is chapter 11 of Shlomit Schuster's book *Philosophy Practice*. Westport, Conn.: Praeger, 1999.

5. Freud, Sigmund. "The Interpretation of Dreams" (1900). *The Basic Writings of Sigmund Freud*. A. A. Brill, trans. and ed. New York: The Modern Library, 1995. 192.

6. Squires, Roger. "dreams." Colin Howson. "snow is white." *The Oxford Companion to Philosophy*. Ted Honderich, ed. Oxford, U.K.: Oxford University Press, 1995. 206, 496–511, 829.

7. *The Encyclopedia of Philosophy*. Paul Edwards, ed. New York: Macmillan, 1967. Vols. 4 and 5.

8. Plato. *Timaeus*. 46a.

9. Aristotle. *De Somniis (On Dreams)*. J. I. Beare, trans. *Works of Aristotle*. Oxford, U.K.: Oxford University Press, 1931. 462a.

10. Plato. *Collected Dialogues* (c. 375 B.C.). Edith Hamilton and Huntington Cairns, eds. Princeton, N.J.: Princeton University Press, 1961.

11. Aquinas, Thomas. *Summa Theologiae* (1274), *A Concise Translation*. Timothy McDermott, ed. London: Methuen, 1989. 412.

12. Locke, John. *An Essay Concerning Human Understanding* (1689). Oxford, U.K.: Clarendon, 1975. 113.

13. See the Bible verses at Genesis chap. 40 and Daniel chap. 2.

14. Freud, "The Interpretation of Dreams." 176–184.

15. Quoted in Ernest Hartmann's *Dreams and Nightmares*. Cambridge, Mass.: Perseus, 2001. 173.

16. Freud, "The Interpretation of Dreams." 193, 197, 201, 203.

17. Ibid., 160.

18. Ibid., 161.

19. Freud, Sigmund. "Introduction to Psychoanalysis" (1916). Quoted in *Psychoanalytic Practice*. Helmut Thomä and Horst Kächele. Northvale, N.J.: Jason Aronson, 1994. 141.

20. Freud, "The Interpretation of Dreams." 339.

21. Ibid., 396–397.

22. Rand, Nicholas and Maria Torok. *Questions for Freud: The Secret History of Psychoanalysis*. Cambridge, Mass.: Harvard University Press. 1997. 215–216. Italics are in the original.

23. The term "backward masking" has been used in litigation to describe the supposedly insidious hidden messages in popular music. The theory was that some musicians were recording backward messages into their music in order to subliminally manipulate the unwary public. It has never been proven that such backward masking in fact exists.

24. Freud, "The Interpretation of Dreams." 206.

25. Logically, if there is censorship of thoughts it would require some sort of homunculus (little man) in the brain who decides what thoughts need to be censored. In or-

der to make such a decision the homunculus would have to have a brain which would then require another homunculus to censor its thoughts, and so on ad infinitum. The only way to avoid this infinite regress of homunculi is to argue that the brain just does this and that the use of the word "censor" is metaphorical, which is no explanation at all.

26. See Hartmann, 169–193. See also Helmut Thomä and Horst Kächele's book *Psychoanalytic Practice*. Especially chapter 5, "Interpretation of Dreams." 139–167.

27. Jung, Carl. "On the Psychogenesis of Schizophrenia" (1939). *The Basic Writings of C. G. Jung*. Violet Staub De Laszlo, ed. New York: Modern Library, 1959. 389.

28. Ibid., "On the Nature of Dreams" (1945). 373.

29. Ibid., "The Relations Between the Ego and the Unconscious" (1953). 143–144.

30. Ibid., "On the Nature of Dreams." 370–371, 378.

31. Ibid., 374.

32. Jung, Carl. *Dreams*. R.F.C. Hull, trans. New York: MJF Books, 1974. 87.

33. Hartmann draws on 5,000 of his own dreams, over 10,000 dreams in long dream series ("dream logs") supplied to him by various dreamers, several thousand patients' dreams, and dreams from numerous research studies conducted by himself and others. Hartmann, 3.

34. Ibid., 57, 147.

35. Ibid., 92–93.

36. See, for example, Jung's *Dreams*. 4.

37. Jung. "Symbols of Transformation" (1912). *Dreams*. R.F.C. Hull, trans. New York: MJF Books, 1974. 25.

38. It should be noted that not all dreams are experienced as pictures. Chapter 3 of this book came to me while I was asleep, not as a picture but in statements without any imagery whatsoever. But this is in line with Hartmann's contention that dreams are concerned with what is important to the dreamer and what the dreamer feels strongly about. For two days previous to the occurrence of this dream I had been wondering what, if anything, could be said about experimental philosophy. Interestingly, I had been considering writing a completely independent essay about it; I had not been considering writing about it in relation to philosophical counseling or as a chapter in this book. This demonstrates how dreams connect various, and often unrelated, items from waking life, thereby contributing to the waking creativity of the dreamer.

39. Hartmann, 3–4.

40. This theory of dreams is also a reasonable hypothesis concerning the function of flashbacks experienced by victims of severe trauma (such as those who have been diagnosed as having Post Traumatic Stress Disorder [PTSD]). A flashback is like a waking dream or nightmare, and is the victim's attempt to make sense of a seemingly senseless violent act.

41. Greenberg, Ramon and Chester Pearlman. "An Integrated Approach to Dream Theory: Contributions from Sleep Research and Clinical Practice." *The Functions of Dreaming*. A. Moffit, M. Kramer, and R. Hoffman, eds. Albany, N.Y.: State University of New York Press, 1993. See also Lüders, W. "Traum und Selbst" (The Dream and the Self). *Psyche 36*. 1982. 813–829.

42. Boss, Medard. *The Analysis of Dreams*. New York: Philosophical Library, 1958. 113–177, 262.

43. Hartmann, 55, 64.

44. Ibid., 136.

45. Ibid., 99.

46. Ibid., 101.

47. Freud often writes as though the unconscious has a mind of its own. For example, he states that the unconscious "is certain" about some things. See Freud, "Interpretation of Dreams." 516.

48. Ibid., 442.

49. Raabe, Peter B. *Philosophical Counseling: Theory and Practice*. Westport, Conn.: Praeger, 2001.

50. Aristotle. "On Prophesying by Dreams." *The Basic Works of Aristotle*. R. McKeon, ed. New York: Random House, 1941.

51. Hartmann, 154.

52. Ibid., 21, 23.

53. For a discussion of the importance of locating a dream within the context of the client's life see Stefan de Schill's book *Crucial Choices—Crucial Changes*. Amherst, N.Y.: Prometheus Books, 2000.

54. Jung, *Dreams*, 89.

55. Ibid.

56. Jung writes "Circumstances prevented me from treating the patient further, nor did my view of the case satisfy him." Jung, *Dreams*, 90.

57. Ibid., 89–90.

58. Hartmann, 141–144.

Chapter 20

Duty to Oneself

Anyone who has studied early modern philosophy will be familiar with Immanuel Kant. Even those who have never studied philosophy will probably have heard some version of this eighteenth-century German philosopher's famous moral pronouncement that you should never treat another person as only a means to an end. In his *Groundwork for a Metaphysics of Morals* Kant writes,

Now I say that man, and in general every rational being, exists as an end in himself, not merely as a means for arbitrary use by this or that will. He must in all his actions, whether they are directed to himself or to other rational beings, always be viewed at the same time as an end.[1]

Kant formulates this normative assertion into what he calls his practical imperative: "Act in such a way that you always treat humanity, whether in your own person or in the person of any other, never simply as a means, but always at the same time as an end."[2] This practical axiom of Kant's is not very radical or even terribly original. In fact it's similar to the principle of respect for others found in many sacred texts. But what is unusual, and what is often overlooked in reading these passages, is that Kant says not only that we should not treat others as merely a means to our own ends, but also that one has "a duty to oneself" to not treat *your own person* that way. But what would constitute treating "your own person" as merely a means to an end?

In philosophical counseling it is not unusual to see clients who are being treated as nothing more than the means to some other person's ends. A male client may talk about how his boss treats him as though he is just a means for reaching the company's goal of maximizing profits; a female client may explain that while she supported her husband through graduate school and in his career she now feels she has only been used by him as a means for reaching his own goals. These are clearly situations that contravene Kant's dictum of not using others as merely a means. But when Kant speaks of "duty to oneself" he is not addressing the perpetrator's actions; that is, he is not commenting on the actions of the one who uses others as a means to his own ends. Rather, Kant is commenting on the actions (or lack of action) of those individuals who are in fact the victims of someone else's selfish intentions.

Kant intends his duty to oneself to include the duty one has to not allow others to victimize oneself; to not allow others to treat oneself as only a means to their ends. More subtly, and perhaps more in line with what Kant meant, duty to oneself also includes not treating yourself as merely the means to some external end. One example of an external end is financial success. But why is financial success called an external end? And if it is an external end, what would constitute an internal end for whose achievement one could not be said to have used oneself as merely a means?

One goal that has often been considered an internal or intrinsic end, because it is directly experiential rather than the necessary antecedent of some other end, is happiness. Happiness may be defined as the experience of significant emotional well being that is the result of other factors. Despite the fact that happiness can in turn lead to other benefits such as improved physical and emotional well being, it would seem odd to say that a person looking for happiness is only looking for happiness in order to have it lead to some other goal, some external end. It would be even more odd to say that a person could use himself merely as the means to the end of personal happiness because when happiness is reached that person is always already benefiting.

On the other hand financial success is an external end for which a person definitely can use herself as only a means. Financial success is an end from which one can benefit only indirectly: if, for example, it results in a feeling of personal security or happiness. Some individuals believe that for them financial success is necessary if they are to attain happiness. This external end can turn the means-and-end relationship on its head. Rather than perceiving financial success as only the instrumental means by which to achieve other ends, such as security or happiness, an individual comes to perceive himself instead as the instrumental means by which financial success is to be achieved. A person can use himself as a means to financial success by offering up his physical health, his time, his emotional resources, his ethical principles, and his spiritual integrity, among other things, as a means to its achievement. The original intention of achieving security or personal happiness is simply lost somewhere along the way. The term "workaholic" is an appropriate designation for the person who uses himself in this manner. This word applies equally as often to women as it does to men, and to those working in the home as well as to those working elsewhere.

In being external-end oriented a client may become so absorbed in doing for others—again whether in the home or outside the home—that the way she sees herself lacks any real sense of self as the justifiable focus of attention and care. In other words, a person's sense of self may not include herself at all. Instead the word "myself" may be merely a designation for the embodiment of useful-to-others. In his book *The Sickness Unto Death* Søren Kierkegaard warns that

> the greatest hazard of all, losing one's self, can occur very quietly in the world, as if it were nothing at all. No other loss can occur so quietly; any other loss, an arm, a leg, five dollars, a wife, etc., is sure to be noticed.[3]

Losing one's self is not an unexpected consequence when one's personal identity has been based in large part on the principle of giving oneself to others. In most societies losing oneself through one's usefulness to others—by treating oneself as merely a means—is an experience more familiar to women than to men.

Treating oneself as merely a means includes what has been called "self-denying benevolence." Feminist writer Rosemarie Tong explains that the concept of self-denying benevolence was defined by nineteenth-century thinker Catherine Beecher as the "grand peculiarity of the character of Christ" and yet, curiously, as personified primarily in women. Tong says it has been portrayed as "both a feminine psychological trait—that is, a nonmoral virtue in which women specialize—and a required human moral virtue." She goes on to explain that Christian society requires men as well as women to practice the virtue of self-denying benevolence in theory. Yet because men supposedly have a harder time than women emulating Christ, Christian society expects far less in the way of self-denying benevolence from men in practice.[4] But while Beecher's Christian society may not have expected men to practice self-denying benevolence as a moral virtue as readily as it expected this of women, men in her day (and still today) often forgot their duty to themselves when the task of being the ideal provider for their families overwhelmed them.

Unfortunately, talk of duty to oneself can raise the specter of the excessive self-indulgence of the so-called me-generation of the 1970s or of the consumer society of the 1980s during which, it is said, self-interest came to be considered the greatest good. Ayn Rand's philosophy is often used as an example of how extreme self-interest can become, and how it can easily be transmuted into selfishness. In an interview Rand explained that her Objectivist ethics holds that "man exists for his own sake, that the pursuit of his own happiness is his highest moral purpose, that he must not sacrifice himself for others."[5] Rand gives the example of stepping in the way of a bullet aimed at her husband to illustrate how she believes that what is termed self-sacrifice is completely self-serving. "It is not self-sacrifice to die protecting that which you value. If the value is great enough, you do not care to exist without it. This applies to any alleged sacrifice for those one loves."[6] But Kant's call for duty to oneself is not intended to promote such a self-serving philosophy. Kant's emphasis on not treating oneself as merely a means highlights the need for the sort of self-regard that is essential for self-preservation. British philosopher Herbert Spencer explains that a very important type of egoism is in fact necessary for personal survival. Spencer puts in print what is clearly obvious: "Unless each duly cares for himself, his care for all others is ended by death."[7] This kind of care for and duty to oneself is far from mere selfishness.

For the philosophical counselor this issue of duty to oneself is significant not only because it may arise as an area of concern for a client within the discussion of a client's life experiences, but also because it is of vital importance to the counselor's own well-being in her private life and within her profession. It is important for a counselor to recognize that she has a duty to care adequately not only for the welfare of her clients but also for herself. This means that a counselor has the duty to herself to charge a reasonable fee for her services, she has a duty to take time off from counseling practice for the purpose of both professional development and personal well-being, she has the duty to seek counseling for herself if the need arises, and she has the duty to refuse to work with a client who is hostile, abusive, controlling, or manipulative, or who purposely sabotages the counseling process. The necessary element of trust in a counseling relationship means not only that the client must be able to trust that the counselor has the sincere desire to help, but also that the counselor must be able to trust that the client has the sincere desire to be helped. Furthermore, the philosophical counselor has the duty to herself and to her profession to allow the client only what she has offered the client in the first place. That is, she has the duty to herself to refuse the client who makes demands of her beyond what she considers reasonable, morally permissible, appropriate for her professional expertise, and contrary to her self-image as a philosophical counselor. She also has the duty to recognize that sometimes the client freely chooses to continue the behavior which caused his predicament in the first place. And she has the duty to herself to draw a clearly defined line between her private life and her life as a practitioner. The philosophical counselor's duty to herself is a vital element of any practice if the counselor wishes to remain an independent philosopher.

NOTES

1. Kant, Immanuel. *Groundwork of a Metaphysic of Morals.* New York: Harper & Row, 1964. 95–97.

2. Ibid.

3. Kierkegaard, Søren. *The Sickness Unto Death* (1849). Princeton, N.J.: Princeton University Press, 1941.

4. Tong, Rosemarie. *Feminine and Feminist Ethics,* Belmont, Calif.: Wadsworth, 1993. 38.

5. Published as a pamphlet titled "The *Playboy* interview with philosopher Ayn Rand." Oceanside, Calif.: Second Renaissance Books, 1964. 5.

6. Ibid., 10.

7. Spencer, Herbert. *The Principles of Ethics* Vol. 1. London: Appleton, 1896.

Chapter 21

The Independent Philosopher

Real life has a wonderful way of intruding on philosophy. It makes philosophers realize that, contrary to their pet theories, this world is in fact not a dream, animals do indeed have feelings, and it's not possible to live as though there is no free will no matter how determined a person may be to do so. Unfortunately real life also demands of philosophers that they have enough money for food, clothing, and shelter regardless of the fact that they would rather be engaged in the 'pursuit of Truth' than in worrying about such mundane matters. But what is a philosopher to do with a philosophy degree if he or she can't get hired to teach? What if he or she only gets hired as a part-time or sessional instructor, with no job security and poor pay? Because academic philosophy offers no career opportunities for philosophy students besides teaching philosophy, and with many universities and colleges cutting back on philosophy courses because of philosophy's seeming uselessness to students hoping to get a job in "the real world," there is always very stiff competition among graduates of philosophy departments for the few teaching positions available. But what else is there to do, other than give up the dream of philosophy as a life-long career? Some philosophers have turned their professional gaze in the direction of becoming independent, perhaps as philosophical counselors.

Unfortunately, at the time of this writing most North American philosophical counselors I know are finding it very difficult, if not impossible, to survive financially on the income they receive from the few clients who are willing to pay for their services. Perhaps foremost among the reasons why there are not yet any line-ups in front of their office doors is because it is such a new field. An individual who is suffering and in distress will typically look for comfort and relief in the familiar. And while there is a profusion of familiar therapies to choose from on this continent, philosophical counseling is not counted among them. Added to this is an even greater problem: not only are North Americans not familiar with philosophical counseling, but also the majority have either no idea or they have a negative conception of philosophy per se. For those who have taken one of the many dull academic philosophy courses offered in colleges and universities, the word "philosophy" is a euphemism for "useless mind games." People still think of philosophers the way they did in 1748 when British philosopher David Hume wrote,

The mere philosopher is a character, which is commonly but little acceptable in the world, as being supposed to contribute nothing either to the advantage or pleasure of society; while he lives remote from communication with mankind, and is wrapped up in principles and notions equally remote from their comprehension.[1]

Many people today, when they think of philosophy and philosophers, cannot imagine the possibility that either it or they might be able to help them mitigate their suffering from real-life personal problems.

The combined effect of the fact that philosophical counseling is a new field together with the fact that most people believe philosophy is completely impractical makes it a fool's gambit at present to open a philosophical counseling practice with the expectation that immediate financial security or even survival is possible on the income from its practice alone. Still, while philosophical counseling may not yet allow a philosopher to completely avoid financial dependence on some academic institution, it is a step in the right direction.

For the philosopher whose courage and desire to be independent are so strong that she is willing to turn her back on a full-time academic teaching position in favor of private practice, a number of practical issues must first be taken into consideration. For example, there must be a willingness to give up notions such as 'pure philosophy,' 'knowledge for its own sake,' and philosophy as the 'pursuit of Truth.' In fact if morality is an operant element of philosophical counseling then the philosophical counselor must recognize that there are far more important goals to its practice than the mere 'pursuit of Truth.'

Iain Hamilton Grant was writing about the quest for 'pure knowledge' in science, but his perspective fits philosophy perfectly when he says,

In the postmodern condition, owing to the collapse of grand narratives, [philosophy] can no longer justify itself or legitimate its practices by appealing to the innate value of 'knowledge in itself,' since knowledge in itself is not a salable commodity.[2]

The question for every philosopher wishing to become independent is whether he or she is prepared to view philosophy as a salable commodity. Until around the middle of the nineteenth century when philosophy became an academic profession, "interesting philosophers were all independent men of letters."[3] Talk of making a living with philosophy, and philosophy as a salable commodity, is likely to immediately remind most twenty-first-century philosophers of Socrates' reproach of the Sophists. Socrates' main criticism of the Sophists, however, was not that they were charging money for doing philosophy, but rather that many of them were in fact mercenaries who were willing to take either side of an issue under dispute, and argue in defense of anyone who was willing to pay for it. In other words, according to Socrates, the Sophists did not particularly care about whether they were defending a moral or an immoral position as long as there was money to be made.[4]

Besides not being mercenary, Socrates also said that the *true* philosopher has courage.[5] One of the ways a philosopher who wishes to become independent must show courage is in truthfully answering some important questions regarding the issue of making money with philosophy, such as, Why do I want to be in private practice? Is private practice the best situation in which to do the kind of work I want to do? Do I even like the idea of being an entrepreneur? Do I feel comfortable about promoting my own services? Do I feel comfortable charging for my services? and Will the money I bring in from a private practice afford me the kind of lifestyle I want to live?[6]

Even if these questions have failed to dampen the burning desire to become an independent philosophical counselor, other difficult but important issues still need to be considered. As mentioned earlier, the general public tends to see philosophy as purely academic, and academic philosophy has a powerfully negative reputation as being highly objective (and therefore impersonal and heartless) argumentation, so that few suffering individuals will consider calling a philosophical counselor as their first choice. In other words, a philosophical counselor will typically see individuals who come to philosophical counseling as their last resort either because other therapists were unable to help them resolve their problems or because they are hoping to be rescued from a previous diagnosis (such as when a woman told me her psychotherapist had diagnosed her as suffering from "demon possession"). It also means potential clients may come with very low expectations. Of course this may help, but it can seriously hinder a beneficial counseling outcome.

The philosopher wishing to become a philosophical counselor must also learn to overcome any professional jealousy and competitiveness acquired in academic institutions and the combative attitude so prevalent within philosophy faculties and associations. This may seem like an obvious point, but it is not easy to shift from the aggressive and challenging stance of those who desire to gain status by winning arguments in academic disputations to the genuinely caring stance of the philosophical counselor for whom empathetic listening is the most rewarding activity.

It may also prove challenging to sustain one's self-respect and credibility as a legitimate philosopher when primary employment is outside the academy. This involves not only having to contend with personal attacks on one's professional credibility from both psychotherapists and philosophers, but also having to deal with professional criticism that philosophical counseling is neither a legitimate form of counseling—because it is not yet generally recognized by psychotherapeutic counseling associations—nor a credible form of philosophy—because its practice is not located within the highly rationalistic discourse of some academic institution's philosophy department. This denial of a philosopher's legitimacy and credibility may be exacerbated if written works are self-published rather than presented in academic journals. It may appear that the best response to this is to say, Then why not simply submit your essays and articles only to academic journals? But academic journal publication reveals a "Catch 22" situation in that many journals are reluctant to accept items from authors not affiliated with an institution because of their perceived lack of professional credibility, while professional credibility comes in part from being published in academic journals. The independent philosopher must ask herself whether she can tolerate having journals refuse or even ignore her written work simply because she is not a member of some institution's teaching faculty.

Aside from credibility, perhaps the biggest problem for any independent philosopher is income. Being independent means not having the security of being on an academic payroll, and not having the satisfaction of automatically receiving a regular paycheck every month. With the issue of the certification or licensing of philosophical counselors still a controversial and unresolved debate in most areas, the philosophical counselor also does not have access to the government healthcare funding available to other healthcare providers. This means a practice in philosophical counseling will have to rely exclusively on individuals who are able and willing to pay for services out of their own pockets. In addition to a lack of access to public funding, the philosopher who wants to become a philosophical counselor must be prepared to deal competently with such crucial business matters as filing tax returns, buying insurance, renting office space, distributing business cards and other promotional materials, and making adequate personal preparations for retirement. To survive financially the independent philosopher must treat the practice of philosophy in a businesslike manner, and not merely as a passion, a pastime, or a public charity.

Being an independent philosopher doesn't have to mean being caught in an either/or dilemma, however. It doesn't have to mean making a choice between being either a full-time instructor (or a tenured professor) in an academic institution *or* a philosophical counselor. There are other ways to make money with philosophy. For example, a philosopher may facilitate a philosophy café on a regular basis; he may offer lectures and seminars to the public; she may sell academic books she has written and published; he may write books, essays, and articles meant for the general public; she may take a part-time or sessional teaching position; he may offer consulting work; she may provide private tutoring; he may do philosophy with elementary school children and high school students; she may teach philosophical counseling to psychiatrists, psychoanalysts, counseling psychologists, social workers, and other mental healthcare providers (as opposed to teaching philosophical counseling as a discrete approach); he may host a radio broadcast or televised philosophical discussion program; and so on. Separately these can bring a modestly rewarding income. Several of them in combination can add up to respectable earnings.

It is also important to note that the independent philosopher cannot rely on a single pedagogic approach, such as the one required in lecturing, to serve for all occasions. The various situations in which a philosopher may find herself require a variety of approaches. Lecturing to a class of students, speaking to a public audience, being interviewed by a reporter or media host, hosting a seminar (where comments or questions are directed to the philosopher), facilitating a group discussion (using a community of inquiry approach, in which participants direct comments and questions to each other), counseling a suffering client, and counseling a group of people in distress all require the philosopher to adopt different communication or discursive styles if each meeting is to be successful. In fact teaching philosophy in a classroom environment can have a negative effect on a philosopher's ability to counsel because of the different approaches required. The philosopher wishing to become and remain independent should keep in mind that it is not easy to shift back and forth between a didactic, a dialectic, and a counseling style of discourse.

To offer the best service, the independent philosopher must also keep up with the latest developments in the field, which means she must access various journals, books, academic seminars, professional conferences, e-mail discussion groups, and so on. E-mail discussion groups that are cooperative rather than competitive can be a valuable place to gain insights into issues that arise in counseling, where difficult or stressful cases can be discussed, and where the negative emotional impact of a problematic client suffered by the counselor can be diffused. What will also help is keeping in touch with a network of like-minded philosophers, those who are actively trying to succeed on their own, and not simply theorizing, pontificating, or daydreaming about it.

Finally, one of the primary abilities a philosopher must have if he wishes to remain independent is to value his own work, whether it is writing, counseling, or teaching outside the academy. The independent philosopher will go through times when money is scarce and clients are few. Self-esteem may dwindle as self-doubt increases, unless the counselor has the unshakable personal conviction that what he has to offer is indeed valuable.

Logically, one of the best ways to learn more about how to be a successful independent philosopher is simply to ask some of them. I contacted three of them—Christopher Phillips, Vaughana Feary, and Colin Clayton—to ask them for their perspectives on the joys and hardships of being an independent philosopher, and for some practical suggestions on how to make philosophy profitable. Following are their responses.

Christopher Phillips is founder and executive director of the nonprofit independent Society for Philosophical Inquiry in the United States, and author of *Socrates Cafe: A Fresh Taste of Philosophy* and the children's book *The Philosophers' Club.*

1. ADVICE TO INDEPENDENT PHILOSOPHERS

I prefer the term "autonomous" philosophers, by the way. I suggest you dare to go your own way. Don't let those who see the great feat of bringing philosophy out of academia as a moneymaking scheme be the only game in town. There are all too many philosophers, most from formal academic backgrounds, who primarily want to bring philosophy out of the university cloister, but they bring the same stilted hierarchies out of academia with them. They tend to frown upon creative and critical thinking, and they want to be "the" philosopher in any setting in which they engage with people outside of academia, instead of recognizing that philosophizing par excellence is all about "co-inquiring" with people, learning just as much, if not much more, from them than they could ever hope to learn from you. So stand up to such people. Offer a viable alternative. Pooh pooh these ridiculous certification programs that are started by those who treat philosophy like a Fortune 500 corporation and are motivated by money and a skewed sense of grandeur. Look to great autonomous individuals like Socrates as your role model, and don't just emulate his method of inquiry but his ethos; he was willing to live in poverty to practice his heretical brand of philosophy. Don't let money be your motive for philosophizing. Let passion, and dedication, be your primary motivation. You may end up being able to make a living at some point by philosophizing in an autonomous way, but if you start out doing this without even thinking of making money, then your passion and integrity will always be at the forefront. Perhaps, like I have, you eventually will form a nonprofit group that truly is nonprofit and that isn't just a front to make money. Hopefully you'll come across philanthropic groups that will be touched by your endeavors and will want to support you and help you subsist while you continue with your labor of love. It's also exhilarating, I find, to recognize that you are part of a tradition of people who throughout human existence have lived on a shoestring budget and less, people of deep acute social and intellectual conscience who were committed to making the world a better place than it was when they got here, and were willing to put it all on their line to realize their ideals. So, be willing and ready to survive for a good while on a shoestring budget and less, and look for other ways to subsist financially while you pursue your dreams. Just as many great creators past and present have had to survive by other means while they pursued their loftier aspirations, you should be prepared to do the same. I think it's just about the only way to go if you hope to maintain your autonomy and integrity.

2. MEMORABLE EXPERIENCES

By philosophizing with people in an egalitarian way, I recognized that a certain method of inquiry such as the Socratic method enables me to learn much more from others than they can learn from me, as we help one another articulate and clarify our unique perspectives on life and living. Every experience can be a singularly memorable one. I call it the "wow factor." Always, always, when I philosophize with people, I find that their insights are so exhilarating that I can't help but say "wow." This is especially true, I find, when I philosophize with at-risk children who essentially have been cast off by society. To be sure, their abilities with the traditional three R's can be lacking, but their grasp of the fourth R—reasoning—is breathtaking. The Socratic method of philosophical inquiry lends itself to enabling those who typically are voiceless in our society to break through the culture of silence that has oppressed them and to better articulate answers to those questions of questions, "Who am I?" and "Who can I become?" I also find that philosophizing with seniors in nursing homes is particularly redeeming. Like children, they have been marginalized by society, and like children, they are inordinately honest and probing critical and creative thinkers who are more than willing to pursue a line of inquiry as far down the Socratic path of enlightenment as possible.

3. BE COURAGEOUS

Stand up to the Sophists of your day. Recognize, as Schopenhauer did, that few philosophers have ever come from the ranks of academic philosophy professors, who tend not to come from a tradition of critical and creative thinking and who have abrogated the original intent of philosophical thinking, which was tantamount to the methodical exploration of everything over and under and through the sun. Recognize that as an independent scholar and philosopher, you can chip away at the artificial divides that exist in the academic disciplines, and that not only will you NOT dilute philosophy by bringing it out to the public, but you can enrich and enhance and deepen its range of inquiry. Do away with the stilted hierarchies, the stifling and needless attempts at "certifying" those who want to philosophize. Be autonomous, like all the great thinkers and people of social conscience, past and present! By standing up to the snake oil salesmen of your time, you'll help ensure that this latest attempt to resuscitate philosophy won't fail.

Vaughana Feary is an independent philosophical counselor in New Jersey, and vice president of the American Philosophical Practitioners Association. She offers the following suggestions:

Pointers on Starting a Practice

- Don't restrict yourself to only doing philosophical counseling.
- Get APPA certification for counseling; it includes some training on practical issues.
- Recognize you are starting a business and leave academic thinking behind.
- Who you know and how you market yourself are more essential than what you know at least in getting established, so network!
- Most philosophers are solitary types, who don't have a clue how to network, so buy some books on the subject, start giving talks for the Rotary Club and support groups, facilitate some philosophy cafés, join your local golf club, etc.
- Many consultants have held corporate jobs. Try to teach Business Ethics, preferably in the College of Business.
- Recognize that most areas where mental health professionals and Human Resources/Management consultants work are areas in which you can work too.
- Decide where you want to specialize; you can't do it all, e.g., doing Ethics and Compliance training for an oil company is very different from doing it for a hospital.
- Develop multidisciplinary skills or combine degrees: a Master of Business Administration (MBA) and a Master of Social Work (MSW) work well with philosophical training; alternatively get certificates from institutes in management, Rational Emotive Behavior Therapy (REBT) or other counseling techniques, etc.

- Have a business plan, good office services (which turn out vanilla-perfect training/marketing materials) and a good accountant; incorporate and carry insurance.
- Develop brochures, business cards, a web site, and different sorts of resumes for different sorts of clients.
- Hot areas for me have been corporations (Ethics and Compliance, Sexual Harassment, and Diversity), Corrections, Nonprofit organizations; now moving into more consulting work with healthcare issues and staff.
- Emphasize *group* counseling and *group* facilitation for corporate settings—it is more lucrative.
- Write articles for corporate newsletters, trade journals, etc.—you don't get work or money from writing academic articles.
- Get, or keep, some academic affiliation—it reassures your clients.
- Don't hammer new clients with philosophy if you have a Ph.D.
- Market yourself as an organizational consultant/trainer, etc. It works better, although the American Philosophical Practitioners Association (APPA) is beginning to secure more recognition for philosophers and philosophy outside of the academy.
- If you need help, hire and train "trainers," rather than colleagues in philosophy, to complete special projects, unless they are APPA trained. You don't want people who don't know the difference between lecturing, teaching, training, and facilitating.
- Don't support fishing trips by people who are looking for ideas to develop training projects internally. Know how to write up good contracts which are not simply blueprints for others to use your stuff.
- Work from a virtual office and call on clients—leasing office space is expensive.
- Share an office with one or two other professionals and split the cost.
- Do *pro bono* and volunteer work, but be sure to ask if you can use the institution as a reference.
- Don't work for any less than what is made by management/psychology consultants.
- Don't economize on business attire or equipment.
- Most of my clients are referrals from other clients; hand out your business card to every client and anyone else who asks you what you do for a living.
- People tell me that web sites and putting resumes out on the Internet are a good way to get clients.
- Make referrals to other professionals where applicable—they will refer to you in return.
- One of the quickest ways to get hired as a consultant is to bring money with you; for this practitioners really need to know how to write grants and use The Foundation Center (a U.S. granting agency). I took a 5-day grant writing course and it was a very good investment. Philosophers have a big advantage because they know how to write already, and many people working for agencies are terrible. Where possible, however, subcontract the job to spare yourself the hassles.

Colin Clayton has been an independent philosopher in the United Kingdom for quite some time. But when he sent me the following e-mail he was in the process of moving from the United Kingdom to the United States. His comments are therefore instructive to anyone in the early stages of setting up an independent practice regardless of where their office may be located.

When I set up in the U.K. I was lucky; I had an organization, freedom, and financial resources, plus I was working with a client group that is difficult to work with. Hence many professionals were looking toward anything different, new, that could assist them. But for all the ideals, ideas, etc. I had to take a managerial line to enable the work I was doing. I started out using Existential counselling in 1987. I then adapted and implemented Professor Matthew Lipman's Philosophy for Children program to work with addicts, which was fine for group type work. Then I embarked upon exploring the form of 'Socratic discourse,' and then around '92ish what many describe now as one-on-one philosophical counseling.

I am now in the process of coming to a different country (the United States) to set up a philosophical counseling practice. My main partner has a background in marketing, management training, and strategy development; he is also a Reiki healer. The other two individuals also have a background in business. Here are some of the issues we are considering, and our strategy:

Nature of the organization: We will register as a nonprofit organization. Reasons: we will have the best of worlds, fees, sponsors, and donations. Therefore we are able to work with the poor, corporations, etc. and be salaried. It gives us a degree of credibility and respectability, e.g., in obeying legislation governing nonprofit organizations, etc.

Areas of expertise: We have marketing, management, and administration expertise: Essential if the organization is to be successful, e.g., practice management, schedules, policies, marketing, etc. Good secretarial services are a must, which we have.

Operational policy: We are deciding what services to provide to whom, where, how.

Service provision: Clarity of what is provided, well thought out service, and programs for training, groups, etc. are necessary.

Targeting client group: We are targeting addictions, marriage, grief, and "other stress related issues." Also companies: team building, personal development, EAPs (employee assistance programs). Plan to set up Philosophy Cafés. No e-mail, telephone services other than inquiries.

Marketing strategy: Essential; research well, especially potential funders, competition, etc., brochure, advertising, cafés. Presentations: talks, seminars, use of presentation software, etc. Linking with other groups and individuals to provide service, referrals, etc. We believe it is not only essential to get our literature "right" but also we have clear, well thought out practices and policies behind it.

Location: Important; we will be in main downtown location, easily accessible, reasonably respectable.

Premises: The organization is renting a property for one to two years. Two of my partners will be living upstairs, downstairs are the office and other rooms.

Fees and charges: We are developing a sliding scale of charges.

Credibility: We are resting the organization on my experience and knowledge of working with a wide range of issues. E.g., working with addicts is not only counseling for addiction, but marriage, grief, abuse, etc. My book, self-published, again to describe the work and achievements of our organization. I set up a publishing company to do that and took the whole thing through to the end.

Accreditation: Well that's a difficult one. My Ph.D. is not accredited in the United States. Though a hefty tome, it was awarded by, you guessed it, a non-accredited university. Ah well,

I lost out there. But it was written more to express the development of philosophical counseling and my organization here in the United Kingdom, as well as my own development.

Colin Clayton's experience should be understood as a word to the wise: If you are a student wishing to become an independent philosopher or a philosophical counselor, and you are planning to get a doctorate in the field, make sure you do your Ph.D. work through an accredited university. While there is currently a lack of accredited academic programs in philosophical counseling, there is no doubt in my mind that, as it becomes more accepted as a legitimate field of practice in its own right, the number of universities willing to offer postgraduate courses and doctorates in philosophical counseling will steadily increase.

A final word on independent philosophy comes in the form of a rhetorical question posed by the German philosopher Friedrich Nietzsche:

Is there sufficient pride, daring, courage, self-confidence available today, sufficient will of the spirit, will to responsibility, *freedom of will*, for "the philosopher" to be henceforth *possible* on earth?[7]

In my professional opinion I would say that, judging by the number of letters I have received from philosophers asking how they might become independent philosophical counselors, the answer to Nietzsche's question must be a resounding "yes." I hope this book helps you to be such a philosopher.

NOTES

1. Hume, David. *An Enquiry Concerning Human Understanding.* La Salle, Ill.: Open Court, 1991. 55.

2. Grant, Iain Hamilton. "Postmodernism and Science and Technology." *The Icon Critical Dictionary of Postmodern Thought.* Stuart Sim, ed. London: Icon, 1998. 76.

3. French philosopher Henri Bergson quoted in *The Oxford Companion to Philosophy.* Ted Honderich, ed. Oxford, U.K.: Oxford University Press, 1995. 671.

4. Plato. *Collected Dialogues* (c. 375 B.C.). Edith Hamilton and Huntington Cairns, eds. Princeton, N.J.: Princeton University Press, 1961.

5. Regarding the courage of the philosopher see Plato's *Republic* VI, 494b.

6. These questions are adapted from a professional seminar handout titled *Growing a Private Practice* by Dr. Geraldine Brooks, Instructor in the Department of Counseling Psychology at the University of British Columbia. 1998.

7. Nietzsche, Friedrich. "Genealogy of Morals" (1887). *Basic Writings of Nietzsche.* Walter Kaufmann, trans. and ed. New York: Modern Library, 1968. 552.

Selected Bibliography

Adams, Douglas. *The Hitchhiker's Guide to the Galaxy.* London: Pan Books, 1978.

Aiken, Henry D., ed. *Hume Moral and Political Philosophy.* New York: Hafner Press, 1975.

Aires, Elizabeth J. and Fern L. Johnson. "Close Friendship in Adulthood: Conversational Conduct between Same-Sex Friends." *Sex Roles.* 9, 1983, 12.

Alexander, C. N. and E. J. Langer, eds. *Higher Stages of Human Development.* New York: Oxford University Press, 1990.

American Psychiatric Association. *Diagnostic and Statistical Manual of Mental Disorders.* 4th ed. Washington, D.C.: American Psychiatric Association, 1994.

Aquinas, Thomas. *Summa Theologiae* (1274), *A Concise Translation.* Timothy McDermott, ed. London: Methuen, 1991.

Aristotle. *De Somniis (On Dreams).* In *The Works of Aristotle.* J. I. Beare, trans. Oxford, U.K.: Oxford University Press, 1931.

———. "On Prophesying by Dreams." *The Basic Works of Aristotle.* R. McKeon, ed. New York: Random House, 1941.

———. *Ethics.* London: Penguin Classics, 1955.

Aronson, Morton J. and Melvin A. Scharfman, eds. *Psychotherapy: The Analytic Approach.* Northvale, N.J.: Jason Aronson, 1992.

Ayer, A. J. and Jane O'Grady, eds. *A Dictionary of Philosophical Quotations.* Oxford, U.K.: Blackwell, 1994.

Barham, Peter. *Schizophrenia and Human Value.* London: Free Association Books, 1993.

Beauvoir, Simone de. *The Second Sex.* New York: Knopf, 1952.

Bell, Susan Groag. *Women: From the Greeks to French Revolution.* Belmont, Calif.: Wadsworth, 1973.

Benn, Stanley I. *A Theory of Freedom.* New York: Cambridge University Press, 1990.

Ben-Ze'ev, Aaron. "Typical Emotions." *The Philosophy of Psychology.* William O'Donohue and Richard F. Kitchener, eds. London: Sage, 1996.

Binswanger, Ludwig. "Being-in-the-World." *Selected Papers.* J. Needleman, trans. New York: Basic Books, 1963.

Boss, Medard. *The Analysis of Dreams.* New York: Philosophical Library, 1958.

Boswell, John. *Christianity, Social Tolerance, and Homosexuality.* Chicago: University of Chicago Press, 1980.

Camus, Albert. *The Myth of Sisyphus.* J. O'Brien, trans. New York: Knopf, 1955.

Carlson, Nancy L. "Woman Therapist: Male Client." *Handbook of Counseling and Psychotherapy with Men.* Scher, Murray; Mark Stevens, Glenn Good, and Gregg A. Eichenfield, eds. London: Sage, 1987.

Cherniak, Christopher. *Minimal Rationality.* Cambridge, Mass.: MIT Press/Bradford Books, 1986.

Cohn, Hans W. *Existential Thought and Therapeutic Practice.* London: Sage, 1997.

Cooper, John M. and D. S. Hutchison, eds. *Plato: Complete Works.* Indianapolis: Hackett, 1997.

Corey, Gerald. *Theory and Practice of Counseling and Psychotherapy.* Pacific Grove, Calif.: Brooks/Cole, 1996.

Crimshaw, Jean. *Philosophy and Feminist Thinking.* Minneapolis: University of Minnesota Press, 1993.

Curtis, Rebecca C., ed. *The Relational Self.* New York: Guilford Press, 1991.

Damasio, Antonio R. *Descartes' Error.* New York: G. P. Putnam's Sons, 1994.

D'Emilio, John and Freedman, Estelle B. *Intimate Matters.* New York: Harper & Row, 1988.

Dench, Brian. *Homosexuality: Is It Wrong?* Toronto: The Unit on Human Rights, Anglican Church of Canada, 1992.

Descartes, René. *Meditations* (1641). *The Philosophy Source* CD. Daniel Kolak, ed. Belmont, Calif.: Wadsworth, 2000.

———. "Treatise on the Passions of the Soul" (1649). *The Philosophical Works of Descartes.* E. Haladane and G.R.T. Ross, trans. Cambridge, U.K.: Cambridge University Press, 1948.

Deutsch, Barbara G. "Women in Psychotherapy." *Psychotherapy: The Analytic Approach.* Morton J. Aronson and Melvin A. Scharfman, eds. Northvale, N.J.: Jason Aronson, 1992.

Dewey, John. *Reconstruction in Philosophy* (1920). Boston: Beacon Press, 1957.

———. *Democracy and Education. The Philosophy Source* CD. Daniel Kolak, ed. Belmont, Calif.: Wadsworth, 2000.

Dineen, Tana. *Manufacturing Victims: What the Psychology Industry Is Doing to People.* Montreal: Robert Davies Publishing, 1996.

Dittmann-Kohli, F. and P. B. Baltes. "Toward a Neofunctionalist Conception of Adult Intellectual Development: Wisdom as a Prototypical Case of Intellectual Growth." *Higher Stages of Human Development.* C. N. Alexander and E. J. Langer, eds. New York: Oxford University Press, 1990.

Doka, Kenneth J. "The Awareness of Mortality in Midlife: Implications for Later Life." *Awareness of Mortality.* Jeffrey Kauffman, ed. Amityville, N.Y.: Baywood Publishing, 1995.

Eakins, Barbara Westbrook and R. Gene Eakins. *Sex Differences in Human Communication.* Boston: Houghton Mifflin, 1978.

Edwards, Paul, ed. *The Encyclopedia of Philosophy.* New York: Macmillan, 1967.

Eisikovits, Edina. "Girl-talk/ Boy-talk: Sex Differences in Adolescent Speech." *Language and Gender.* Jennifer Coats, ed. Malden, Mass.: Blackwell, 1998.

Ellis, Albert and Raymond J. Yeager. *Why Some Therapies Don't Work.* Buffalo: Prometheus, 1989.

Erwin, Edward. *Philosophy & Psychotherapy.* London: Sage, 1997.

Feinberg, Joel. "Psychological Egoism." *Moral Philosophy.* George Sher, ed. New York: Harcourt Brace Jovanovich, 1987.

Fischer, John Martin, ed. *The Metaphysics of Death.* Stanford, Calif.: Stanford University Press, 1993.

Foucault, Michel. *Madness and Civilization.* New York: Random House, 1965.

———. *Power/Knowledge: Selected Interviews and Other Writings.* Colin Gordon, ed. New York: Routledge, 1980.

———. "What Is Enlightenment." *Foucault Reader.* P. Rainbow, ed. New York: Pantheon Books, 1984.

Frank, Jerome D. and Julia B. Frank. *Persuasion and Healing.* Baltimore: Johns Hopkins University Press, 1991.

Freud, Sigmund. "The Interpretation of Dreams" (1900). *The Basic Writings of Sigmund Freud.* A. A. Brill, trans. and ed. New York: The Modern Library, 1995.

———. "Psychopathology of Everyday Life" (1904). *The Basic Writings of Sigmund Freud.* A. A. Brill, trans. and ed. New York: The Modern Library, 1995.

———. *The Future of an Illusion* (1928). New York: Liveright Publishing, 1949.

Fricker, Miranda and Jennifer Hornsby, eds. *The Cambridge Companion to Feminism in Philosophy.* Cambridge, U.K.: Cambridge University Press, 2000.

Gadamer, Hans-Georg. *The Enigma of Health.* Stanford, Calif.: Stanford University Press, 1996.

Galanter, Marc. *Network Therapy for Alcohol and Drug Abuse.* New York: Basic Books, 1993.

Gallagher, Bernard J., III. *The Sociology of Mental Illness.* Englewood Cliffs, N.J.: Prentice-Hall, 1987.

Geertz, Clifford. *The Interpretation of Cultures.* New York: Basic Books, 1973.

Giddens, Anthony. *Modernity and Self-Identity.* Stanford, Calif.: Stanford University Press, 1991.

Gilbert, Ryle. *The Concept of Mind.* London: Butchison, 1949.

Gilligan, Carol. *In a Different Voice.* Cambridge, Mass.: Harvard University Press, 1982.

Gilliland, Burl E. and Richard K. James. *Crisis Intervention Strategies.* New York: Brooks/Cole, 1997.

Goldfried, Marvin R., ed. *Converging Themes in Psychotherapy.* New York: Springer, 1982.

Goldman, Alvin. *Philosophical Applications of Cognitive Science.* Boulder, Colo.: Westview Press, 1993.

Gould, R. "The Phases of Adult Life: A Study in Developmental Psychology." *American Journal of Psychiatry.* 129. 1972.

Greenberg, Jay R. and Bruce Fisher. *The Limits of Biological Treatments for Psychological Distress.* Hillsdale, N.J.: Lawrence Erlbaum Associates, 1989.

Greenberg, Ramon and Chester Pearlman. "An Integrated Approach to Dream Theory: Contributions from Sleep Research and Clinical Practice." *The Functions of*

Dreaming. A. Moffit, M. Kramer, and R. Hoffman, eds. Albany, N.Y.: State University of New York Press, 1993.

Grimshaw, Jean. *Philosophy and Feminist Thinking*. Minneapolis: University of Minnesota Press, 1986.

Grof, Stanislav. *Beyond the Brain*. New York: State University of New York Press, 1985.

Grollman, Earl A. *Suicide: Prevention, Intervention, Postvention*. Boston: Beacon Press, 1988.

Hadot, Pierre. *Philosophy as a Way of Life*. Oxford, U.K.: Blackwell, 1995.

Hales, Dianne and Robert E. Hales. *Caring for the Mind*. New York: Bantam, 1995.

Hall, Calvin S. and Gardner Lidnzey. *Theories of Personality*. New York: Wiley, 1970.

Hartmann, Ernest. *Dreams and Nightmares*. Cambridge, Mass.: Perseus, 2001.

Hegel, Georg Wilhelm Friedrich. *Lectures on the Philosophy of Religion* (1827). R. F. Brown et al., trans. Peter C. Hodgson, ed. Berkeley: University of California Press, 1988.

Heidegger, Martin. *Being and Time* (1927). Joan Stambaugh, trans. Albany, N.Y.: State University of New York Press, 1996.

Held, David. *Models of Democracy*. Stanford, Calif.: Stanford University Press, 1987.

Hepper, Paul P. and Daniel S. Gonzales. "Men Counseling Men." *Handbook of Counseling and Psychotherapy with Men*. Murray Scher, Mark Stevens, Glenn Good, and Gregg A. Eichenfield, eds. London: Sage, 1987.

Honderich, Ted, ed. *The Oxford Companion to Philosophy*. Oxford, U.K.: Oxford University Press, 1995.

Hume, David. *A Treatise of Human Nature* (1739). New York: Prometheus, 1992.

——— . *An Enquiry Concerning Human Understanding* (1748). La Salle, Ill.: Open Court, 1991.

——— . "Of Suicide" (1779). *Writings on Religion*. Anthony Flew, ed. La Salle, Ill.: Open Court, 1992.

Hyde, Janet Shibley. *Half the Human Experience*. Lexington, Mass.: D. C. Heath, 1991.

Imber, Karl, et al. in the *Journal of Consulting Clinical Psychologists* 58. 1990.

Inwood, Brad and L.P. Gerson, trans. *The Epicurus Reader*. Cambridge, U.K.: Hackett, 1994.

James, William. *The Varieties of Religious Experience* (1902). New York: Penguin, 1958.

——— . *Pragmatism* (1907). New York: Dover, 1995.

Jamison, Kay Redfield. *Night Falls Fast: Understanding Suicide*. New York: Vintage, 1999.

Johnson, Don Hanlon. "The Loneliness of the Male Body." *To Be a Man*. Los Angeles: Jeremy P. Tarcher, 1991.

Jourard, Sydney. *Disclosure: An Experimental Analysis of the Transparent Self*. New York: Wiley, 1971.

Jouvet, Michel. *The Paradox of Sleep: The Story of Dreaming*. Cambridge, Mass.: MIT Press, 1999.

Jung, Carl G. *The Basic Writings of C. G. Jung*. Violet Staub De Laszlo, ed. New York: Modern Library, 1959.

——— . *Dreams*. R.F.C. Hull, trans. New York: MJF Books, 1974.

——— . "Psychotherapy and a Philosophy of Life." *Essays on Contemporary Events*. R.F.C. Hull, trans. Princeton, N.J.: Princeton University Press, 1989.

Kant, Immanuel. *Critique of Pure Reason* (1781). Norman Kemp Smith, trans. New York: St. Martin's, 1965.

——— . *Prolegomena to Any Future Metaphysics That Can Qualify as a Science* (1783). Paul Carus, trans. Chicago: Open Court, 1993.

——— . *Groundwork of a Metaphysic of Morals* (1797). H. J. Paton, trans. New York: Harper & Row, 1964.

Kauffman, Jeffrey, ed. *Awareness of Mortality.* Amityville, N.Y.: Baywood Publishing, 1995.

Kierkegaard, Søren. *The Sickness Unto Death* (1849). Princeton, N.J.: Princeton University Press, 1941.

Kinsey, A. C., W. B. Pomeroy, C. E. Martin, and P. H. Gebhard. *Sexual Behavior in the Human Female.* Philadelphia: Saunders, 1953.

Kirschner, L. A. "Effects of Gender on Psychotherapy." *Comprehensive Psychiatry.* 19, 1978.

Klemke, E. D. *The Meaning of Life.* New York: Oxford University Press, 2000.

Koestenbaum, Peter. *The New Image of the Person: The Theory and Practice of Clinical Philosophy.* Westport, Conn.: Greenwood Press, 1978.

Lazerson, Arlyne, ed. *Psychology Today: An Introduction.* New York: Random House, 1975.

LeBon, Tim. *Wise Therapy: Philosophy for Counsellors.* London: Continuum, 2001.

Leibniz, Gottfried Wilhelm. "Letter to Foucher" (1675). *Philosophical Essays.* Roger Ariew and Daniel Garber, ed. and trans. Indianapolis: Hackett, 1989.

Lewis, Michael. *Altering Fate: Why the Past Does Not Predict the Future.* New York: Guilford Press, 1997.

Lindberg, David C. and Ronald L. Numbers, eds. *God and Nature.* Berkeley: University of California Press, 1986.

Locke, John. *An Essay Concerning Human Understanding* (1689). Oxford, U.K.: Clarendon, 1975.

Lundy, Katherina L. P. and Barbara D. Warme. *Sociology.* Toronto: Methuen, 1986.

Mackie, Marlene. *Constructing Women and Men: Gender Socialization.* Toronto: Holt, Rinehart and Winston, 1987.

Malpas, Jeff and Robert Solomon, eds. *Death and Philosophy.* London: Routledge, 1998.

Maltz, Daniel N. and Ruth A. Borker. "A Cultural Approach to Male–Female Miscommunication." *Language and Gender.* Jennifer Coats, ed. Malden, Mass.: Blackwell, 1998.

Metzger, Bruce M. and Roland E. Murphy, eds. *The New Oxford Annotated Bible.* New York: Oxford University Press, 1989.

Mill, John Stuart. *On Liberty* (1859). New York: Hackett, 1978.

Miller, Nancy E., et al., eds. *Psychodynamic Treatment Research.* New York: Basic Books, 1993.

Millet, Kate. *Sexual Politics.* New York: Doubleday, 1970.

Morgan, Brian S. "Intimacy of Self-disclosure Topics and Sex Differences in Self-Disclosure." *Sex Roles* 2. 1976.

Moss, M. and S. Moss. "The Impact of Parental Death on Middle Aged Children." *Omega.* 14. 1983.

Mulcahy, Gloria A. "Sex Differences in Patterns of Self-disclosure among Adolescents: A Developmental Perspective." *Journal of Youth and Adolescence* 2. 1973.

Nagel, Thomas. *The View from Nowhere.* New York: Oxford University Press, 1986.

Navia, Luis E. *The Adventure of Philosophy.* Westport, Conn.: Praeger, 1999.

Nietzsche, Friedrich. "Beyond Good and Evil" (1886). *Basic Writings of Nietzsche.* Walter Kaufmann, ed. New York: Modern Library, 1968.
——— . "Genealogy of Morals" (1887). *Basic Writings of Nietzsche.* Walter Kaufmann, ed. New York: Modern Library, 1968.
——— . "The Will to Power" (1930). *Basic Writings of Nietzsche.* Walter Kaufmann, ed. New York: Modern Library, 1968.
Nozick, Robert. *Anarchy, State and Utopia.* New York: Basic Books, 1974.
Nussbaum, Martha. *The Therapy of Desire.* Princeton, N.J.: Princeton University Press, 1994.
O'Donohue, William and Jason S. Vass. "What Is an Irrational Belief?" *The Philosophy of Psychology.* William O'Donohue and Richard F. Kitchener, eds. London: Sage, 1996.
Person, E. "Women in Therapy: Therapist Gender as a Variable." *Between Analyst and Patient.* Helen Meyers, ed. Hillsdale, N.J.: Analytic Press, 1986.
Pierce, Charles S. *Selected Writings* (1905). Philip P. Wiener, ed. New York: Dover, 1966.
Plato. *Collected Dialogues* (c. 375 B.C.). Edith Hamilton and Huntington Cairns, eds. Princeton, N.J.: Princeton University Press, 1961.
Pleck, Joseph H. "Man to Man: Is Brotherhood Possible?" *Old Family, New Family.* Nona Glazer-Malbin, ed. New York: Van Nostrand, 1975.
Pletcher, Galen K. "Meaning and Awareness of Death." *Awareness of Mortality.* Jeffrey Kauffman, ed. Amityville, N.Y.: Baywood Publishing, 1995.
Poincaré, Henri. *Science and Hypothesis* (1905). New York: Dover, 1952.
Poole, Ross. "Morality, Masculinity and the Market." *Radical Philosophy.* No. 39, Spring 1985.
Porter, Roy. *The Social History of Madness.* New York: Weidenfeld & Nicolson, 1987.
Raabe, Peter B. *Philosophical Counseling: Theory and Practice.* Westport, Conn.: Praeger, 2001.
Rand, Nicholas and Maria Torok. *Questions for Freud: The Secret History of Psychoanalysis.* Cambridge, Mass.: Harvard University Press. 1997.
Ratey, John J. and Catherine Johnson. *Shadow Syndromes.* New York: Pantheon, 1997.
Rogers, Carl R. *On Becoming a Person* (1961). Boston: Houghton Mifflin, 1989.
Rorty, Amelie Oksenberg. "Socrates and Sophia Perform the Philosophic Turn." *The Institution of Philosophy.* Avner Cohen and Marcelo Dascal, eds. La Salle, Ill.: Open Court, 1989.
Rorty, Richard. *Contingency, Irony, and Solidarity.* Cambridge, U.K.: Cambridge University Press, 1989.
Rosenau, Pauline Marie. *Post-Modernism and the Social Sciences.* Princeton, N.J.: Princeton University Press, 1992.
Ross, C. E. and J. Mirowsky. "Child Care and Emotional Adjustment to Wives' Employment." *Journal of Health and Social Behavior.* 29, 1988.
Russell, Bertrand. *The Problems of Philosophy* (1912). London: Allen and Unwin, 1966.
——— . *Our Knowledge of the External World* (1914). London: Routledge, 1993.
Sartre, Jean-Paul. *Essays in Existentialism.* Secaucus, N.J.: Citadel Press, 1997.
Schaef, Anne Wilson. *Women's Reality.* San Francisco: Harper & Row, 1985.
Schill, Stefan de. *Crucial Choices—Crucial Changes: The Resurrection of Psychotherapy.* Amherst, N.Y.: Prometheus Books, 2000.
Schissel, Bernard and Linda Mahood, eds. *Social Control in Canada.* Toronto: Oxford University Press, 1996.

Sharma, Sohan Lal. *The Therapeutic Dialogue*. Albuquerque: University of New Mexico Press, 1986.

Shlain, Leonard. *The Alphabet Versus the Goddess*. New York: Viking, 1998.

Shusterman, Richard. *Practicing Philosophy*. New York: Routledge, 1997.

Sim, Stuart, ed. *The Icon Critical Dictionary of Postmodern Thought*. London: Icon, 1998.

Singer, J. L. and K. S. Pope. *The Power of Human Imagination*. New York: Plenum Press, 1978.

Sousa, Ronald de. *The Rationality of Emotion*. Cambridge, Mass.: MIT Press, 1987.

Spencer, Herbert. *The Principles of Ethics* Vol. 1. London: Appleton, 1896.

Stebbins, Robert A. *Tolerable Differences*. Toronto: McGraw-Hill Ryerson, 1996.

Stern, James and Tania Stern, trans. E. L. Freud, ed. *Letters of Sigmund Freud*. New York: Harcourt, 1960.

Styron. William. *Darkness Visible*. New York: Random House, 1990.

Szasz, Thomas S. *The Manufacture of Madness*. London: Routledge & Kegan Paul, 1971.

———. *Schizophrenia: The Sacred Symbol of Psychiatry*. Syracuse, N.Y.: Syracuse University Press, 1976.

Tannahill, Reay. *Sex in History*. New York: Stein and Day, 1982.

Tannen, Deborah. *You Just Don't Understand*. New York: Ballantine, 1990.

Taylor, Charles. *The Ethics of Authenticity*. Cambridge, Mass.: Harvard University Press, 1991.

Thomä, Helmut and Horst Kächele. *Psychoanalytic Practice*. Northvale, N.J.: Jason Aronson, 1994.

Tillich, Paul. *The Courage to Be*. London: Collins, 1952.

Tolstoy, Leo. *A Confession and Other Religious Writings* (1879). Jane Kentish, trans. New York: Viking Penguin, 1987.

Tong, Rosemarie. *Feminine and Feminist Ethics*. Belmont, Calif.: Wadsworth, 1993.

Valenstein, Elliot S. *Blaming the Brain: The Truth about Drugs and Mental Health*. New York: Free Press, 1998.

Wade, Wyn Craig. *The Fiery Cross*. New York: Simon and Schuster, 1987.

Wittgenstein, Ludwig. *Philosophical Investigations*. G.E.M. Anscombe, trans. Oxford, U.K.: Blackwell, 1958.

Yutang, Lin. "On Growing Old Gracefully." *The Importance of Living*. New York: William Heinemann, 1931.

Index

About the Author

PETER B. RAABE teaches philosophy and has a private philosophical counseling practice. Dr. Raabe is the author of numerous articles and presentations on philosophical counseling and *Philosophical Counseling: Theory and Practice* (Praeger, 2001).